Giorgio & Dimitrius
LOST in the FUN ZONE

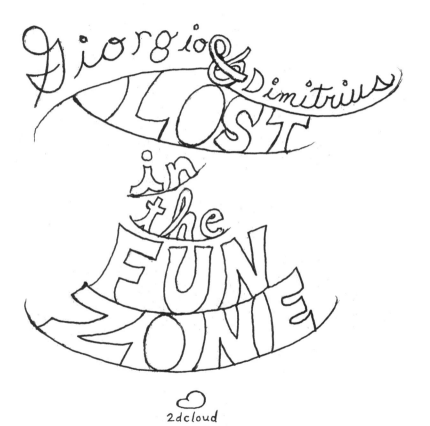

2dcloud

Lost in the Fun Zone
Leif Goldberg
nationalwastecomics.com

Forewarned by Brian Chippendale
Publishers: Maggie Umber, Raighne
Publicity: Melissa Carraher
published by 2dcloud
3364 S. Lituanica Ave #1R, Chicago, IL 60608
2dcloud.com
Distributed TO THE TRADE In the US by Consortium Book Sales
www.cbsd.com   & Distribution
In Canada by Publishers Group Canada - www.pgcbooks.ca
Orders:(800) 283-3572 ♪

First Edition, February 2018 © 2018 Leif Goldberg
10 9 8 7 6 5 4 3 2 1

Library of Congress Control Number: 2017944386
ISBN: 978-1-937541-40-8
Printed In Korea

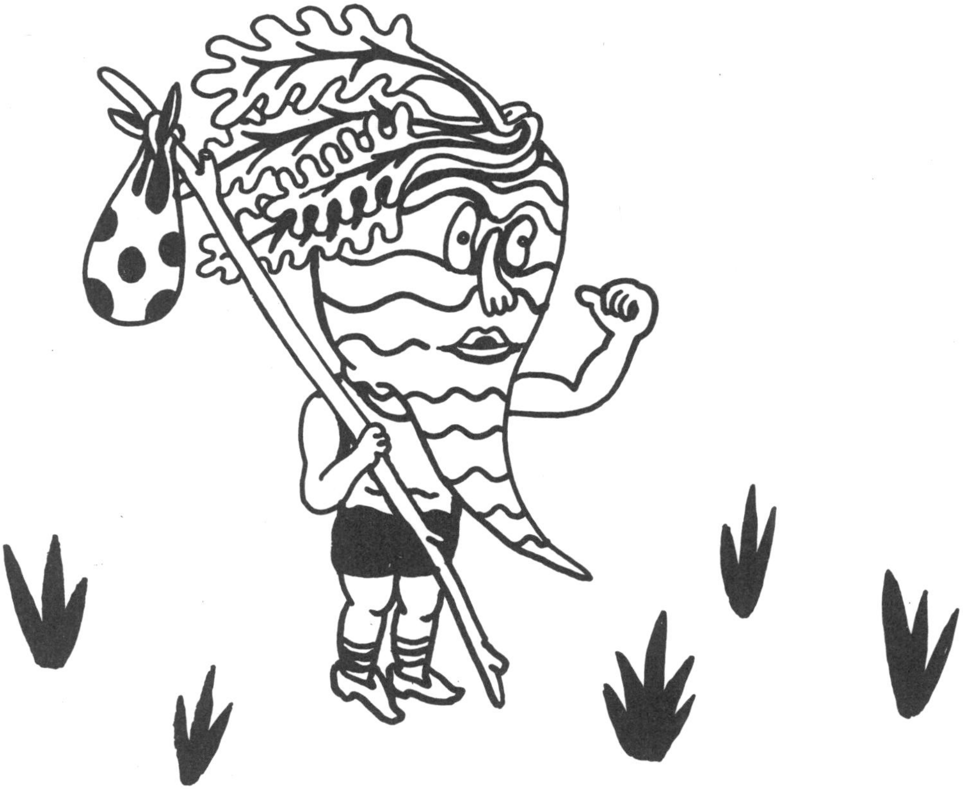

Dimitrius,

It's been a little while since we talked. Moving out of the Hillarious Attic after being here some 15 years has me thinking of you. You left this place maybe 10 years back? I can't go 11 feet without seeing your scrawl on the wall. After you were gone I took your old room and turned it into my drawing room. I call it the Dim-room. It's mainly my winter drawing room cause it's small and it heats up with a x space heater. The regular cats hang out up on your old sleeping loft cause it stays warm up there. How you squeezed yourself up those rickety stairs and onto that loft nightly I have no idea but the cats seem to share your sense of security. I let them pee on the loft floor in your honor.

Moving out of here makes me think of moving out of the Fort back at the beginning of the century. The Beginning. Of The Century. Remember when you hooked up that indoor/outdoor thermometer and it read like 28 outside and 24 inside? those were the days. Lucky you were covered in fur. You and Jim. Fur and muscle. You know I was Always a little jealous of how ripped you were. All of us would be sitting around doing nothing but drawing comics and eating bagels out of a dumpster but somehow you were the only one who got more ripped. I imagine your muscle system was put in place as a kitten building rock walls way up on the northern fringe of Vermont to keep out the invading Canadian hordes who roamed the forest in search of conquest.

Did I ever tell you how cool I thought you and Meerk were after you were in the Whitney Biennial with Forcefield and like a week later you're in Kinkos pulling an all-nighter to get an issue of Paper Rodeo out? For no pay and very little social credit? Like, your New York art world breakout moment happens and you guys zip back to town to edit a free gnarly garbage-comics newspaper that got distributed through video stores and crepe shops. The Wormer is still up in the Attic. He loOks fucking great but if you touch him his hair turns to this horrible sticky dust that rains down death. Forcefield remains untamable. That white christmas-tree headed lady is still here too, weΩl, most of her. Are you still using the Gardeher as a chicken coop?

How's the family? What a handsome team you've gotten yourself involved with. Are you guys still playing as Crude Hill? or did you let anyone join your solo jam Smilax? Smilax is another thing I'm jealous of. If I didn't like you I would steal that band name, put out a record and claim I used it first. It's such a killer name. So wait somebody drew a book about you? Is it that weirdo who draws in the crooked unpredictable energy line? It's a long narrative? Is your nit wit buddy Giorgio in there with you? I still have my copies of those National Waste comics you guys were in. They stay in my "very special heavily guarded items" pile. The guy who made them can layer colors like nobody else man, a true silkscreening hero.

I'm curious has your old drinking buddy Leaf-Ass shown up lately? Leaf-Ass is one of the only guys I have punched in the face. That guy was fucking crazy.

Anyway. Providence hasn't been the same since you flew the coop. I wish I got to see you more. You're really some of the best animals I've ever met. Take care, have fun and I hope to see you and the gang soon.

Love   Brian

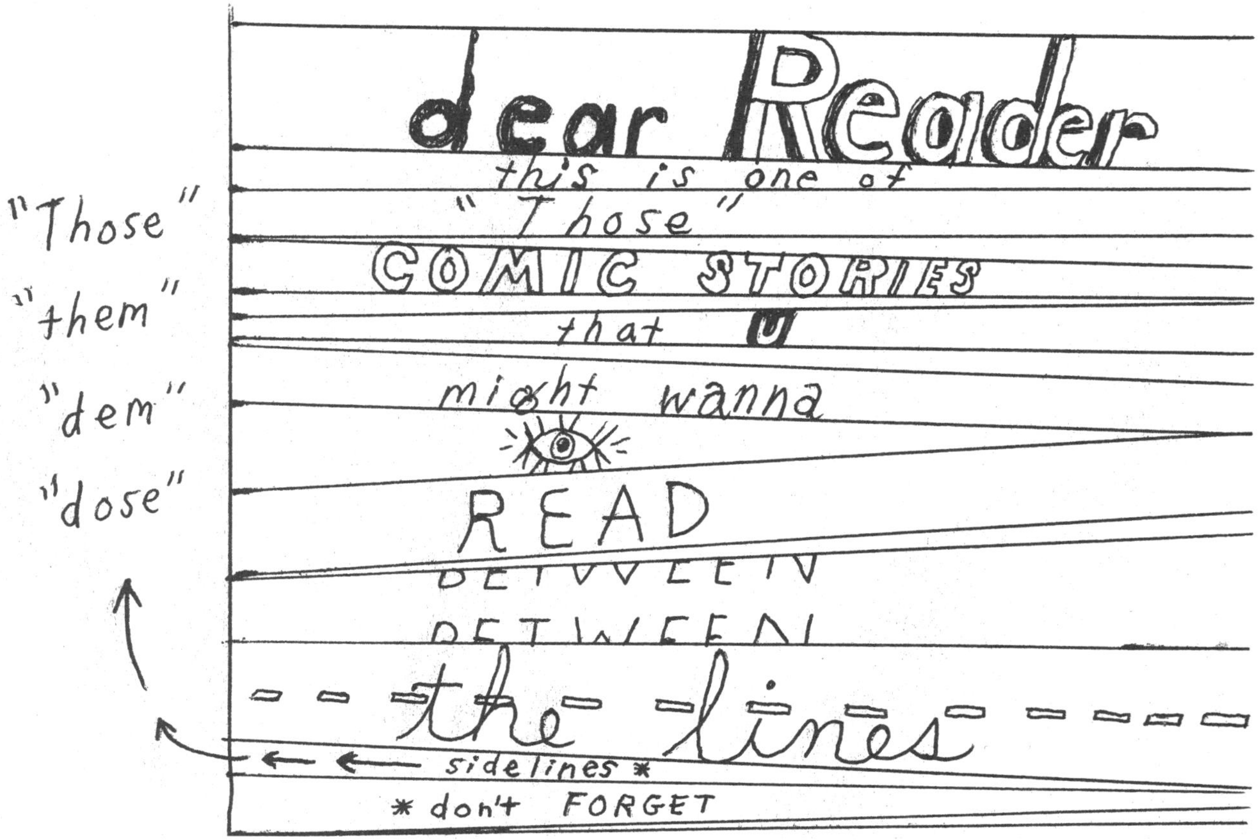

dear Reader
this is one of
"Those"
COMIC STORIES
that U
might wanna
READ
BETWEEN
BETWEEN
the lines
sidelines *
* don't FORGET
"Those"
"them"
"dem"
"dose"

the
flawed
fraud

de
clawed

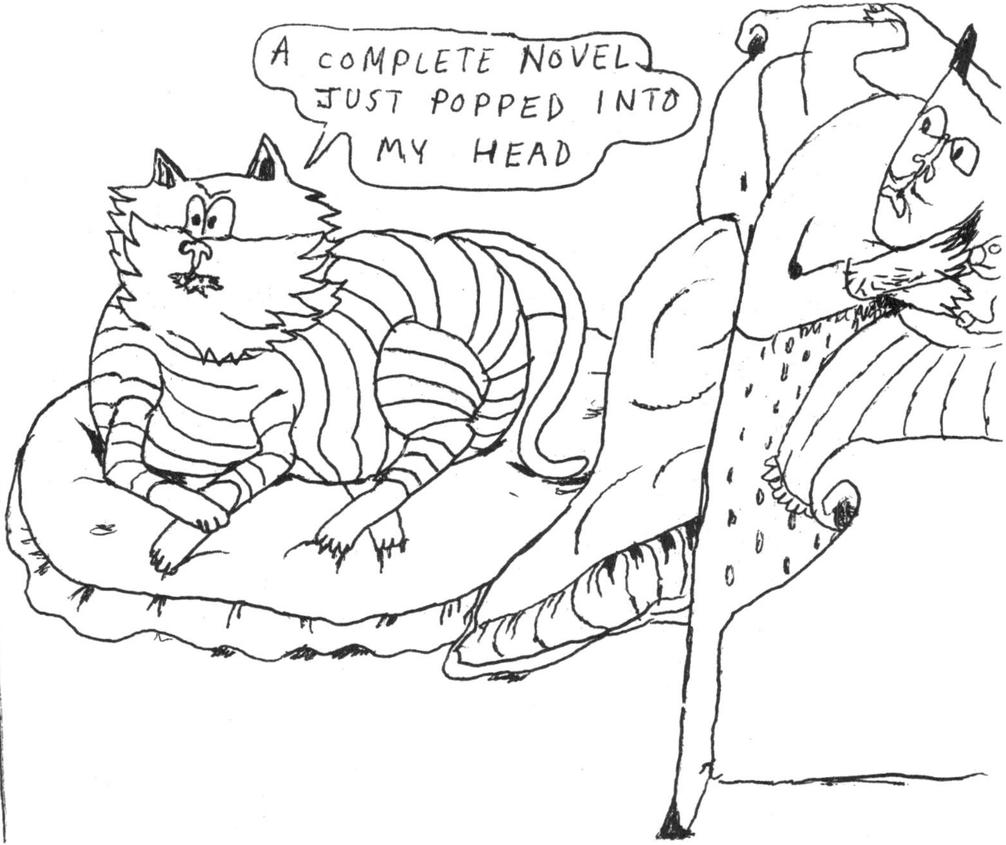
A COMPLETE NOVEL JUST POPPED INTO MY HEAD

burrita rita

pennywhistle yowl

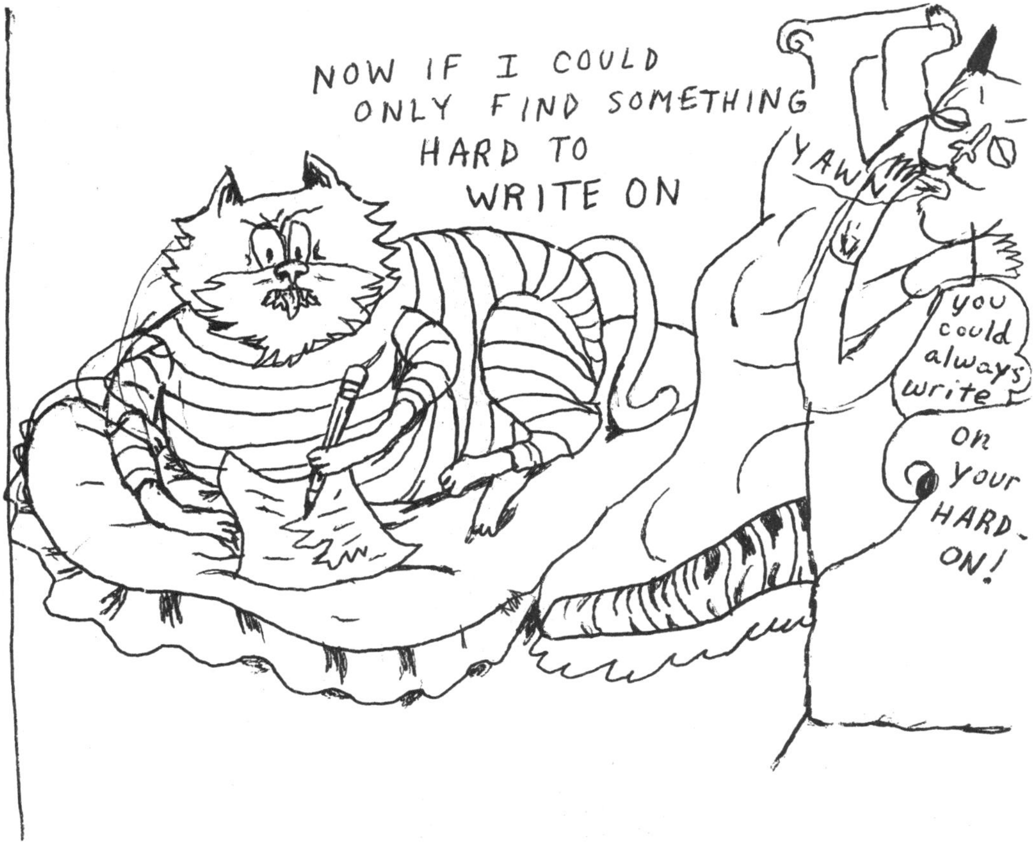
NOW IF I COULD ONLY FIND SOMETHING HARD TO WRITE ON
YAWN
you could always write on your HARD-ON!

ground
story
pencil

high
by
association

witticisms
kitticisms

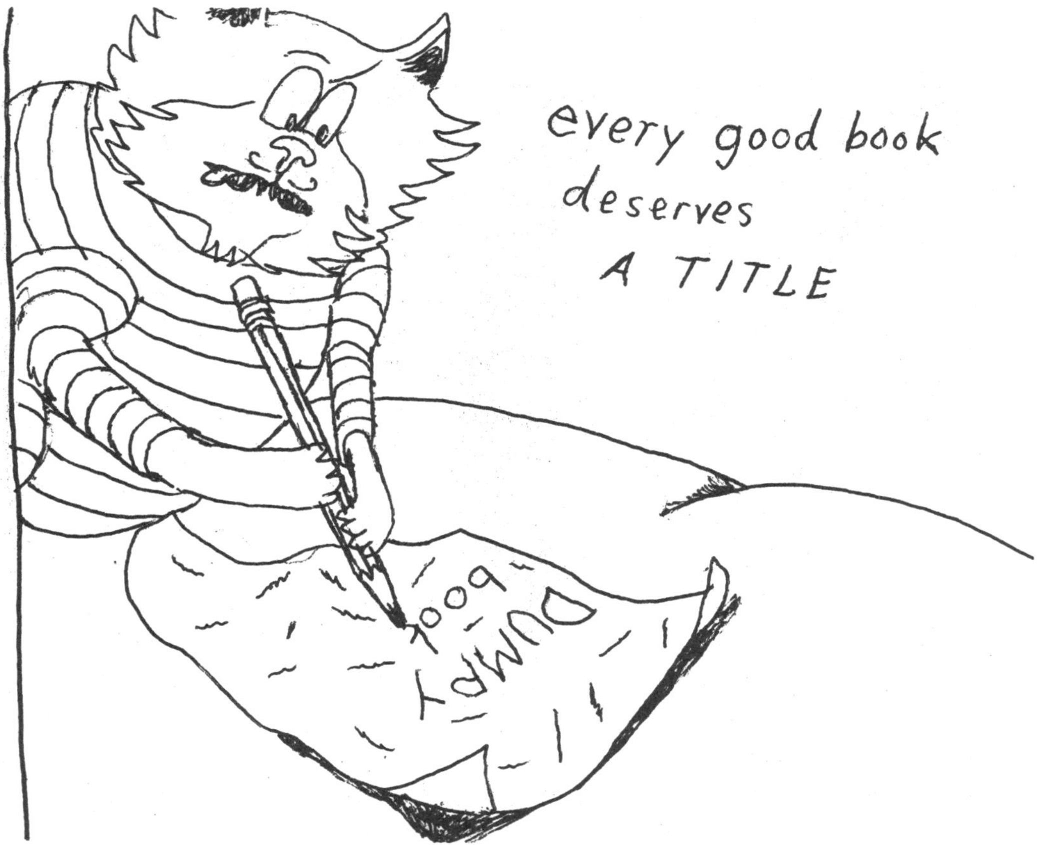
every good book
deserves
A TITLE
DUMPY
boo

a lost
cuz

a

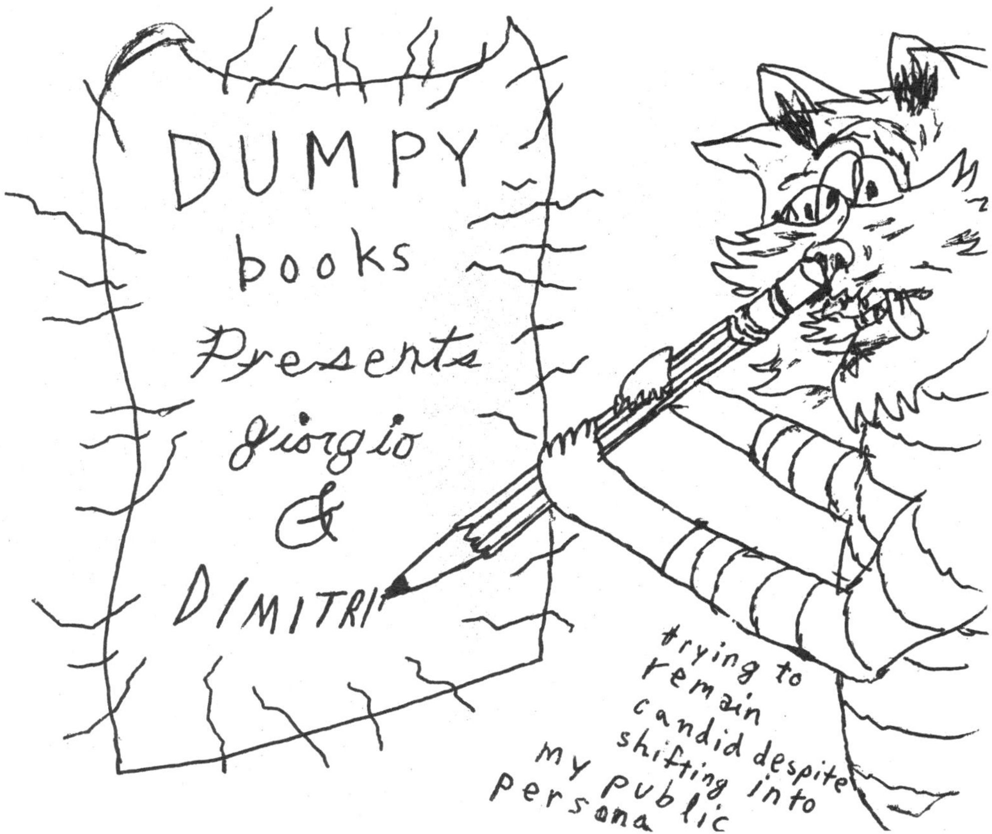
DUMPY
books
Presents
giorgio
&
DIMITRI
trying to remain candid despite shifting into my public persona

disreputable

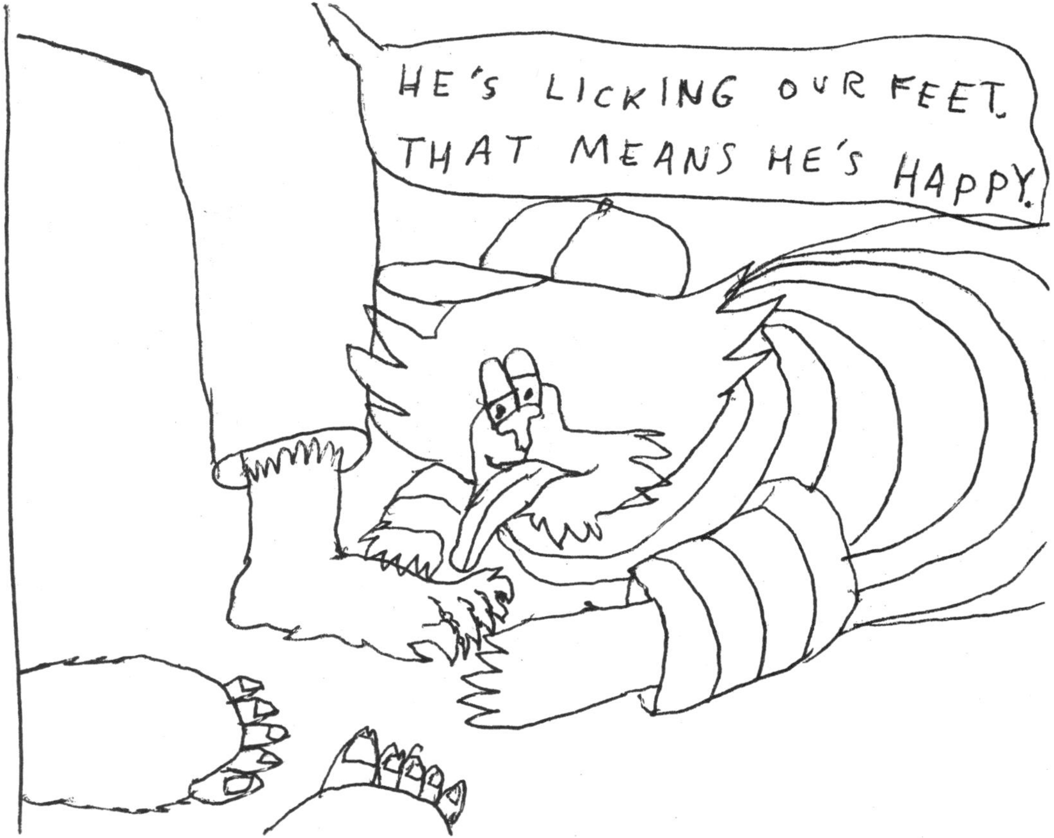
HE'S LICKING OUR FEET. THAT MEANS HE'S HAPPY.

ON
the
road
to UR
de
BOAR!

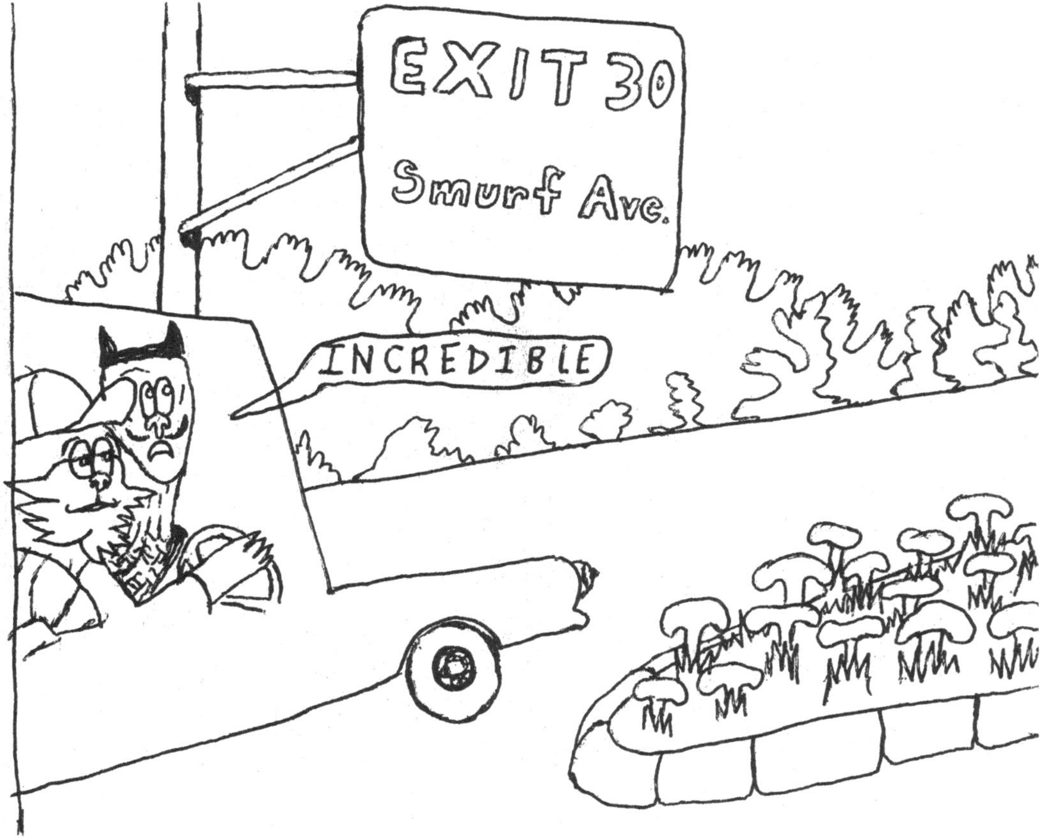

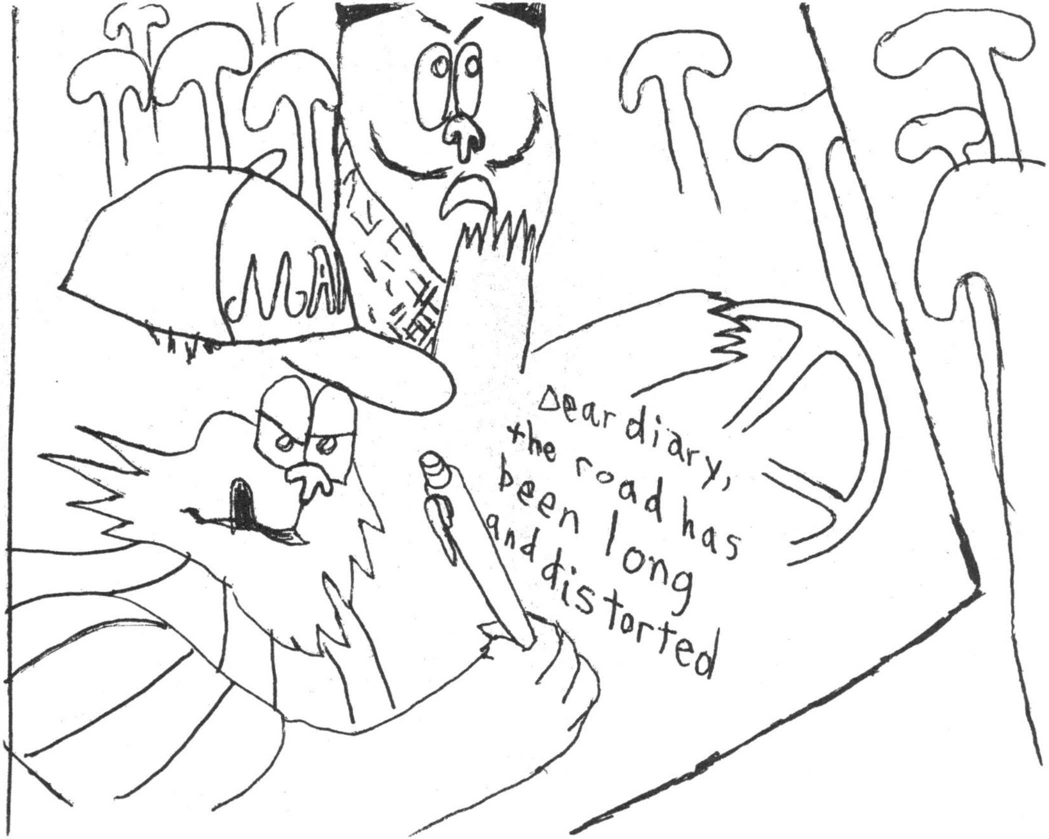
MA
Dear diary,
the road has
been long
and distorted

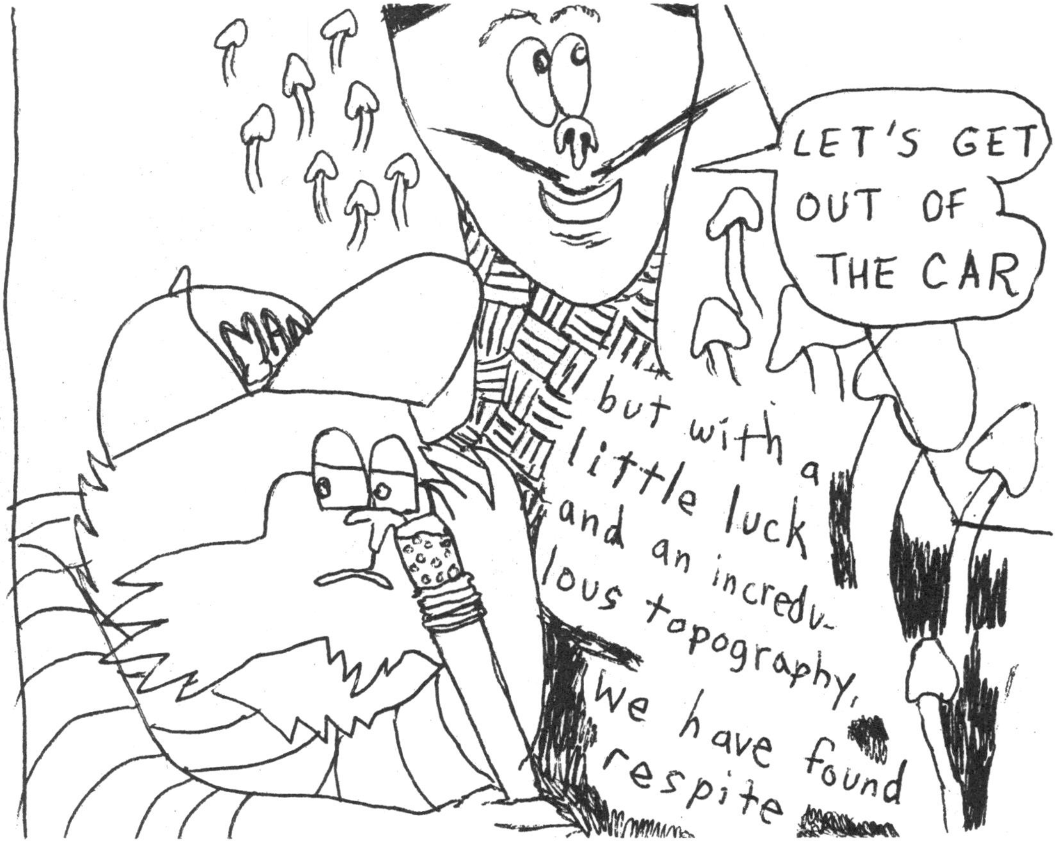

LET'S GET OUT OF THE CAR
but with a little luck and an incredulous topography, we have found respite

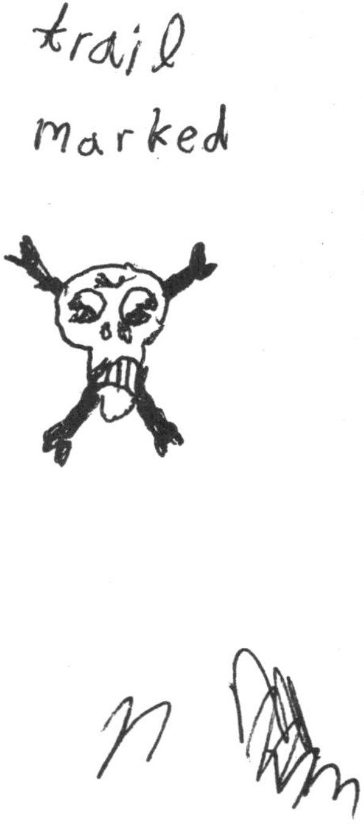
trail
marked

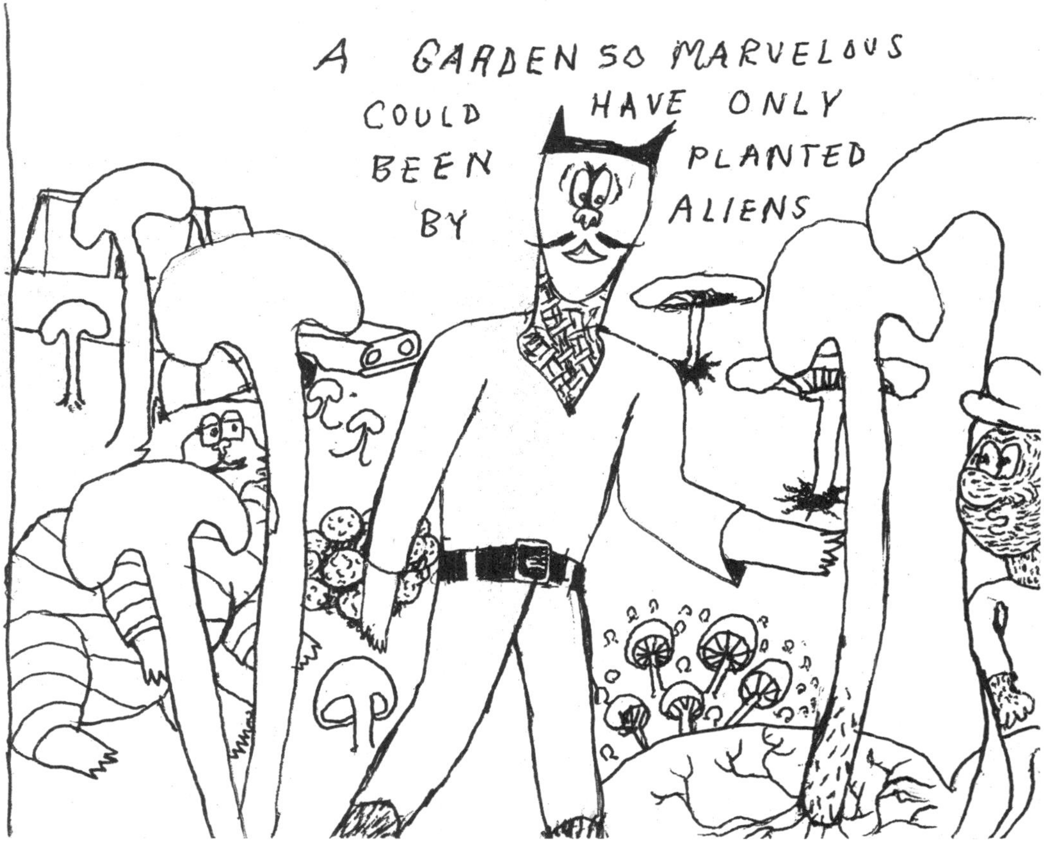
A GARDEN SO MARVELOUS
COULD HAVE ONLY
BEEN PLANTED
BY ALIENS

fun guy

CARPET

"ASIDE"

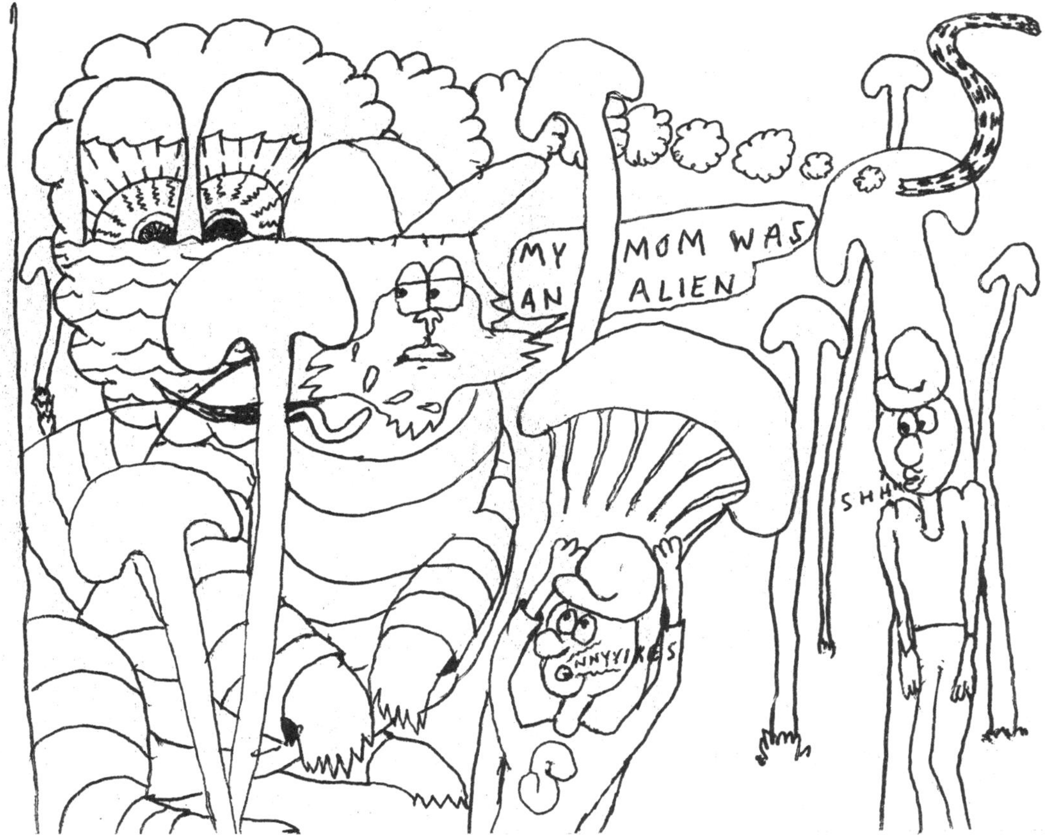
MY MOM WAS AN ALIEN
SHHH
NNYYIKES

Chapter 8: MOREL of the story

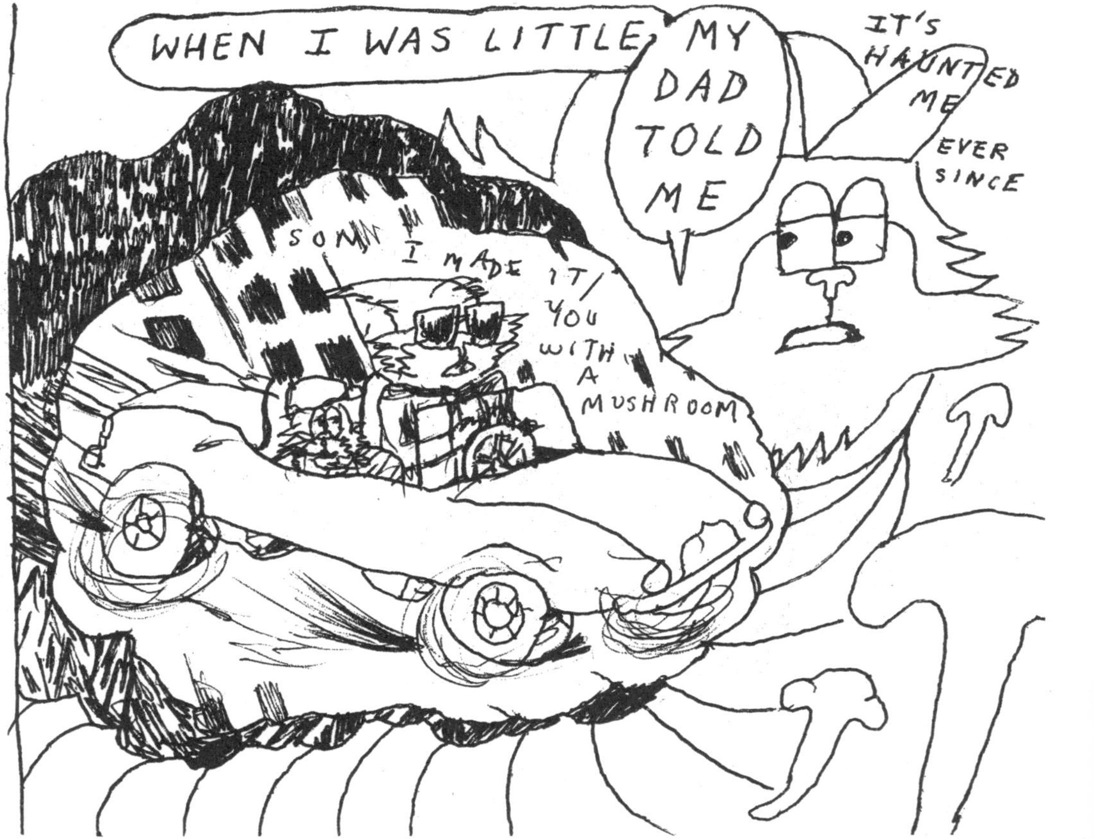
WHEN I WAS LITTLE
MY DAD TOLD ME
SON I MADE IT/ YOU WITH A MUSHROOM
IT'S HAUNTED ME EVER SINCE

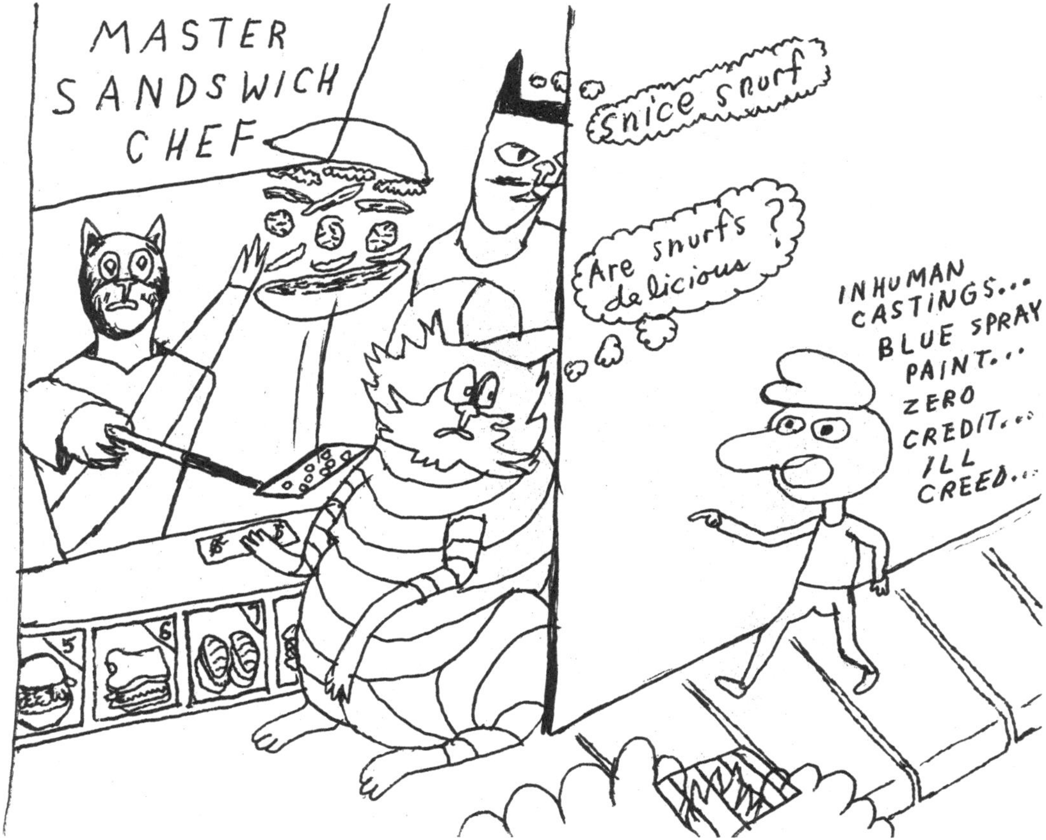
MASTER SANDSWICH CHEF
Snice snurf
Are snurfs delicious?
INHUMAN CASTINGS... BLUE SPRAY PAINT... ZERO CREDIT... ILL CREED...

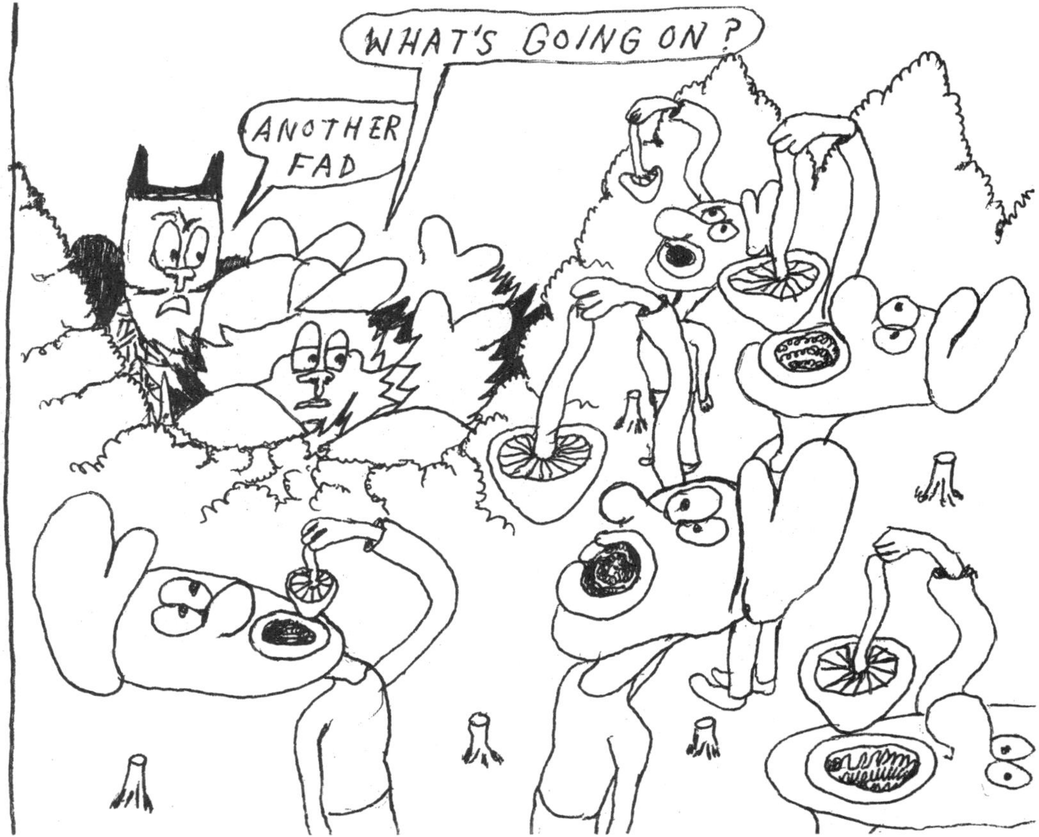
WHAT'S GOING ON?
ANOTHER FAD

Mr Rogers

Nautical

Voyager

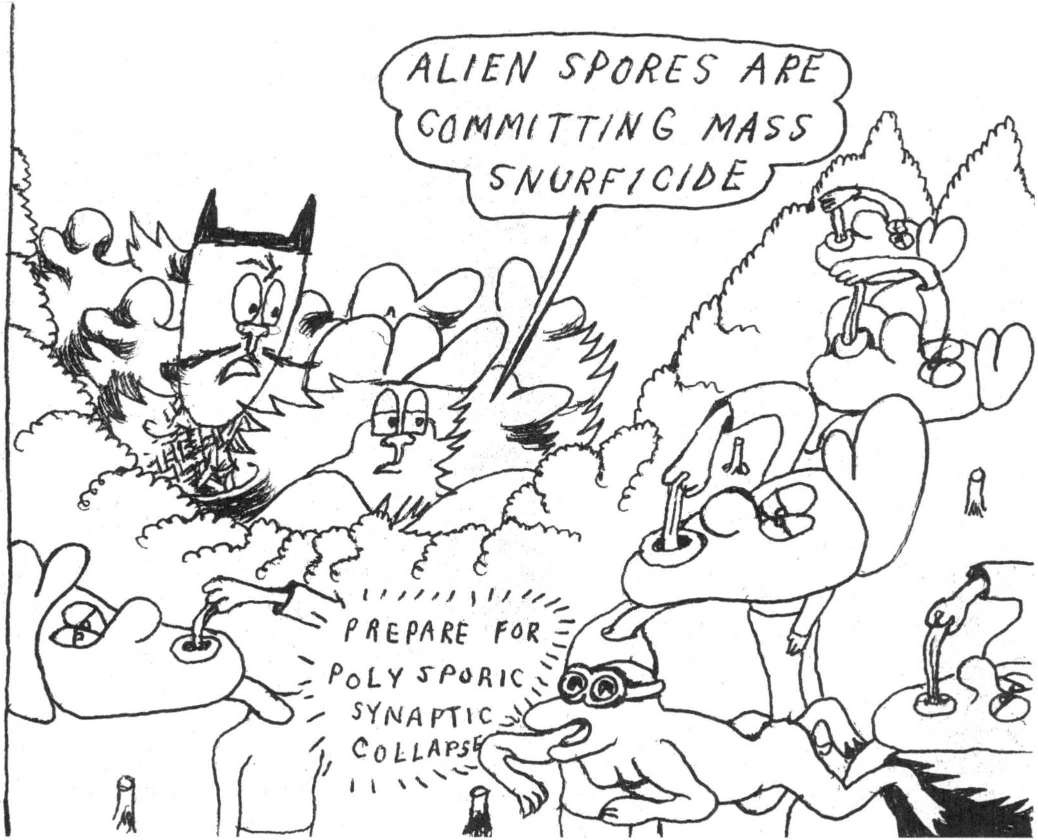
ALIEN SPORES ARE COMMITTING MASS SNURFICIDE
PREPARE FOR POLY SPORIC SYNAPTIC COLLAPSE

escaping

my
clear
conscience

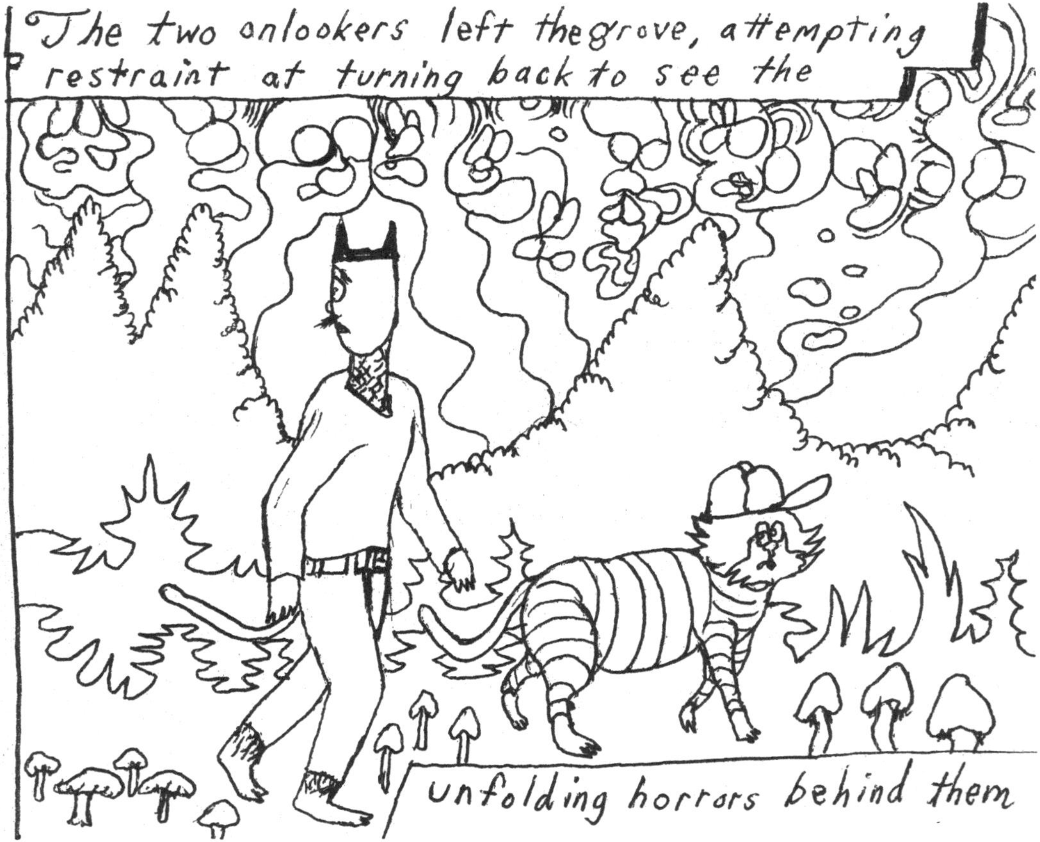
The two onlookers left the grove, attempting restraint at turning back to see the
unfolding horrors behind them

dream wave pillow

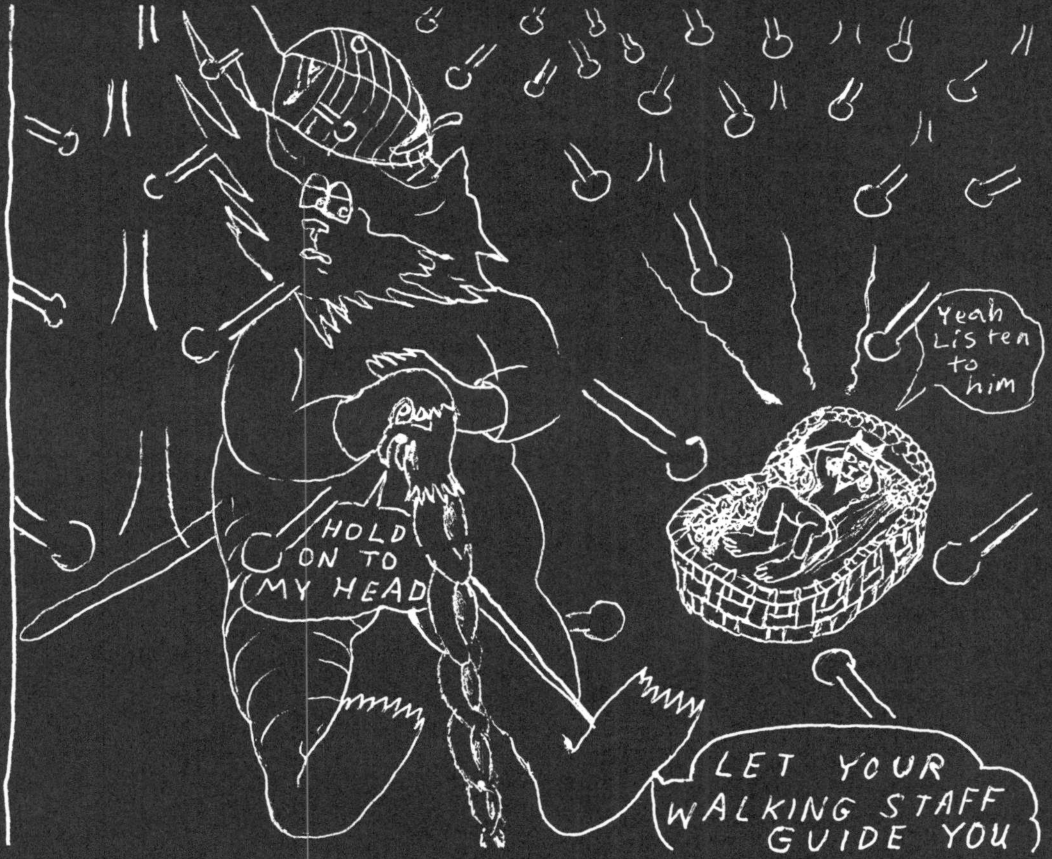
Yeah Listen to him
HOLD ON TO MY HEAD
LET YOUR WALKING STAFF GUIDE YOU

REICHSTAG

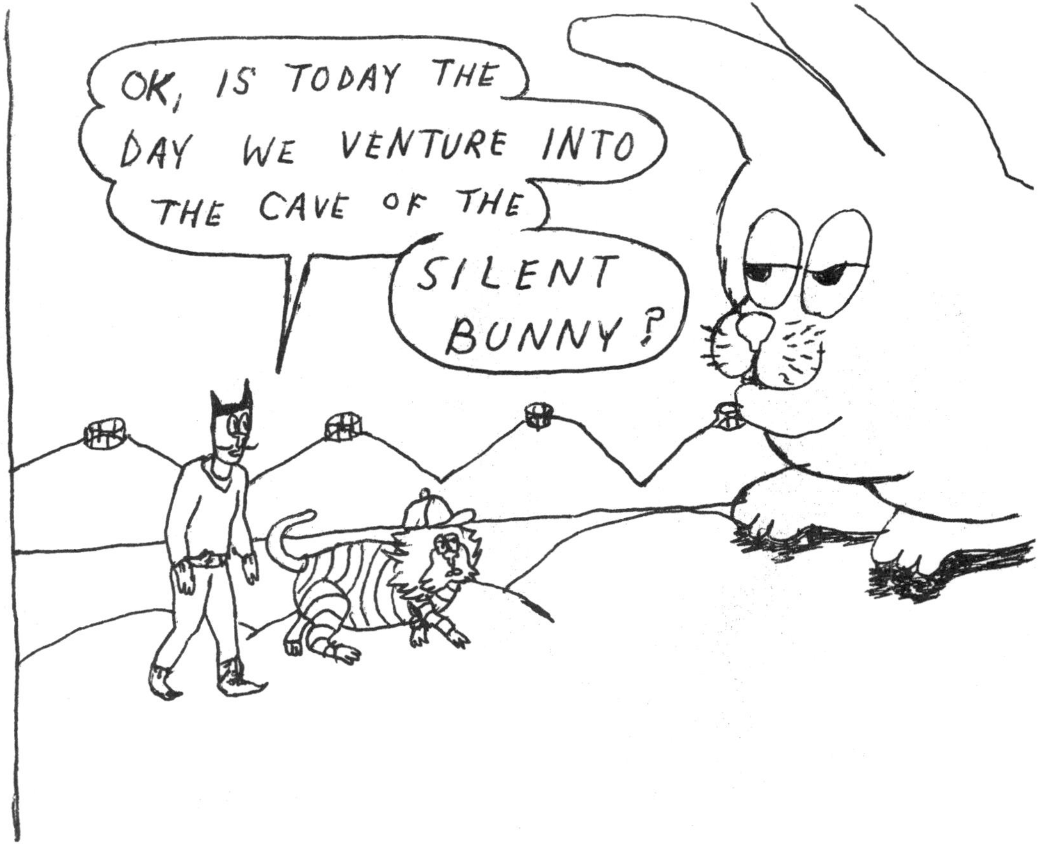
OK, IS TODAY THE DAY WE VENTURE INTO THE CAVE OF THE SILENT BUNNY?

how can such a simple "cartoon" allude to a complex infrequently Konsidered PARALLEL TIME?

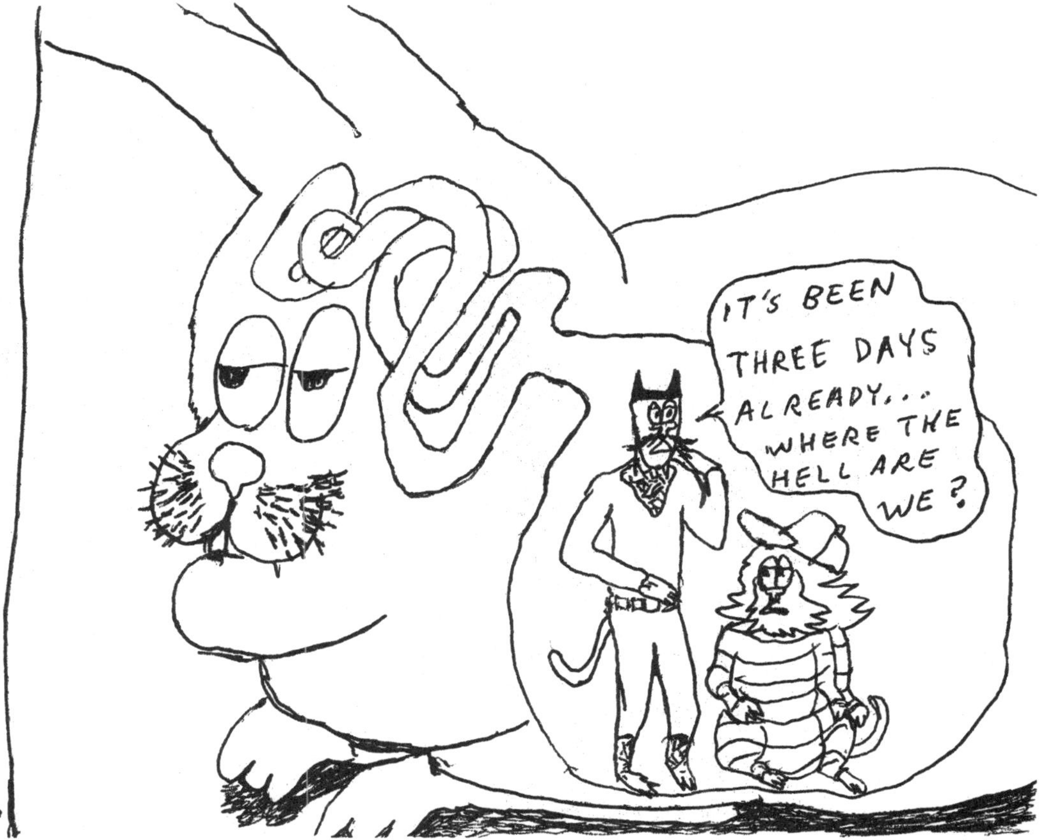

direct
PAY
psychic
tV

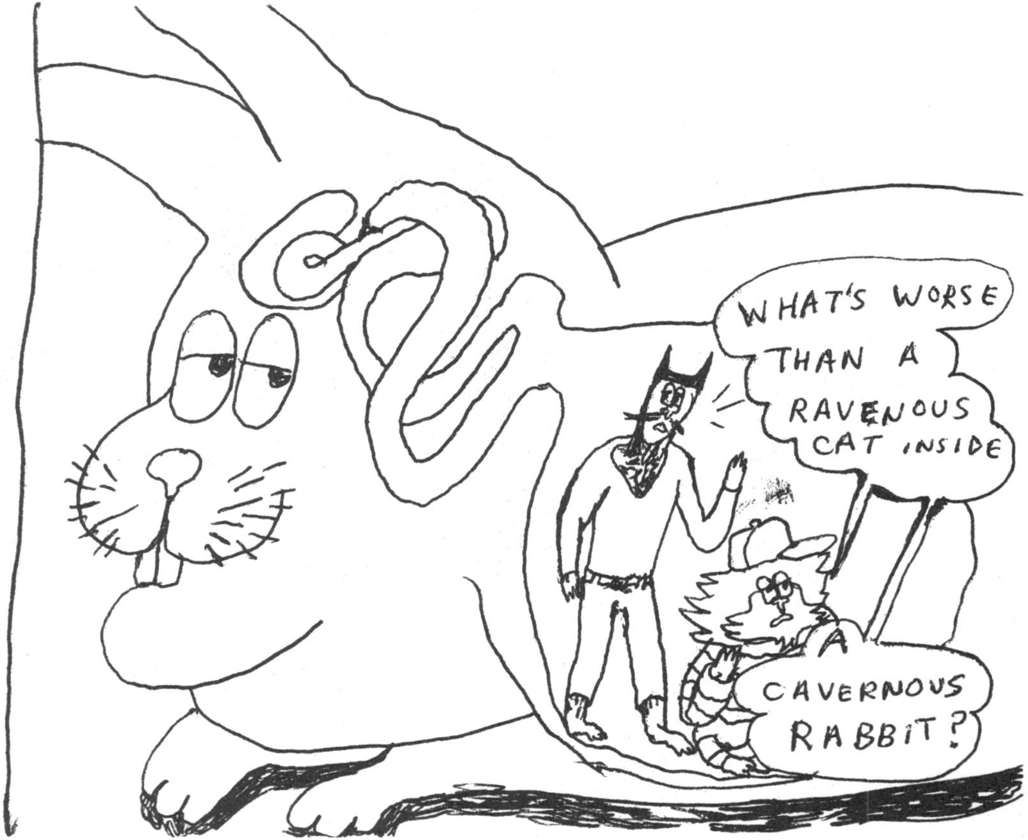
WHAT'S WORSE THAN A RAVENOUS CAT INSIDE
A CAVERNOUS RABBIT?

Disaster strikes

literally scribbled

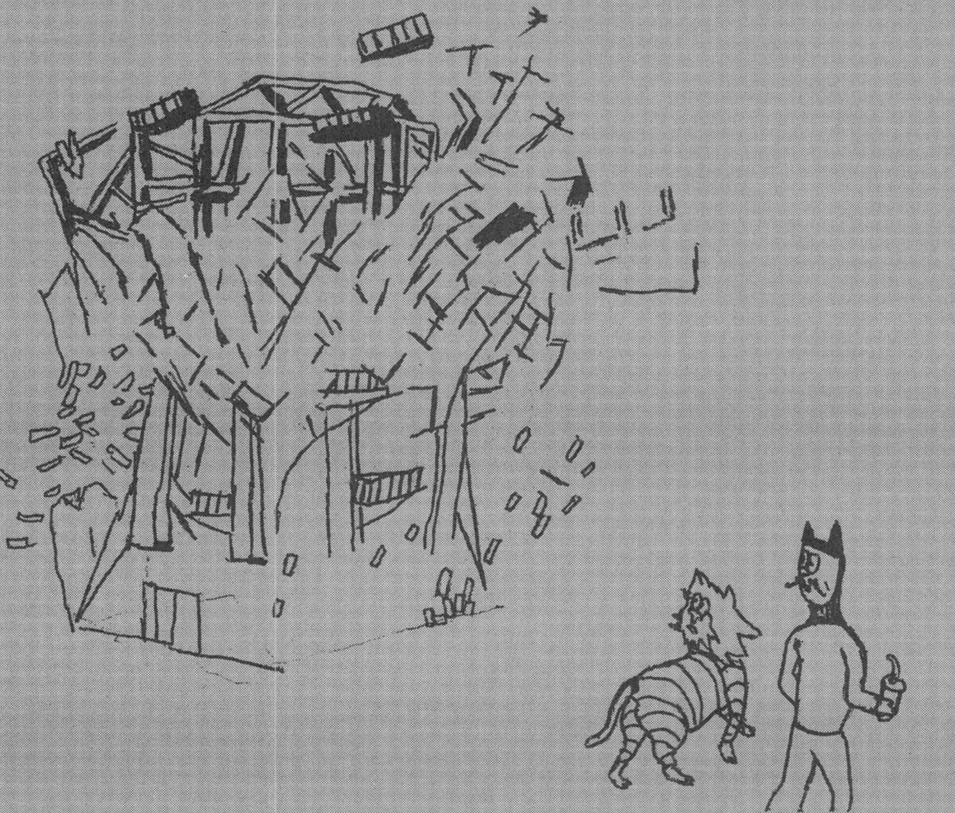

macaroni squid mirage

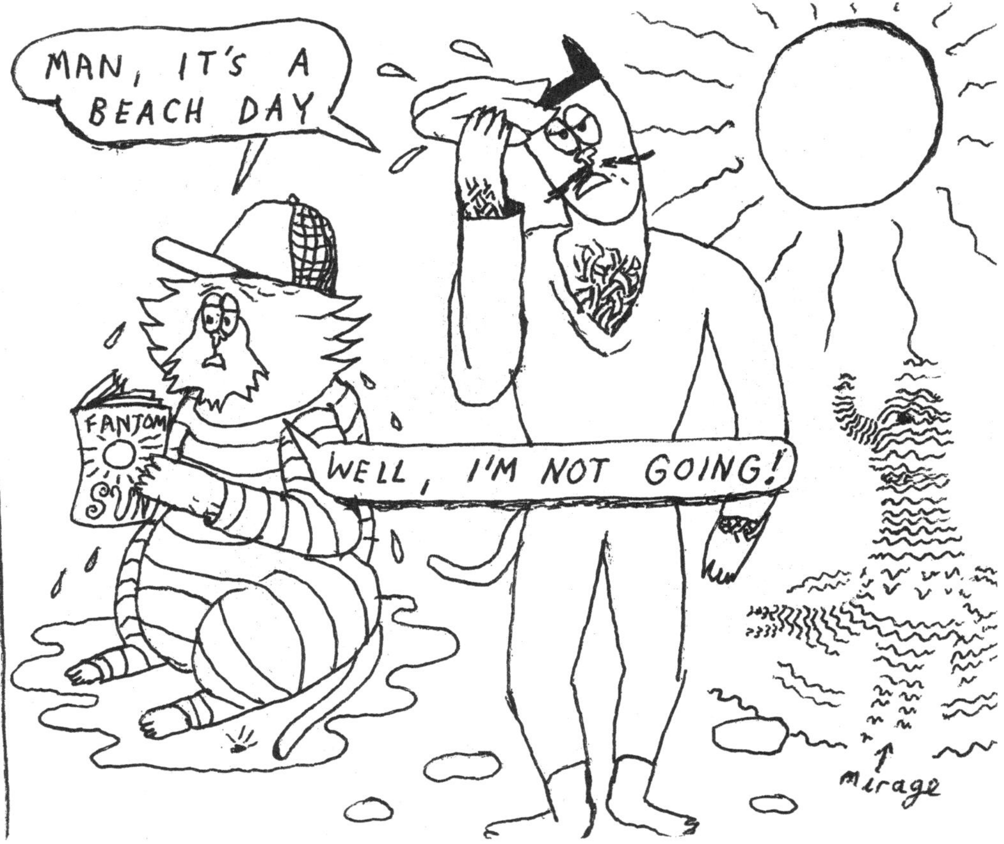
MAN, IT'S A BEACH DAY
FANTOM
SUN
WELL, I'M NOT GOING!
mirage

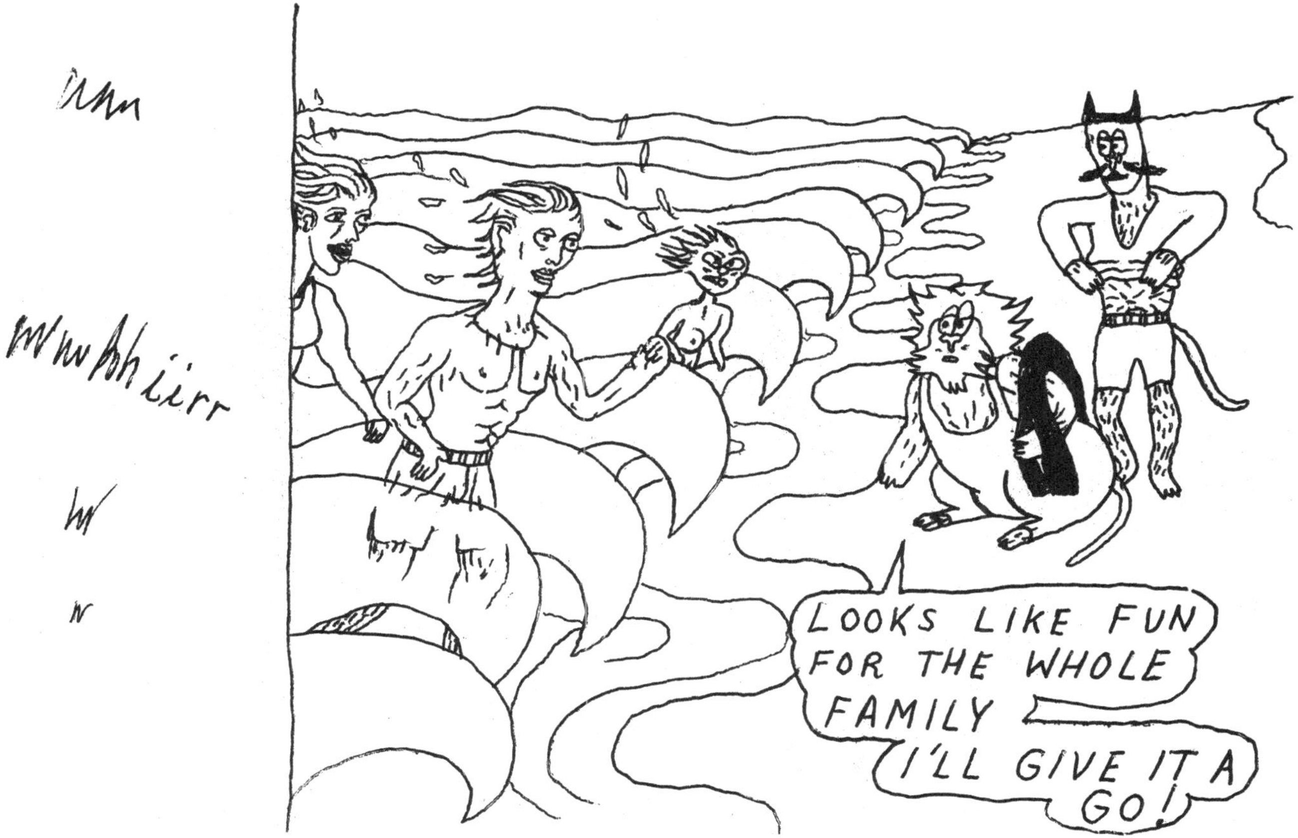
LOOKS LIKE FUN FOR THE WHOLE FAMILY
I'LL GIVE IT A GO!

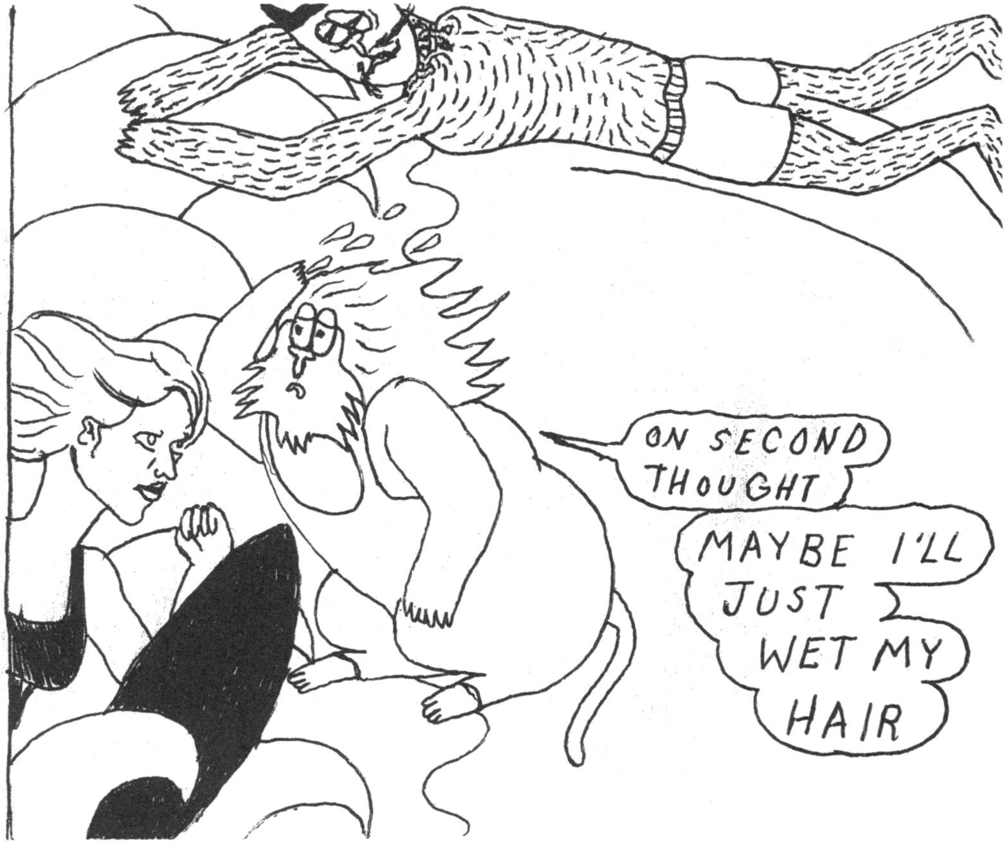
ON SECOND THOUGHT
MAYBE I'LL JUST WET MY HAIR

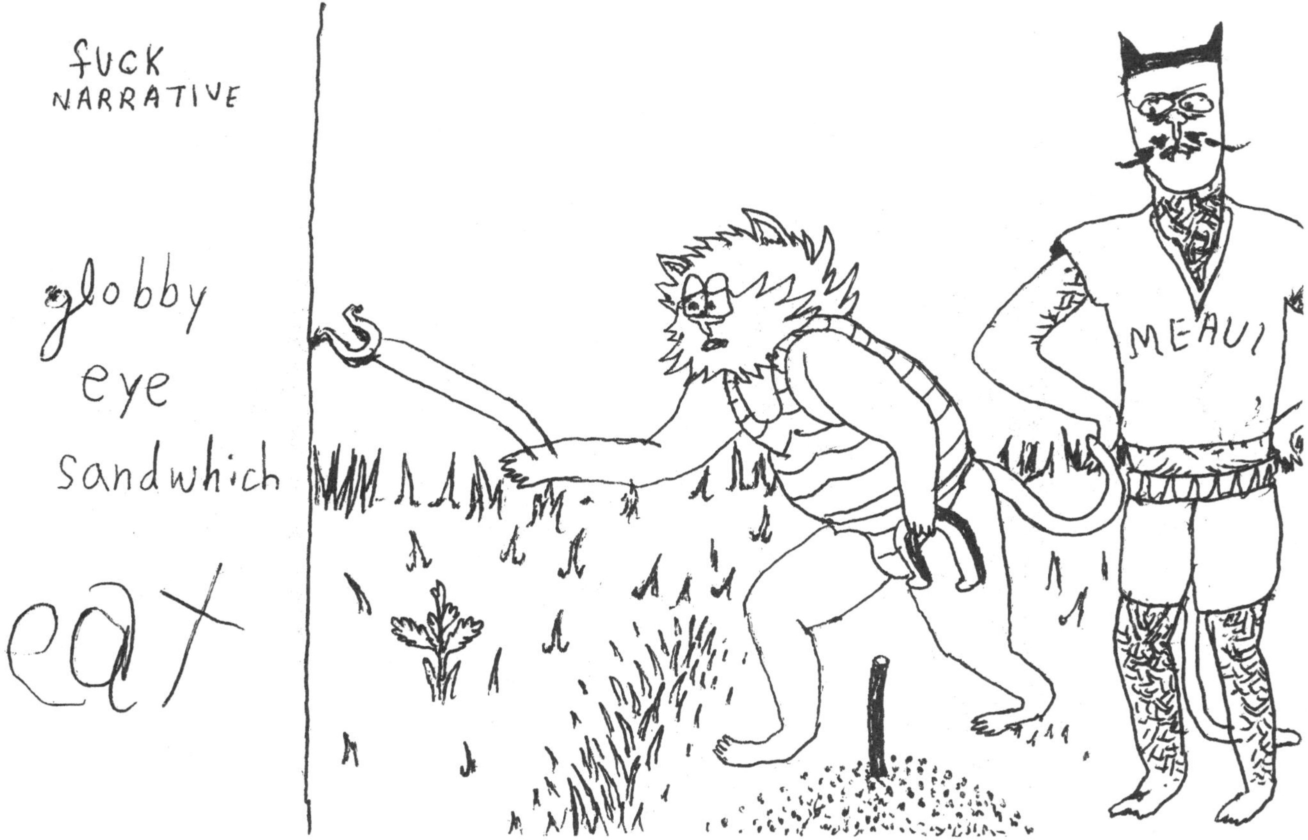
fuck
NARRATIVE
globby
eye
sandwhich
cat
MEAUI

CLOSE though...

GOOD TRY!

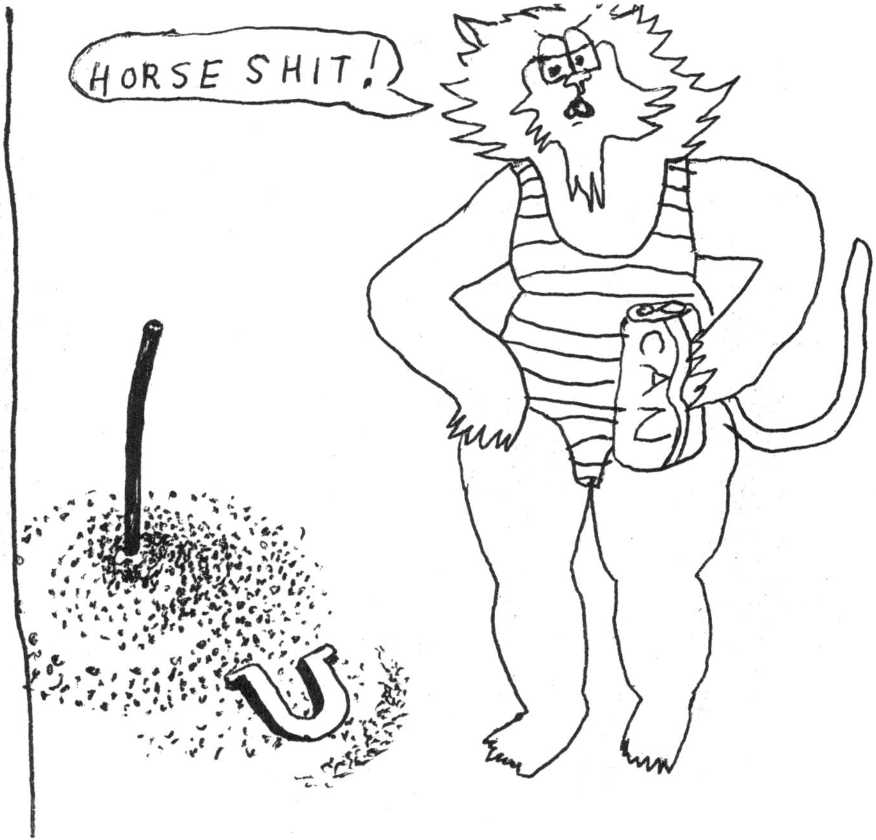

40 year toothpaste tube

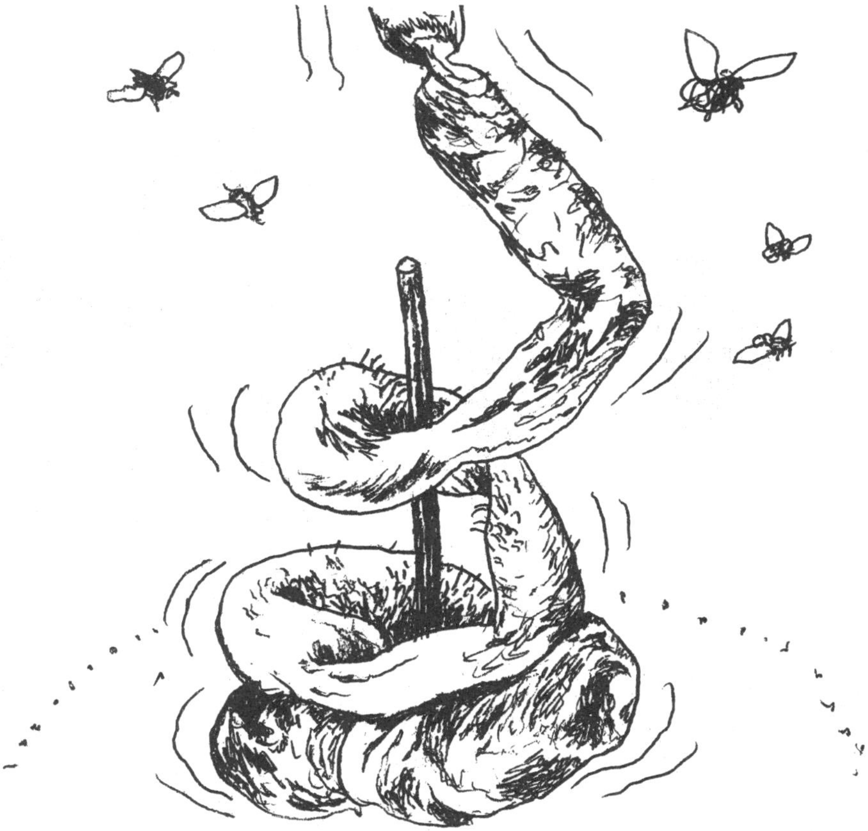

Harry Brainum

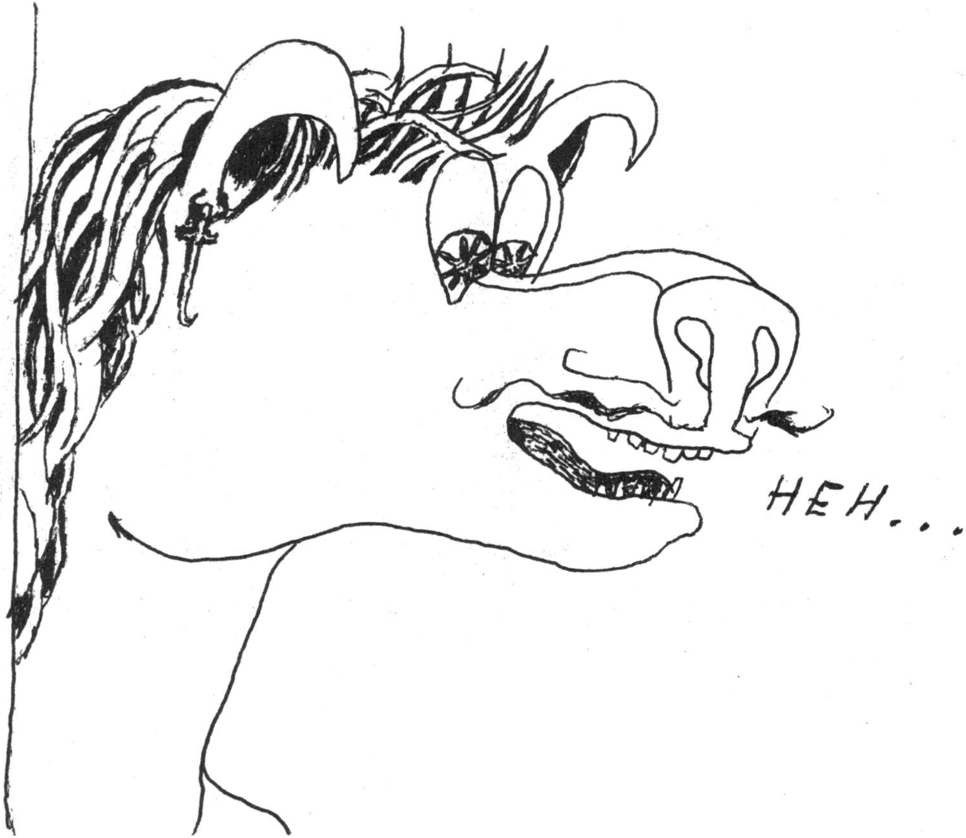
HEH...

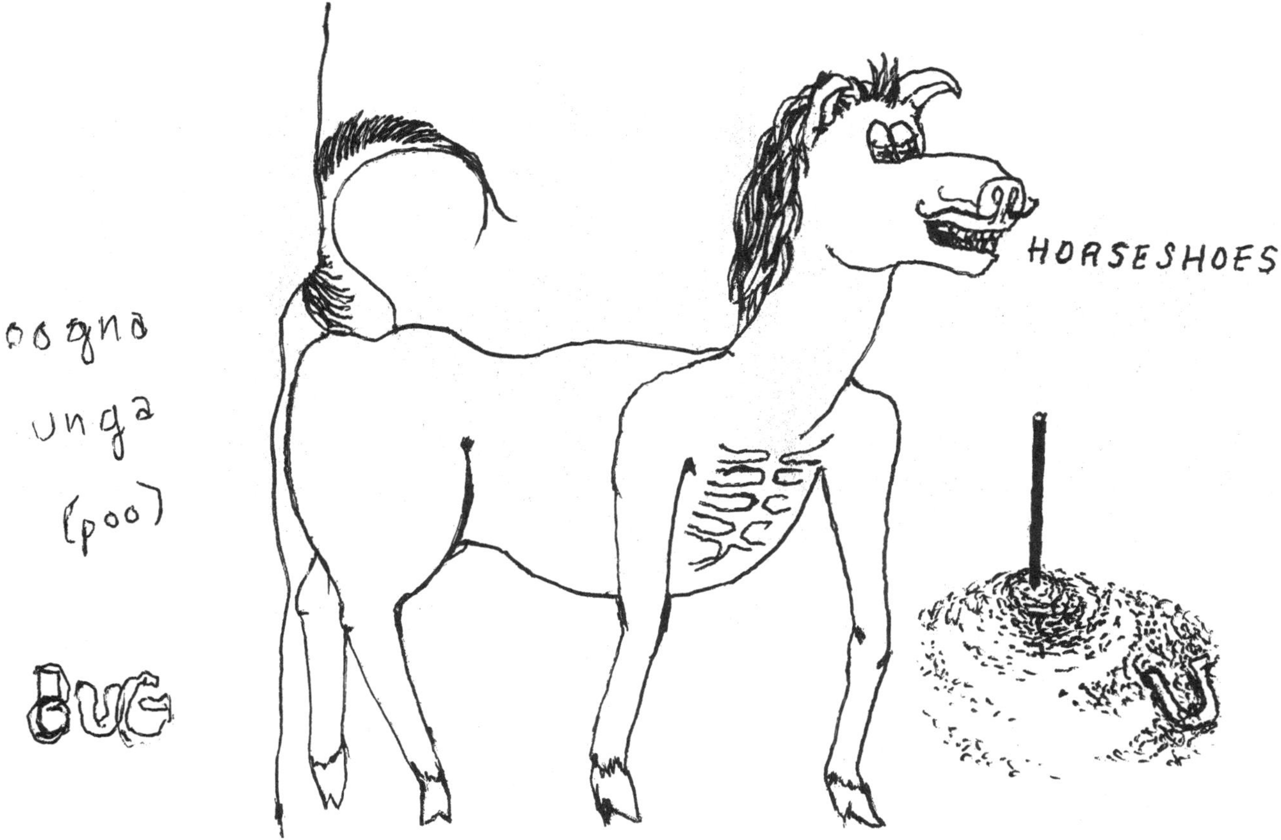

HORSESHOES
oogna
unga
(poo)
BUG

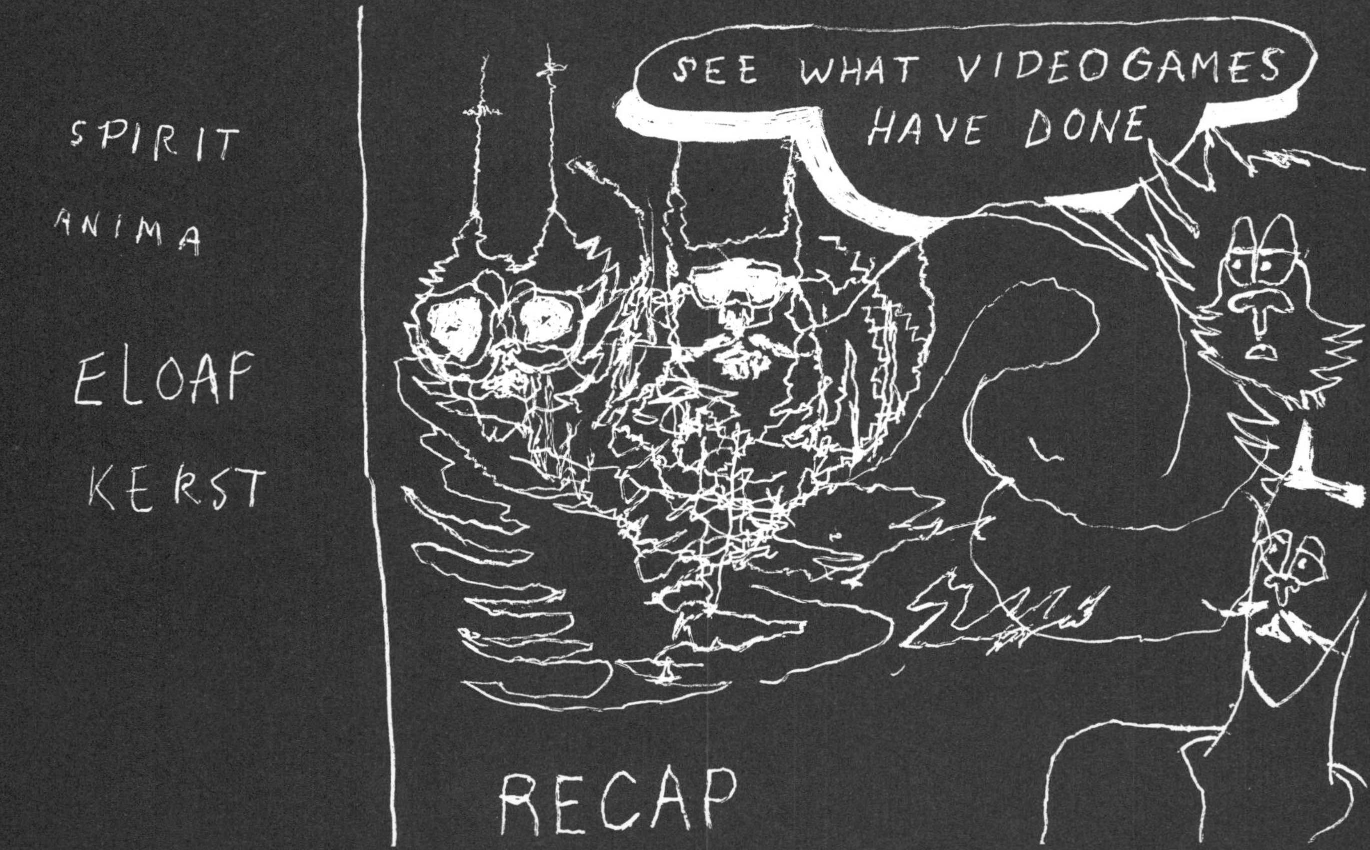
SPIRIT
ANIMA
ELOAF
KERST
SEE WHAT VIDEOGAMES HAVE DONE
RECAP

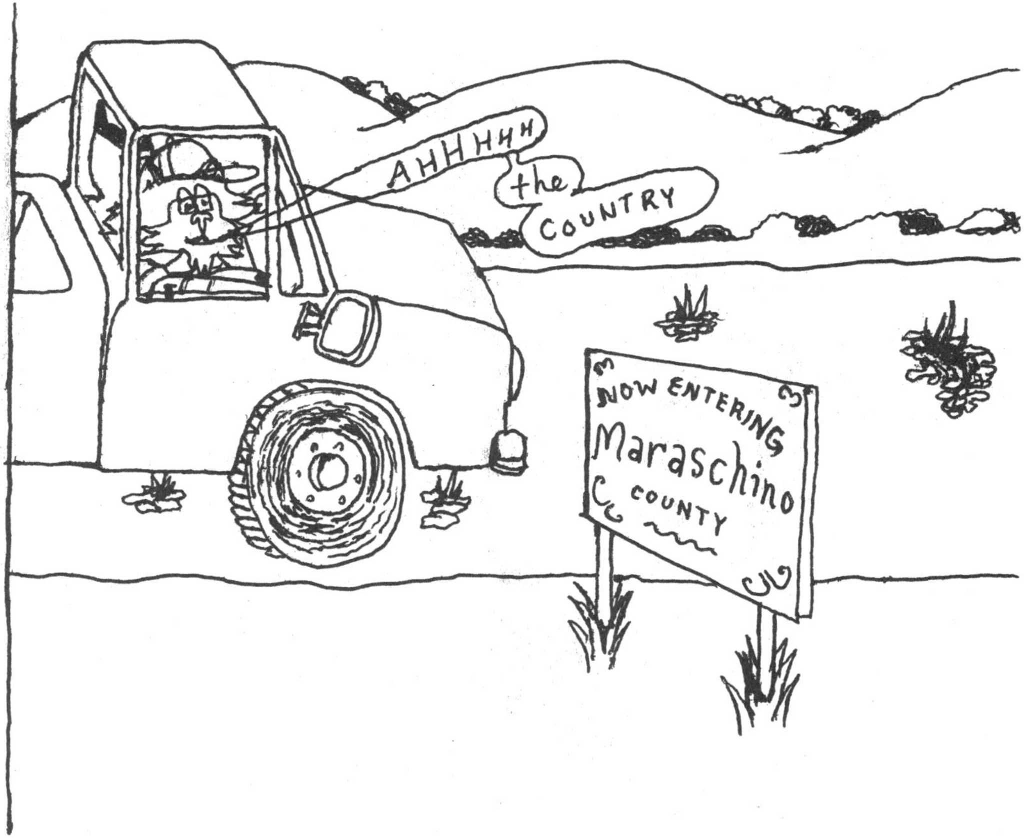
AHHHHH the COUNTRY
NOW ENTERING
Maraschino
COUNTY

John
DEERE
TICKS
nothin' ticks
like A DEERE

the CATS
have befriended
STRIPES

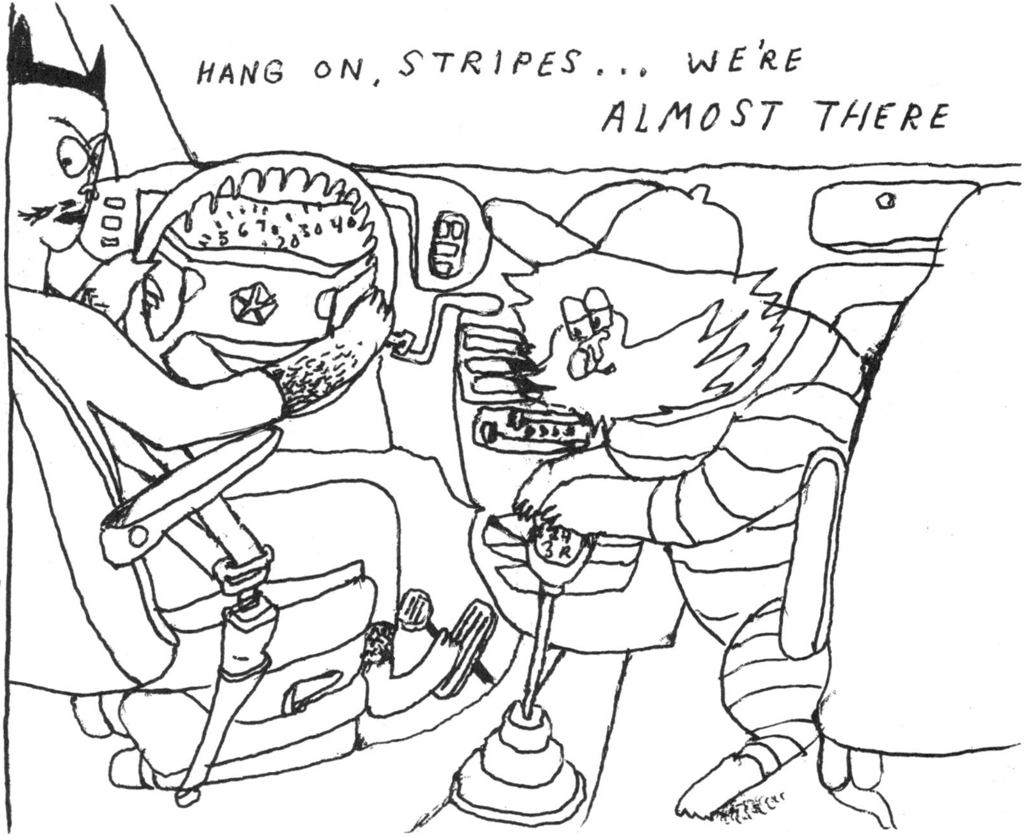

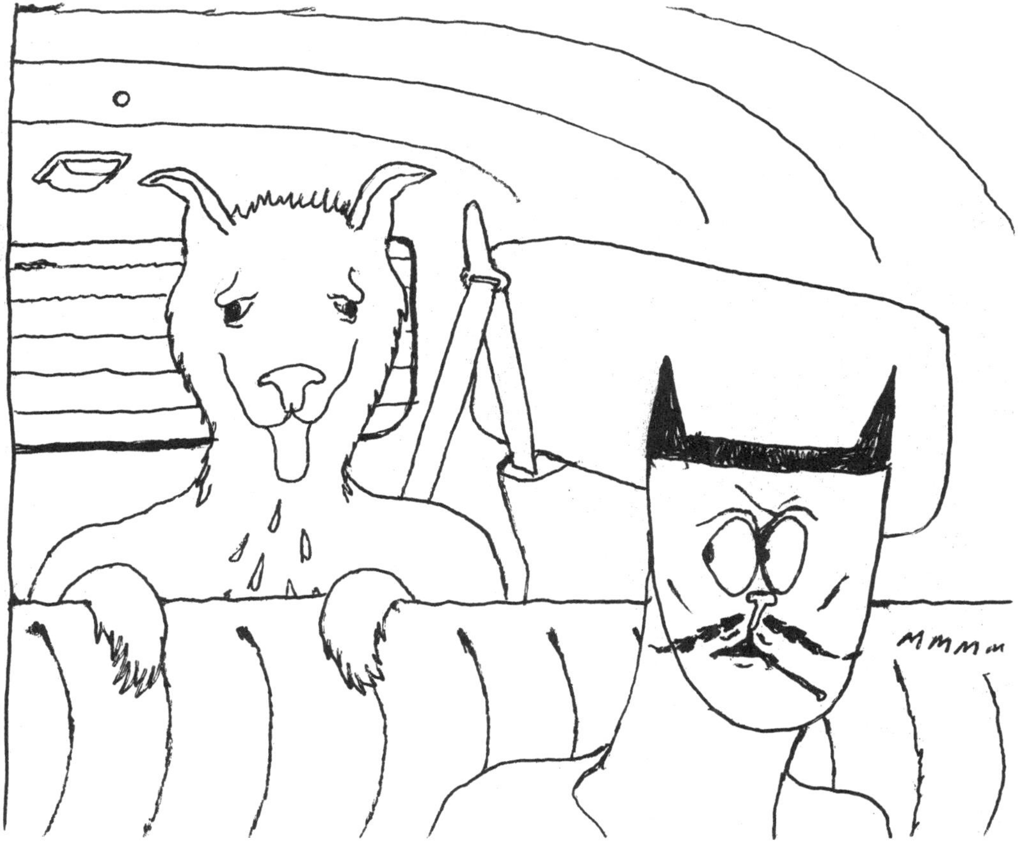
MMMm

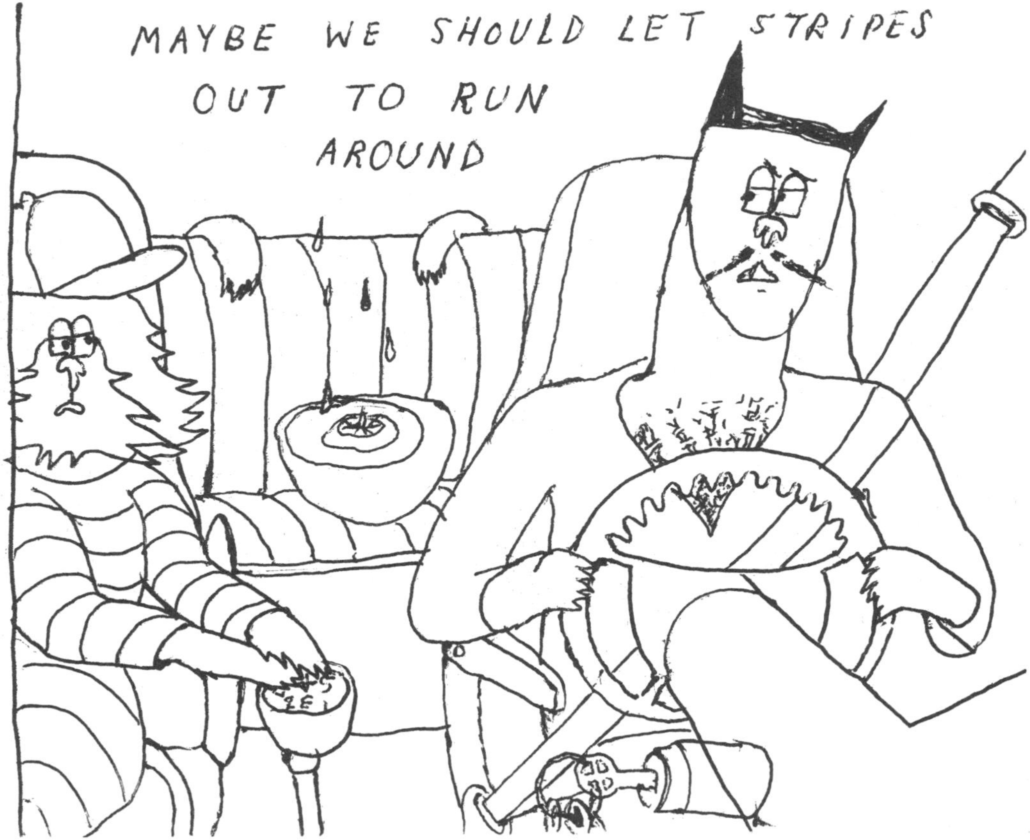
MAYBE WE SHOULD LET STRIPES OUT TO RUN AROUND

RAID

PHARM

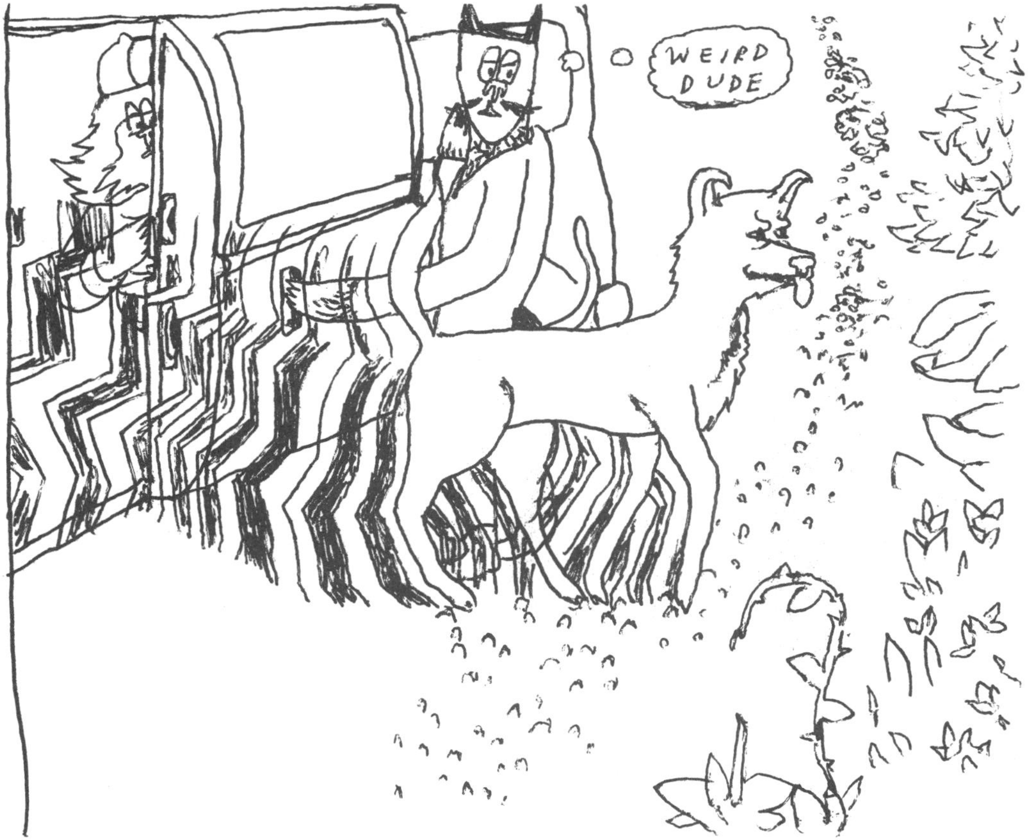
WEIRD DUDE

RESORT TO NOTHING

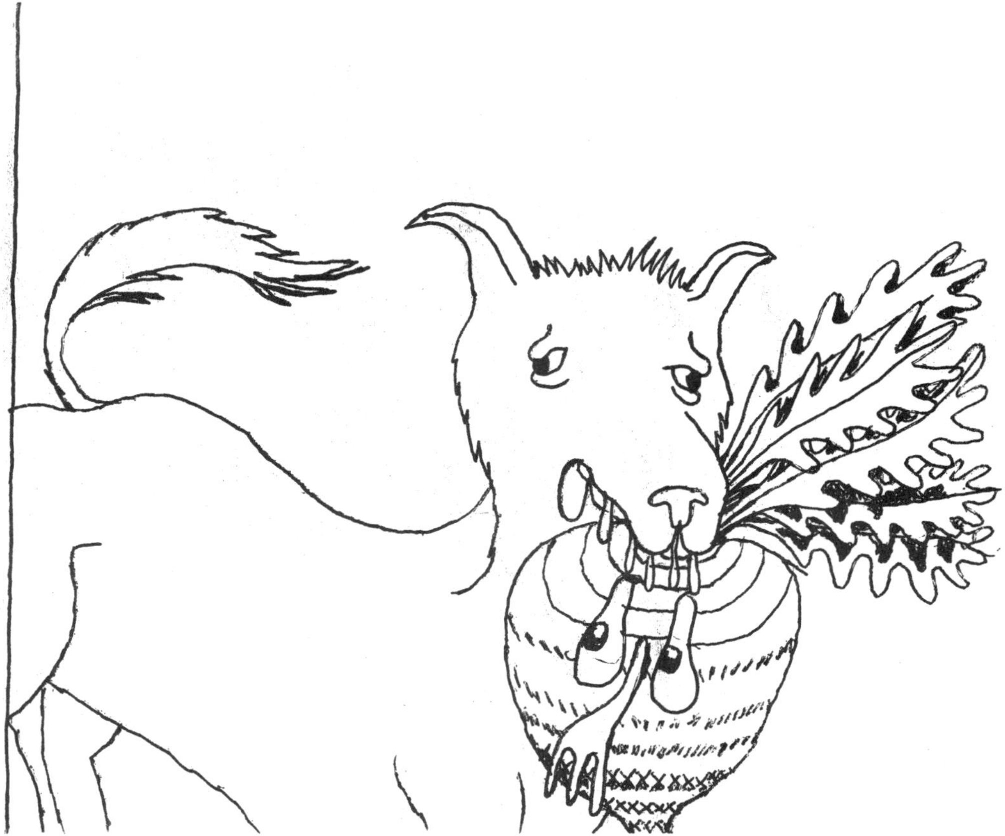

Earth Space
Inhabitants

prunella

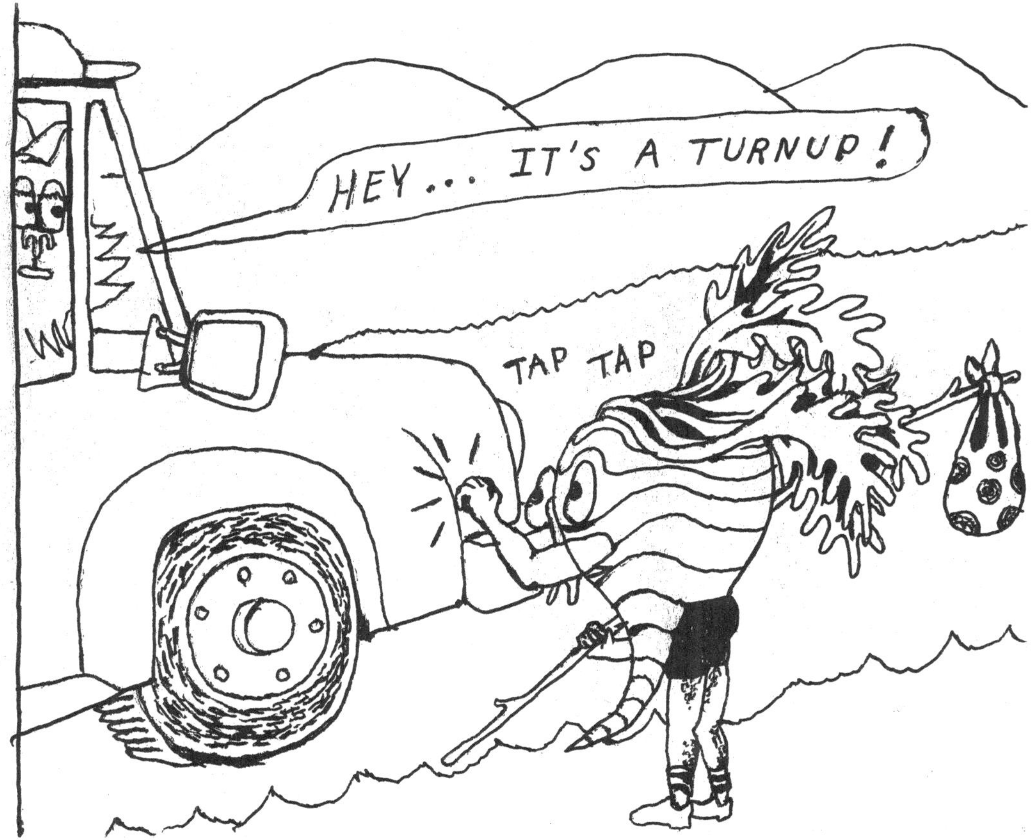
HEY... IT'S A TURNUP!
TAP TAP

y'ears

years
of
re-search

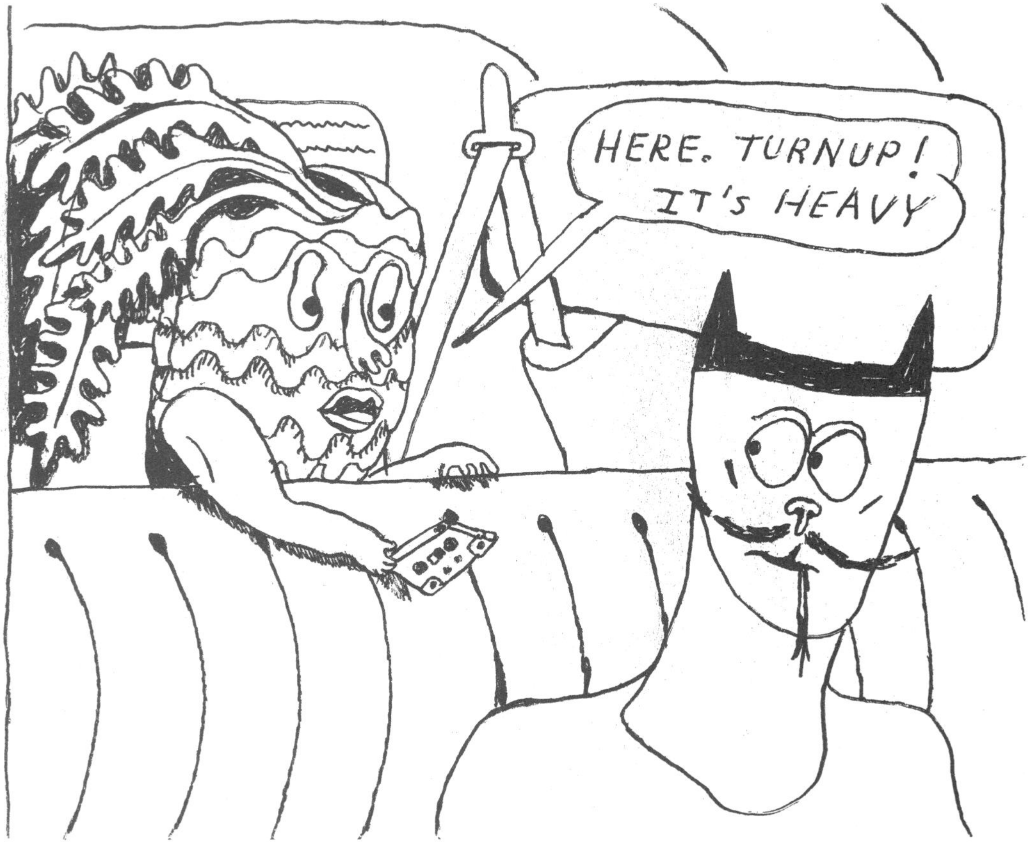
HERE. TURNUP! IT'S HEAVY

Foot
on
the
GAS

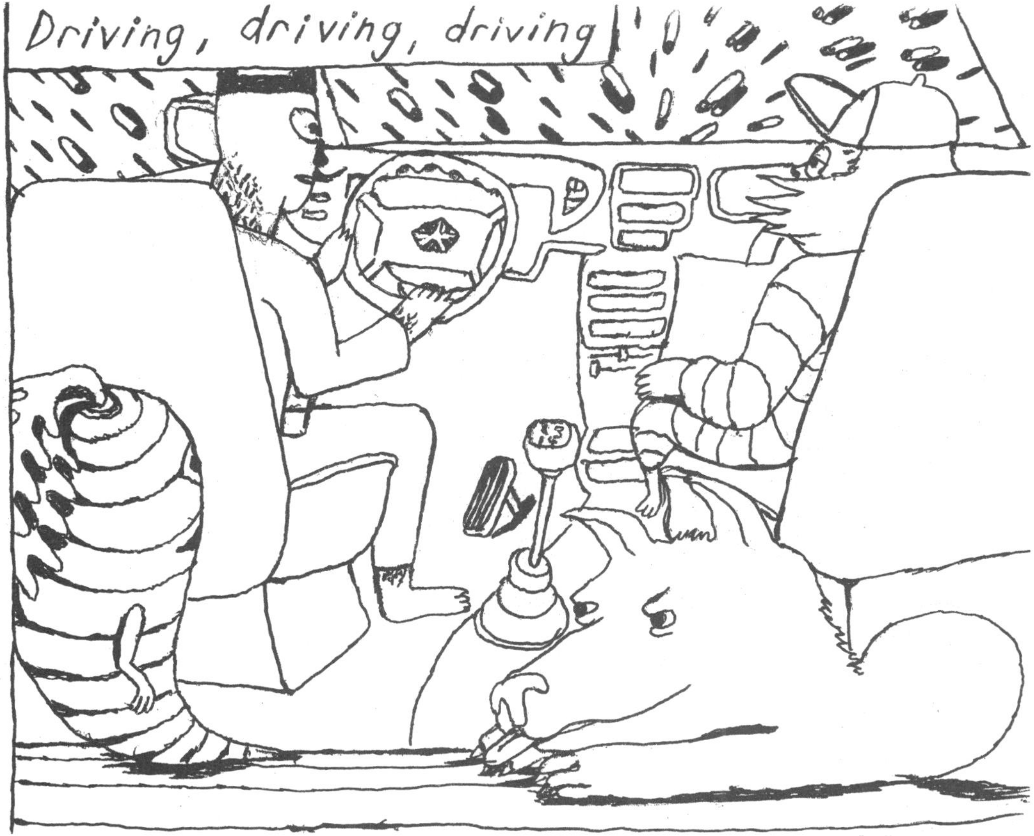
Driving, driving, driving

confetti

+

meat-
blas

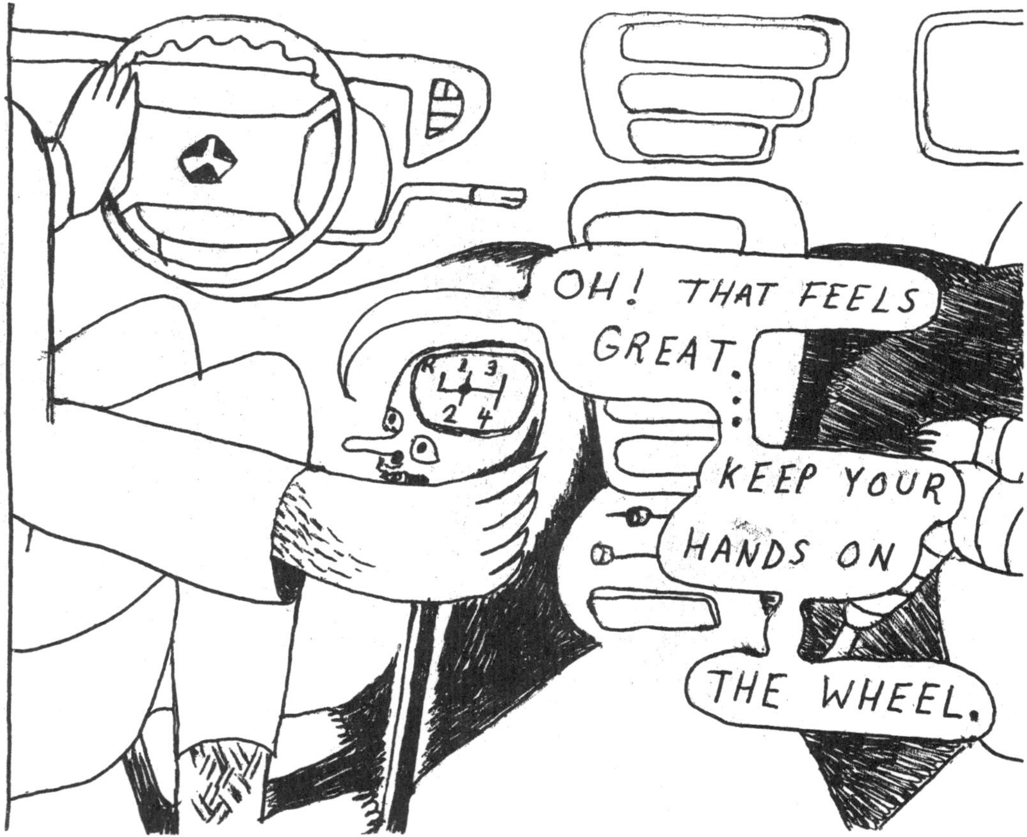
OH! THAT FEELS GREAT.
KEEP YOUR HANDS ON THE WHEEL.

NO PAYOFF !!!

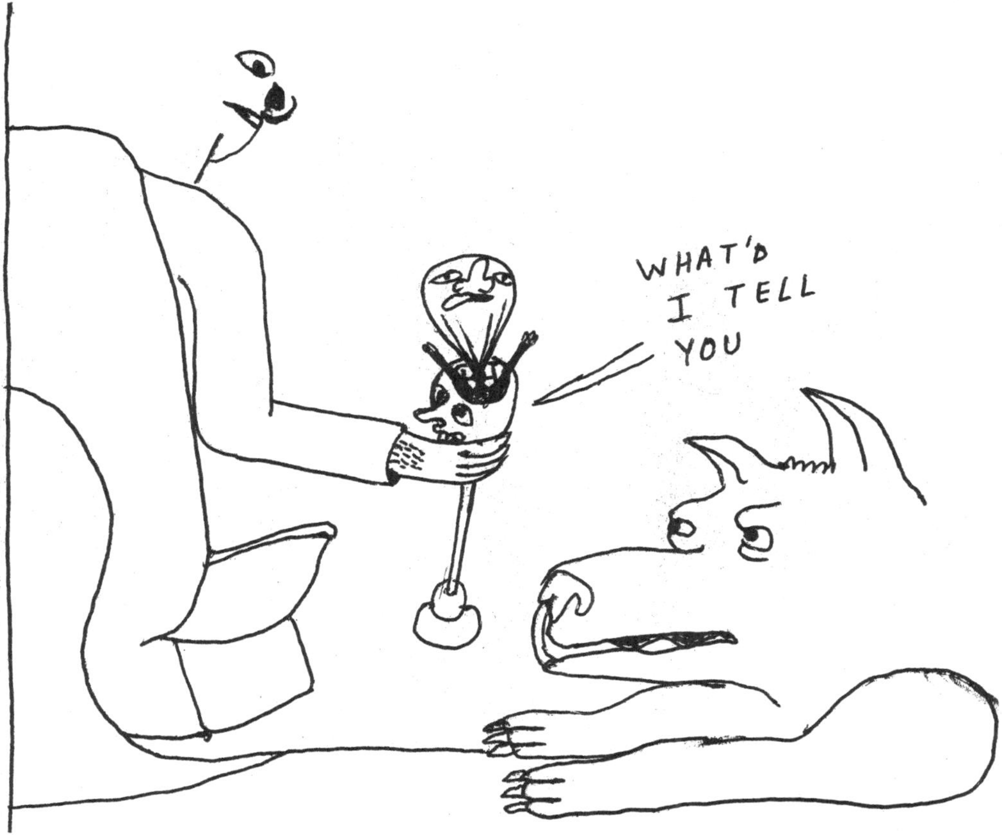

gravel

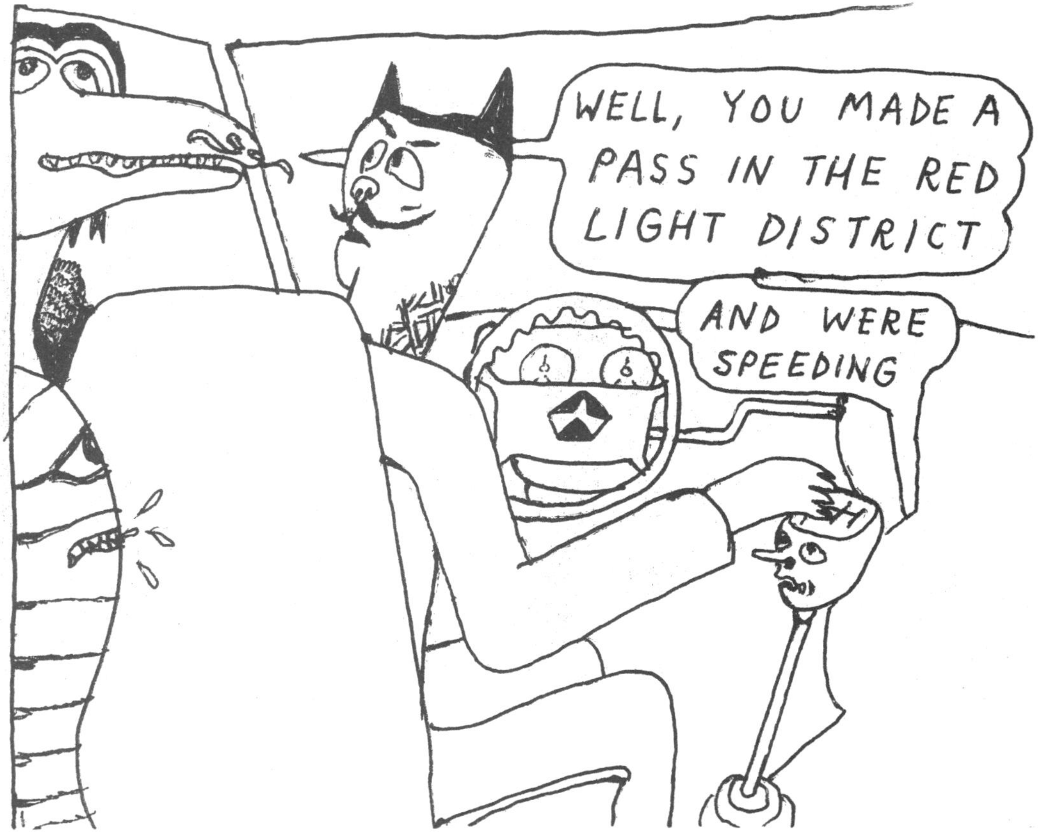
WELL, YOU MADE A PASS IN THE RED LIGHT DISTRICT
AND WERE SPEEDING

HOW CAN YOU GET AWAY WITH THIS SH*T?

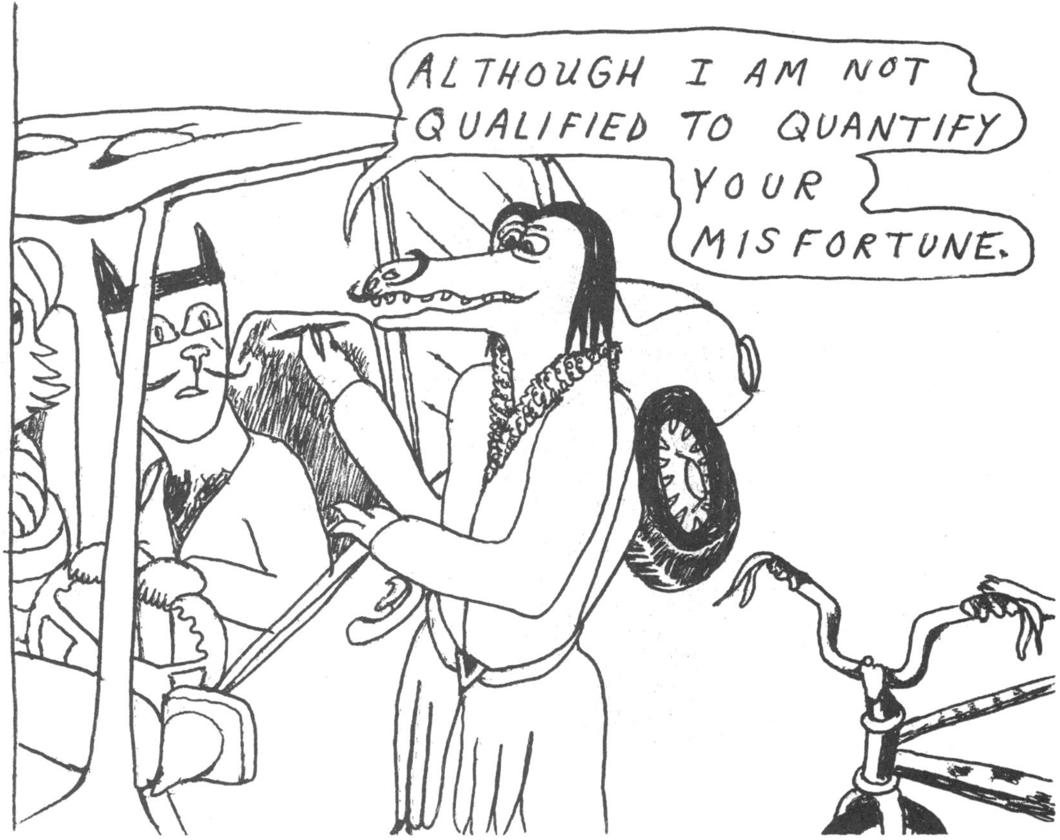
ALTHOUGH I AM NOT QUALIFIED TO QUANTIFY YOUR MISFORTUNE.

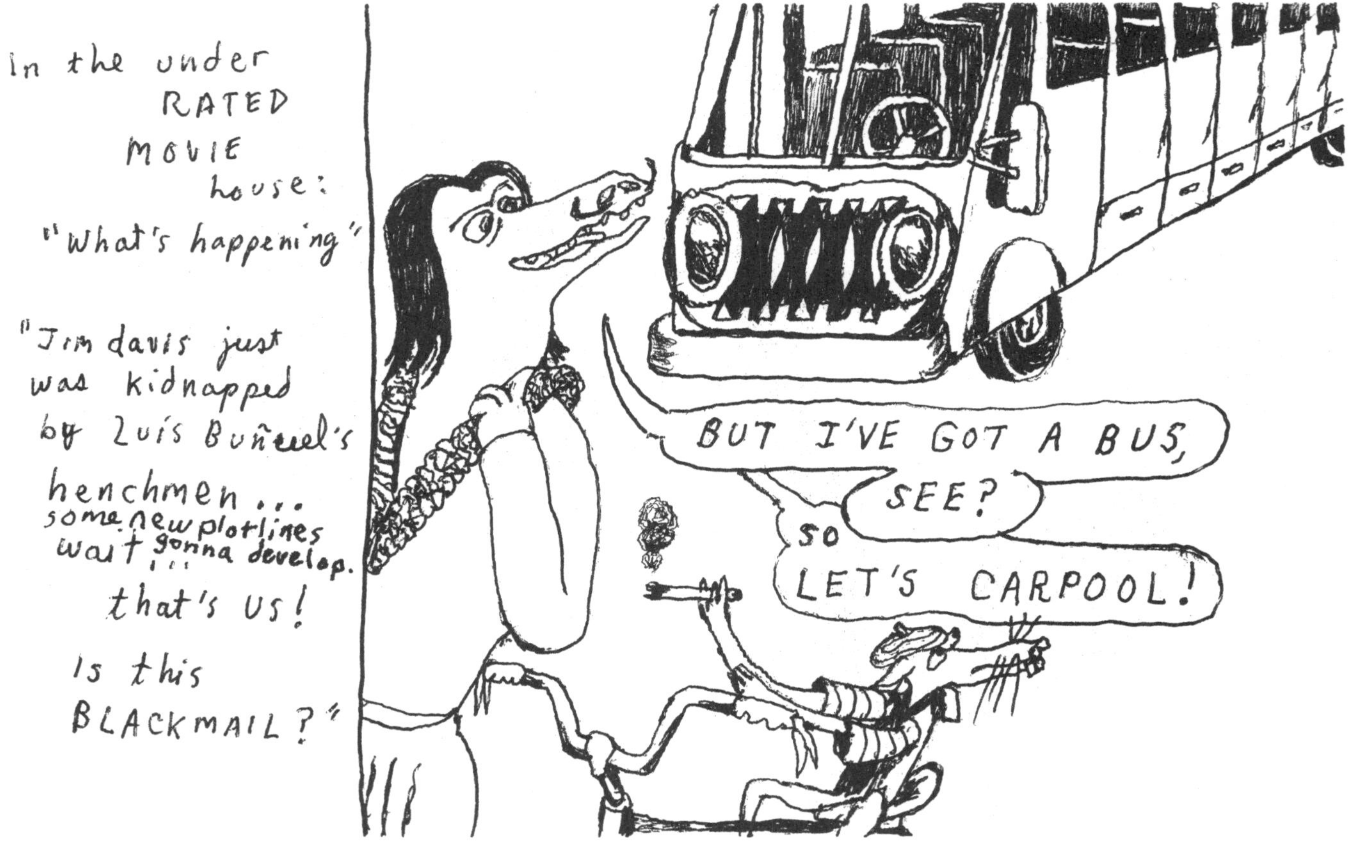
In the under RATED MOVIE house:
"What's happening"
"Jim davis just was kidnapped by Luis Buñuel's henchmen...
some new plotlines gonna develop.
wait...
that's us!
Is this BLACKMAIL?"
BUT I'VE GOT A BUS, SEE?
SO LET'S CARPOOL!

sir
puss

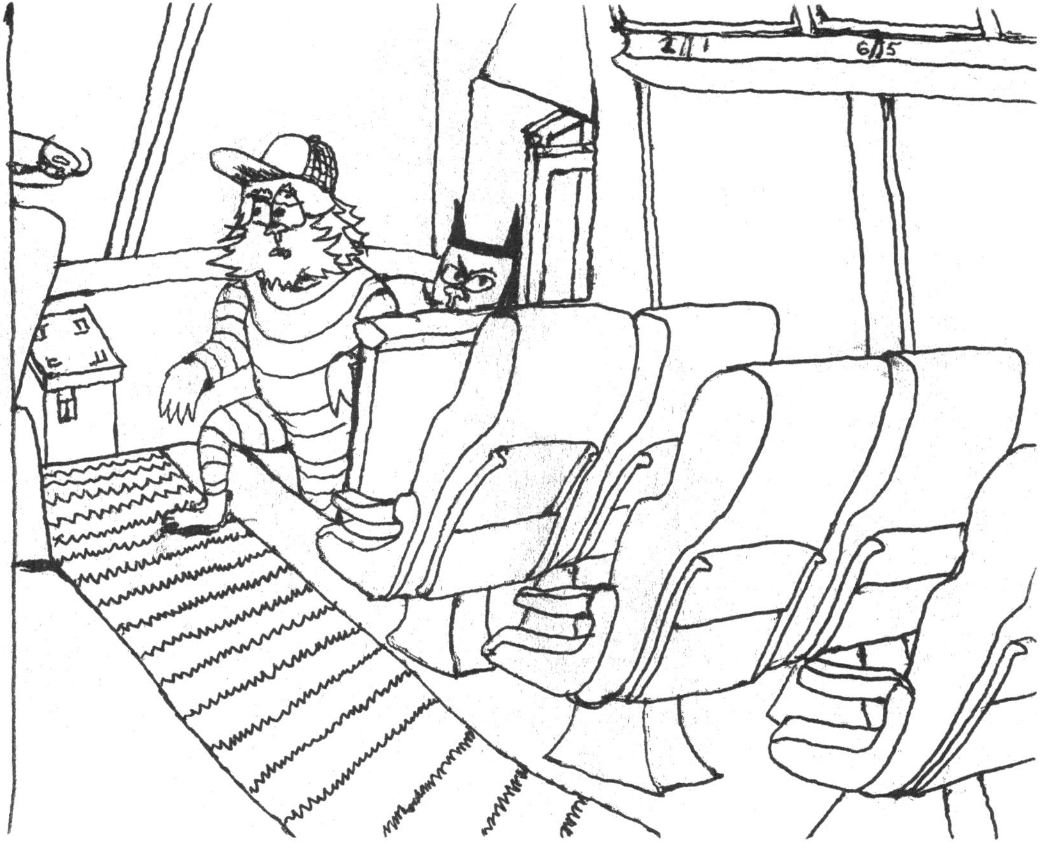
2 1
6 5

situation comedy

a.
f.
u.

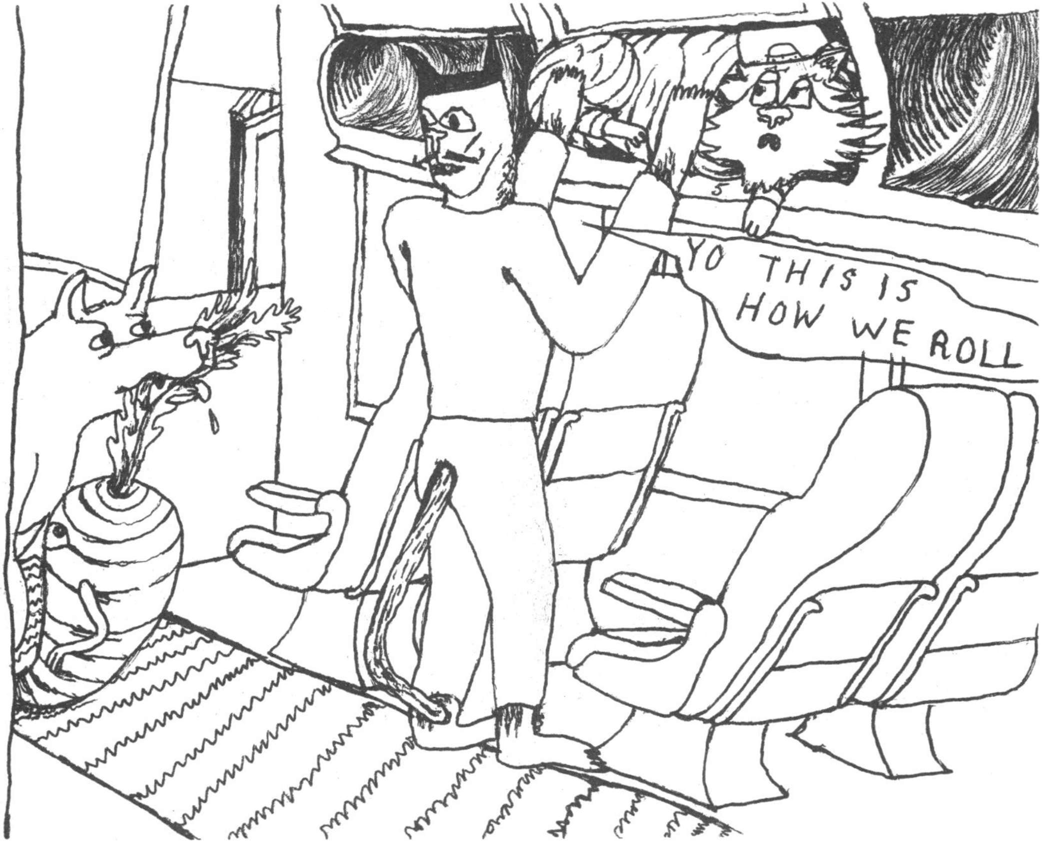
YO THIS IS HOW WE ROLL

Jean Benoît hides inside a hollow tree

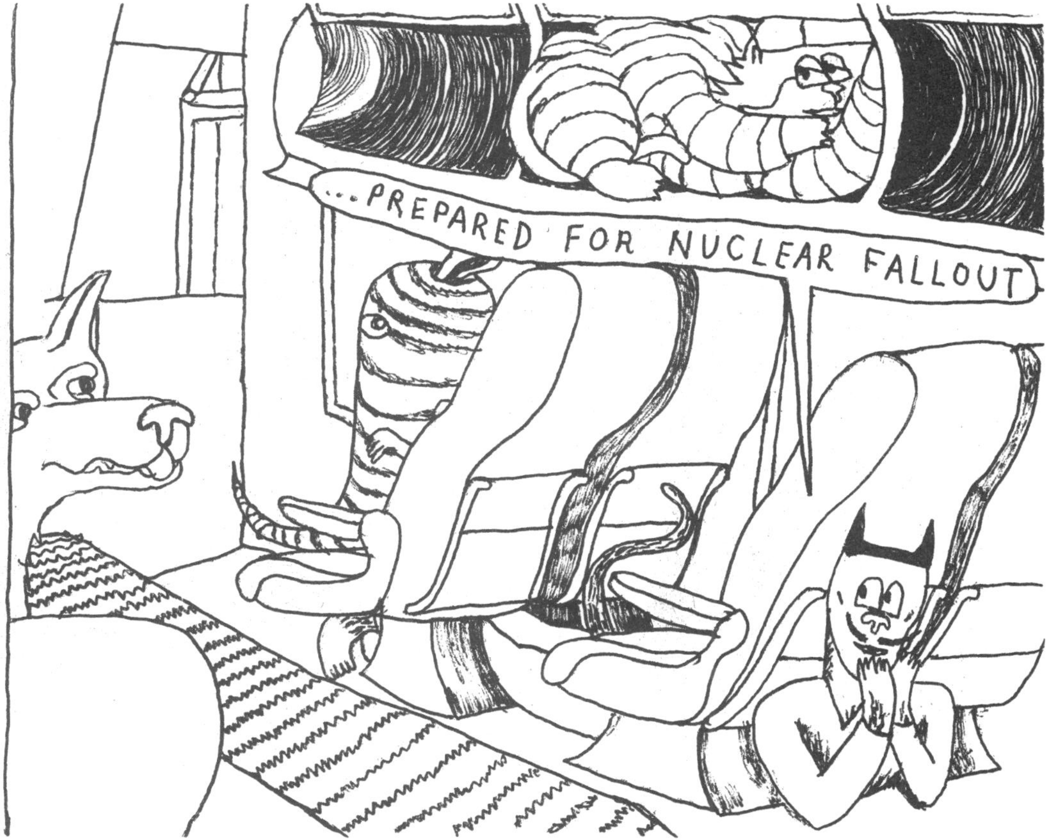
...PREPARED FOR NUCLEAR FALLOUT

Obama

SAID

"NUCULAR"

Love is
a
Battlefield

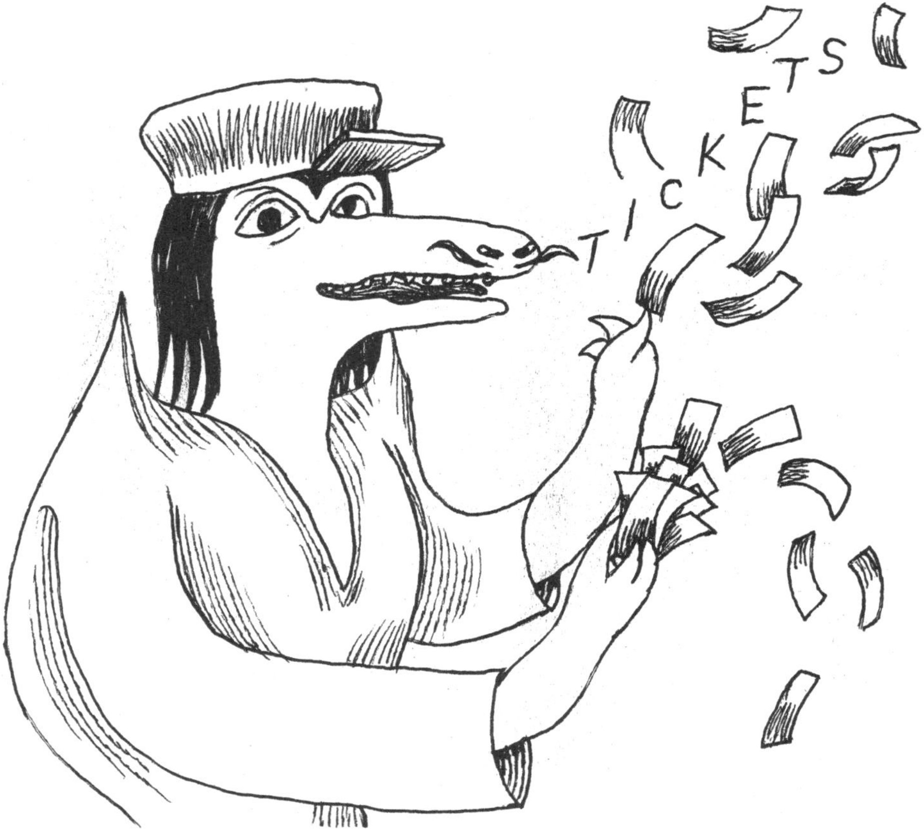
TICKETS

What am I doing?

I can't drive a car!

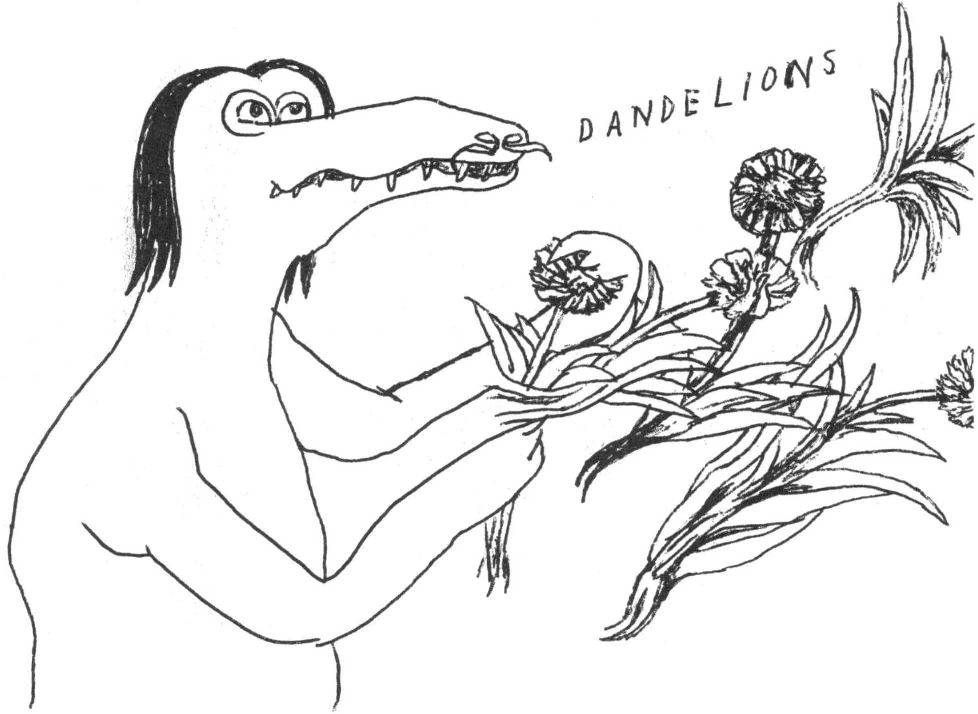
DANDELIONS

"carte blanche"

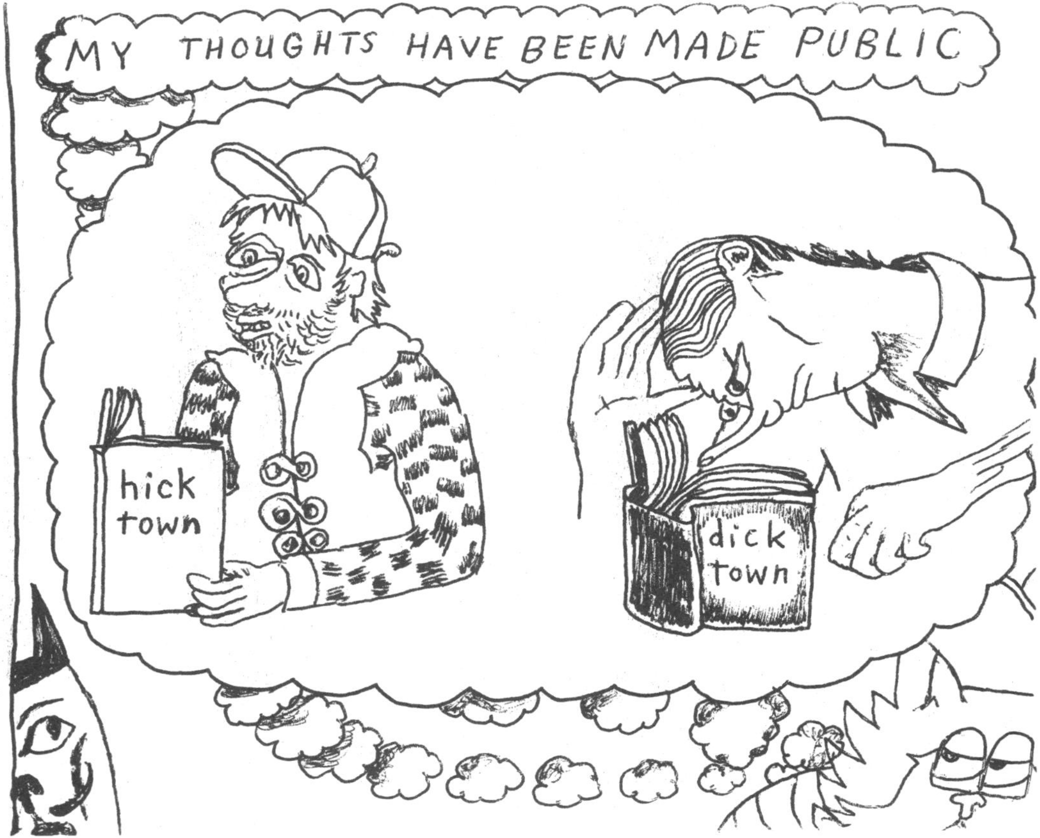
MY THOUGHTS HAVE BEEN MADE PUBLIC
hick town
dick town

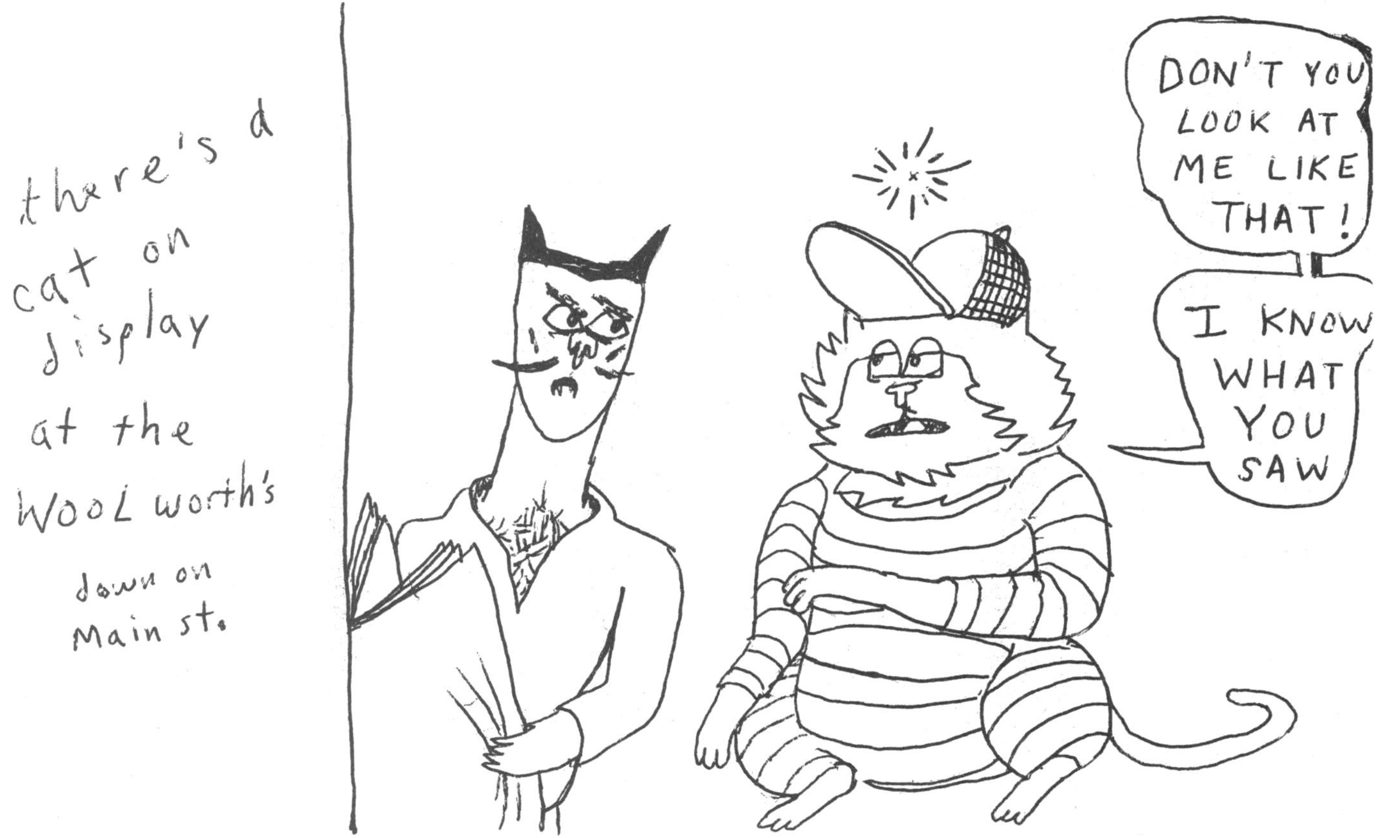
there's a cat on display at the Woolworth's
down on Main st.
DON'T YOU LOOK AT ME LIKE THAT!
I KNOW WHAT YOU SAW

grey matters

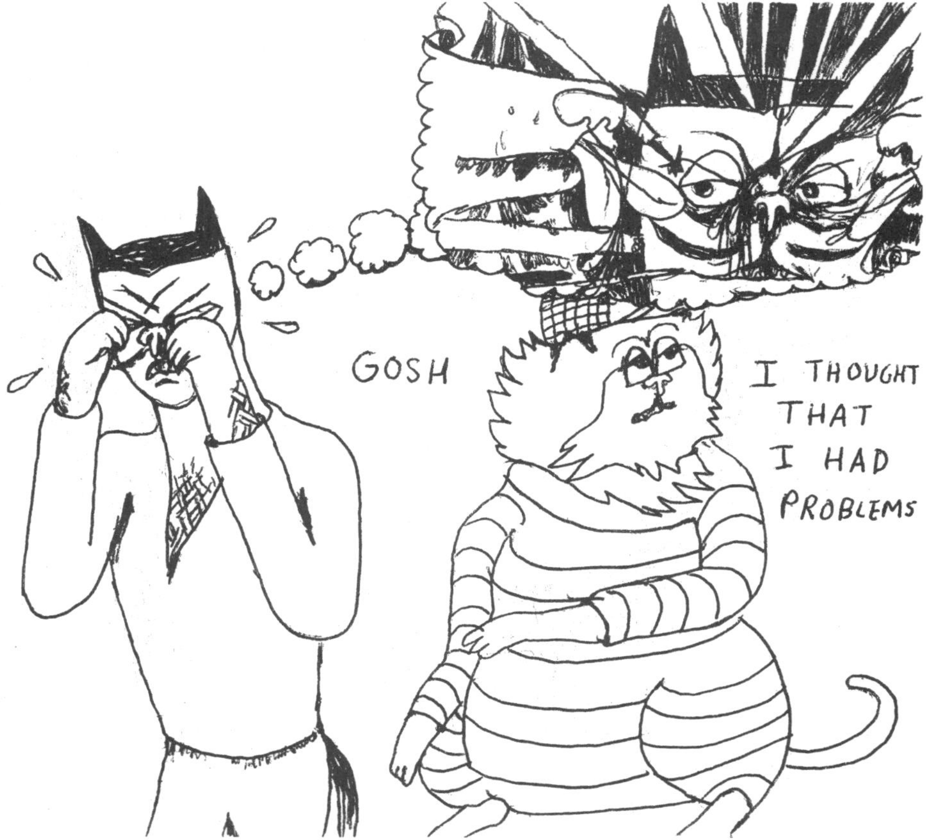
GOSH
I THOUGHT THAT I HAD PROBLEMS

$30 foor a book?

fer re?.

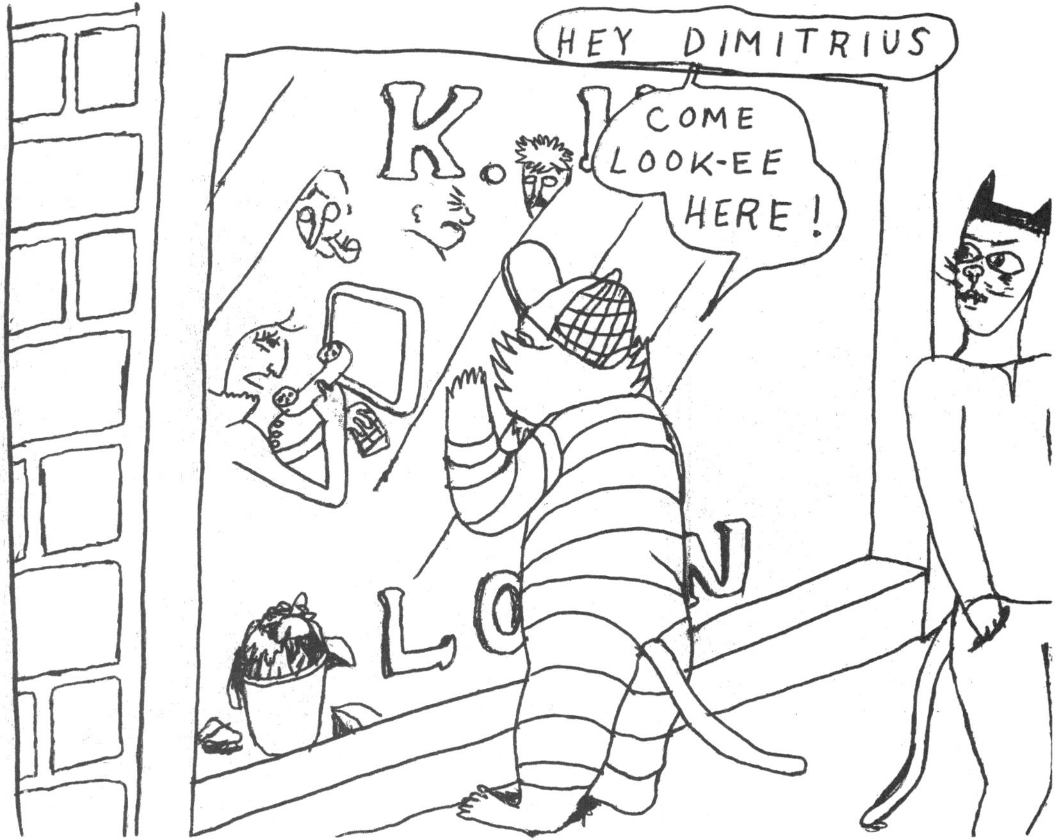
HEY DIMITRIUS
COME LOOK-EE HERE!

CRUD ALL OVER the floor

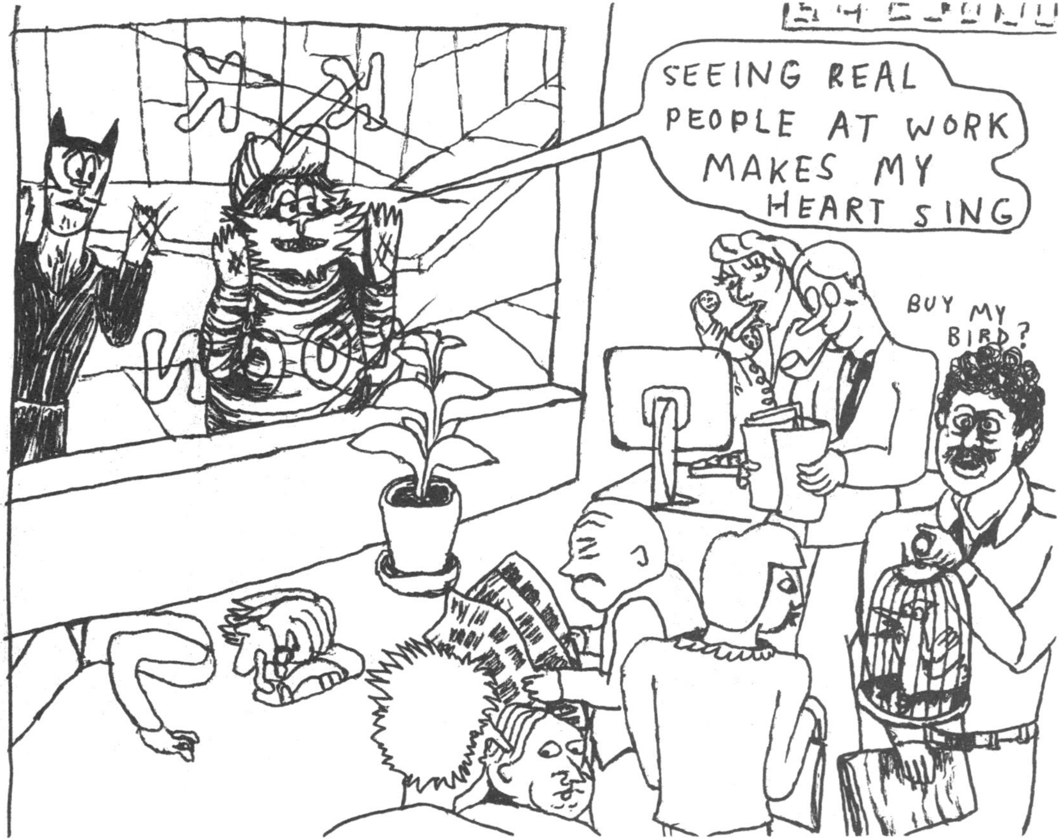

SCAFU

S.C.A.F.U.

* Situation

* comedy

* ALL

* F***ed

* UP

Allegheney
river
theater

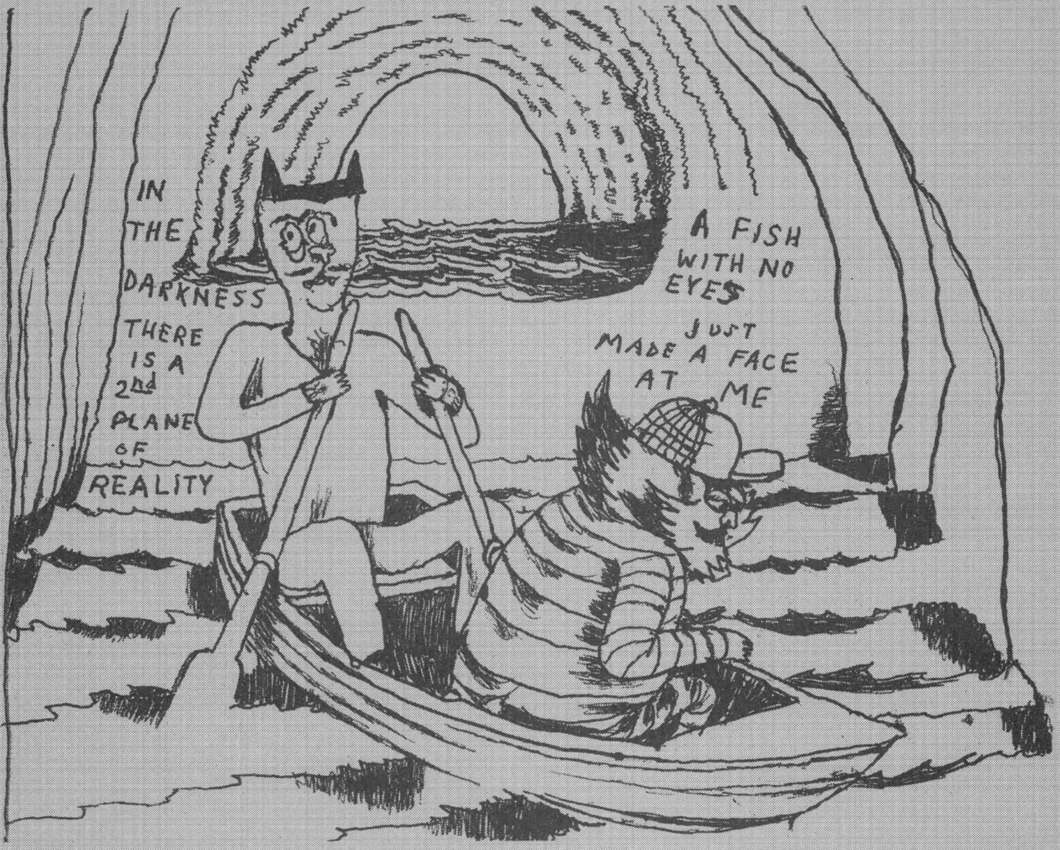
IN THE DARKNESS THERE IS A 2nd PLANE OF REALITY
A FISH WITH NO EYES JUST MADE A FACE AT ME

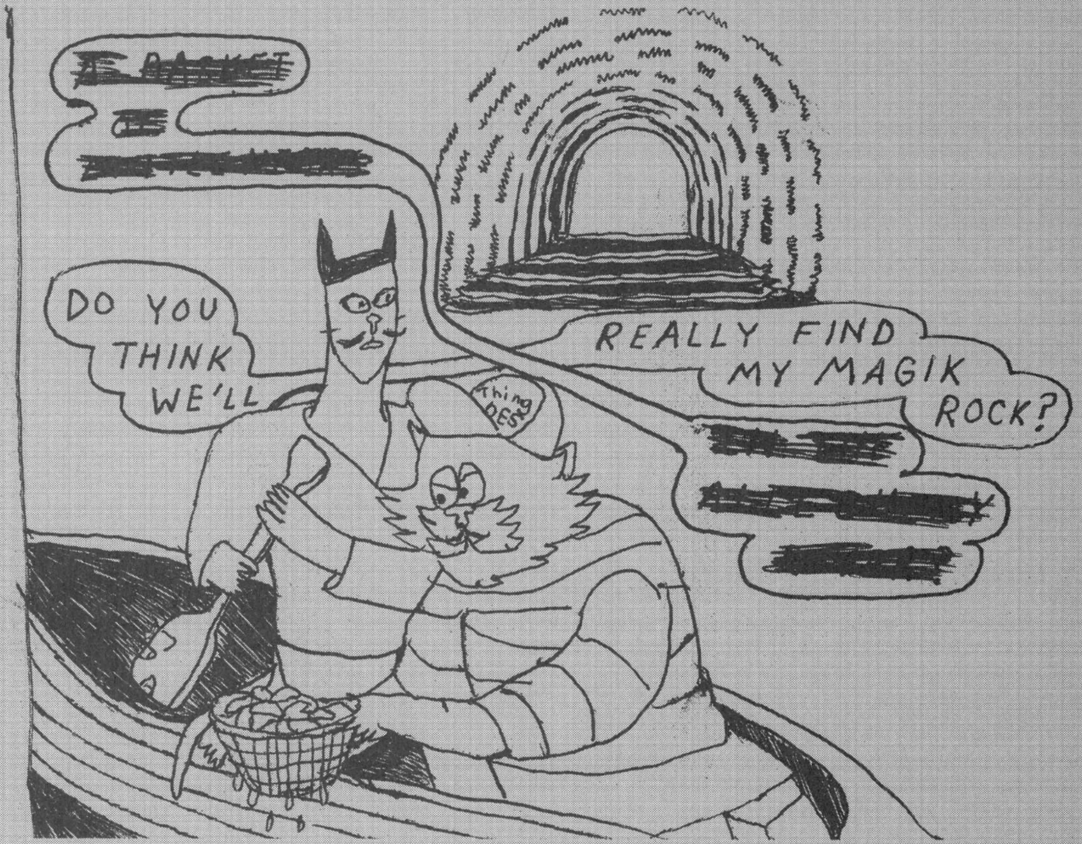
[redacted]
DO YOU THINK WE'LL
REALLY FIND MY MAGIK ROCK?
[redacted]
Thing DES

wit less boards

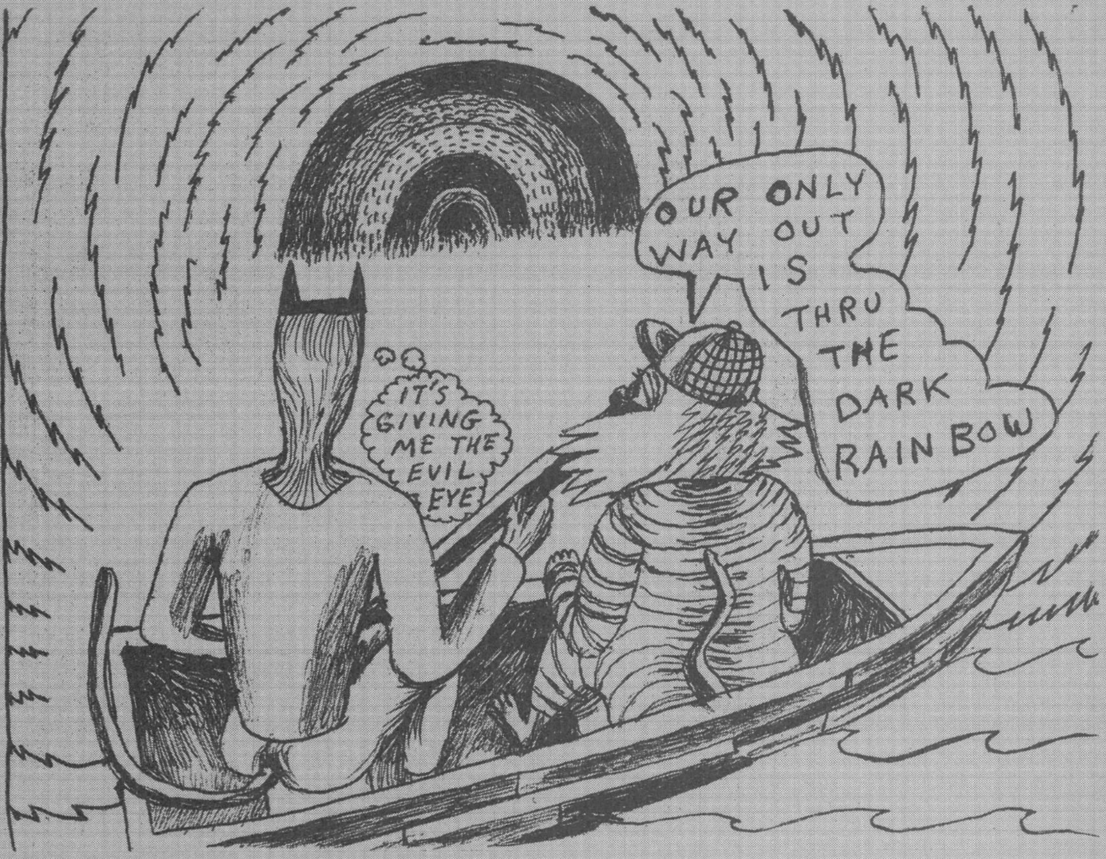
IT'S GIVING ME THE EVIL EYE
OUR ONLY WAY OUT IS THRU THE DARK RAIN BOW

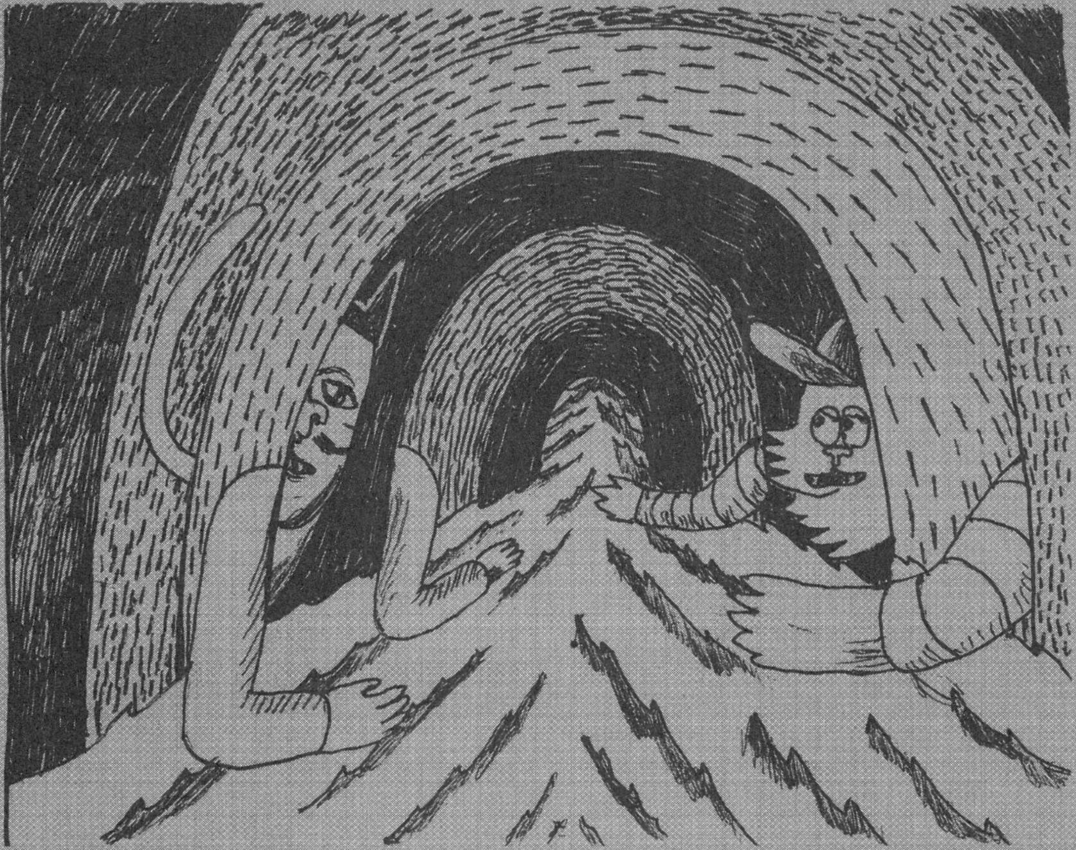

philo

1
oh
1

100%
verified
POTTY
reading

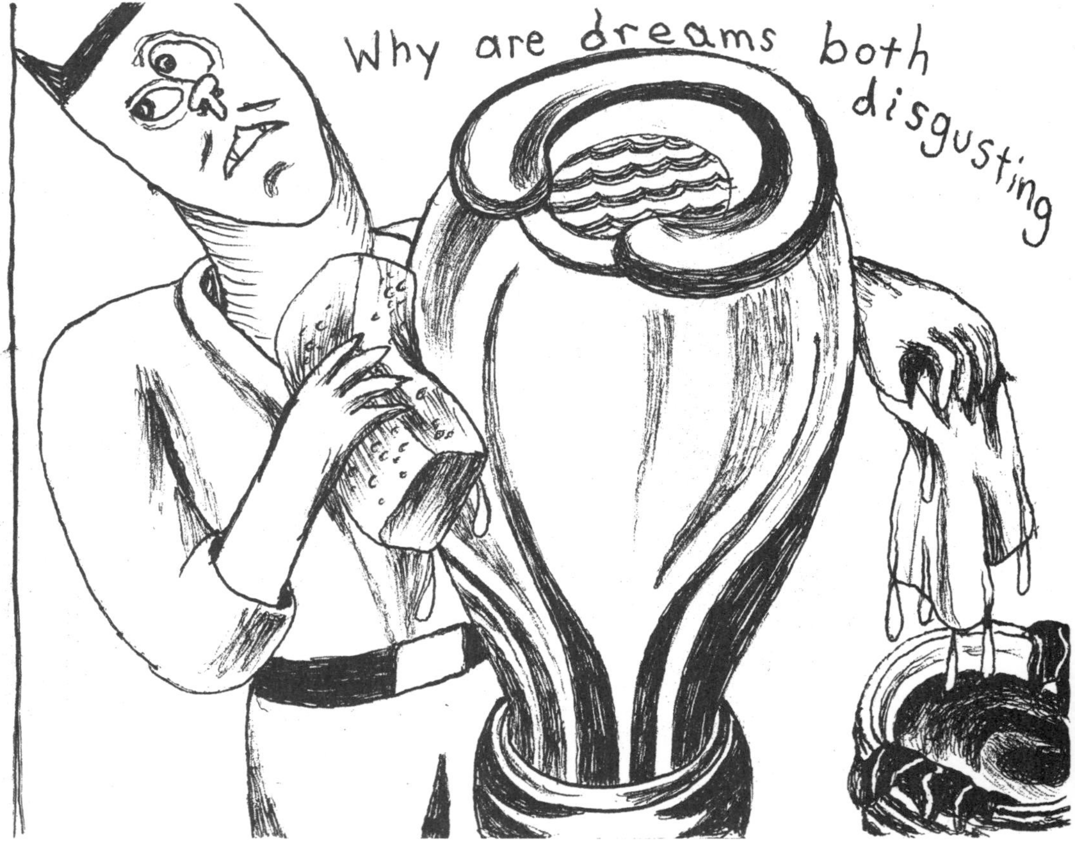
Why are dreams both disgusting

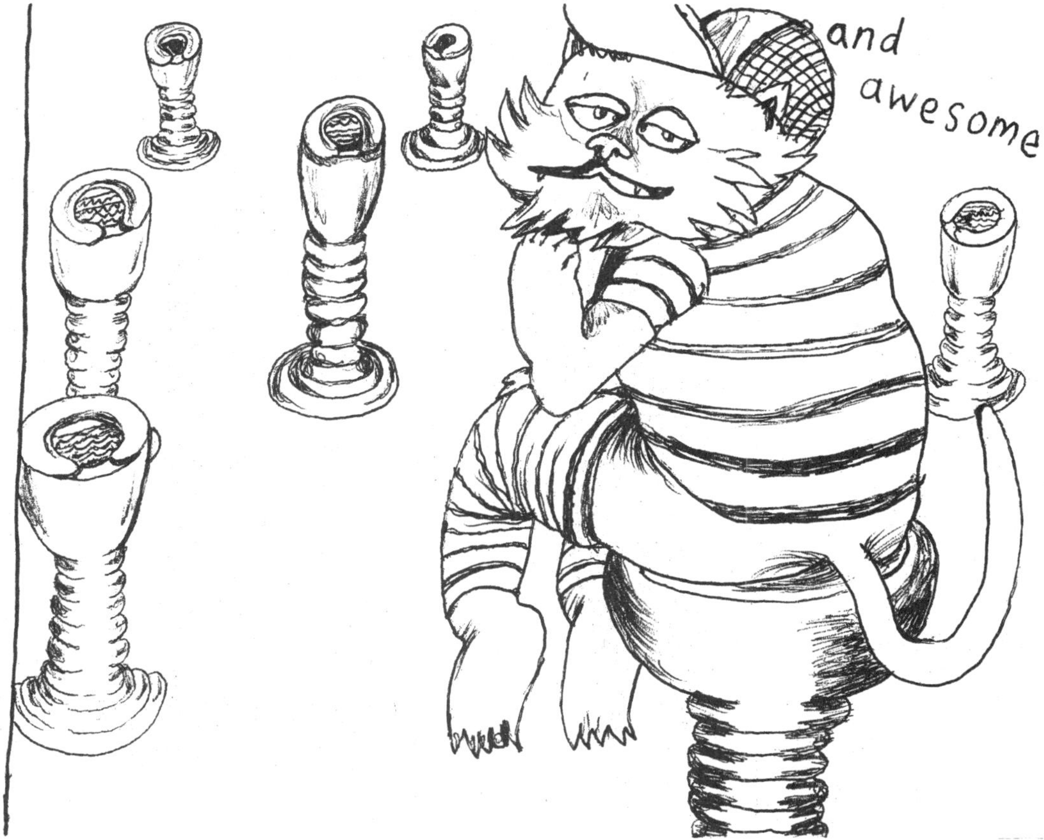
and
awesome

WC

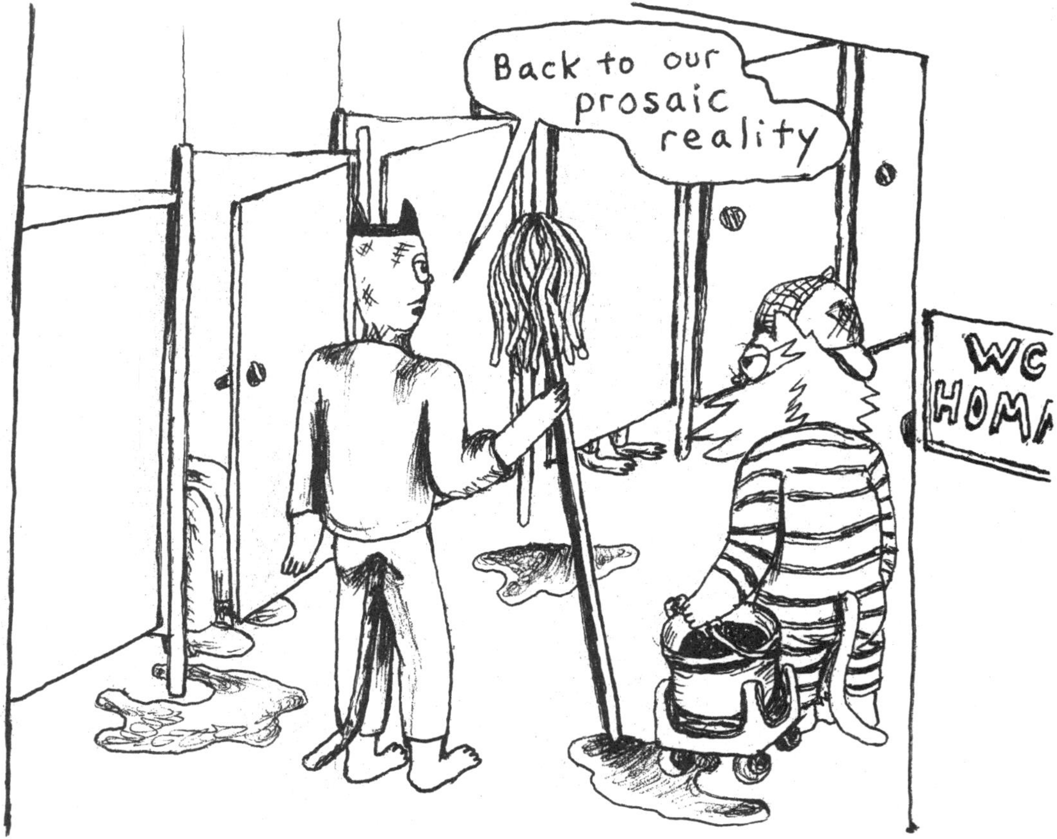

archival
ball
point

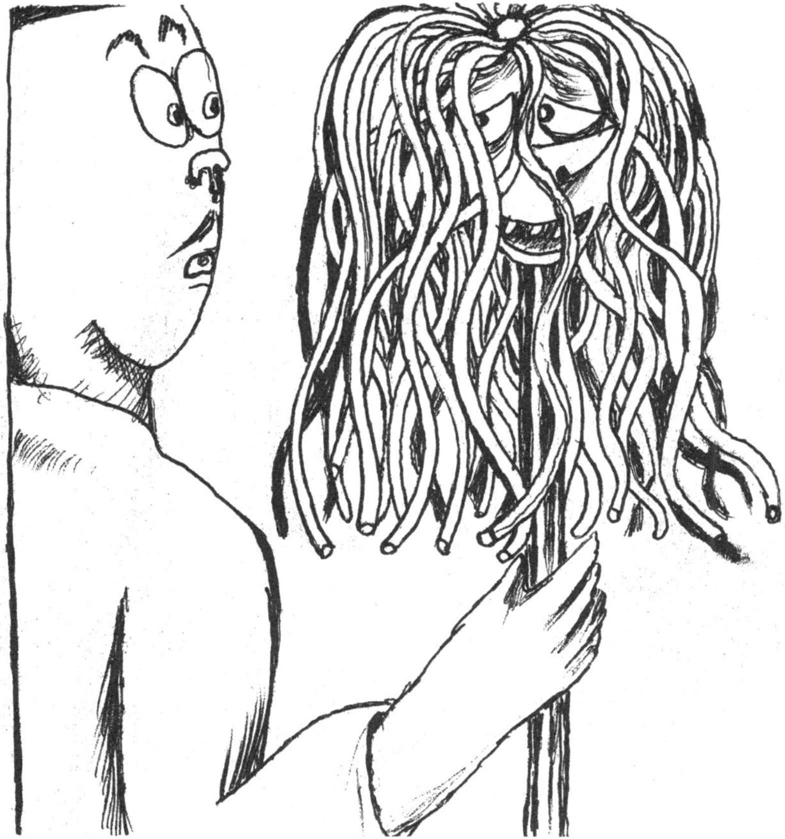

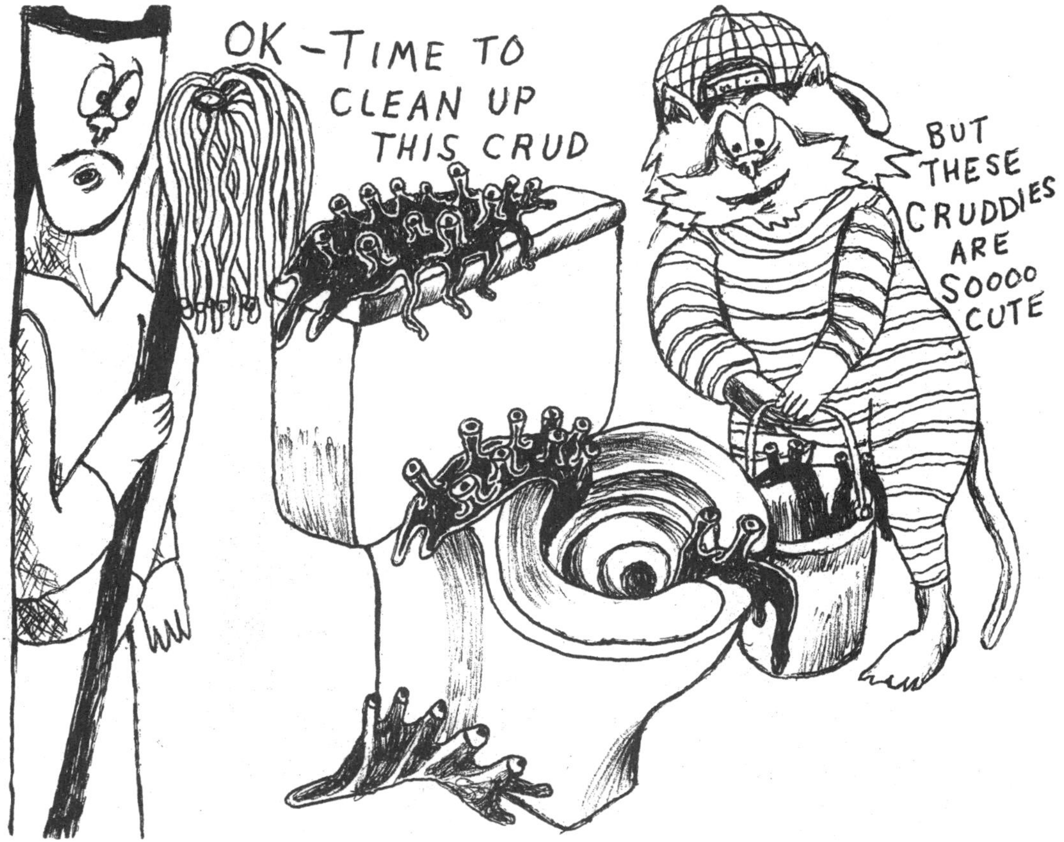
OK - TIME TO CLEAN UP THIS CRUD
BUT THESE CRUDDIES ARE SOOOO CUTE

cruddy helpers

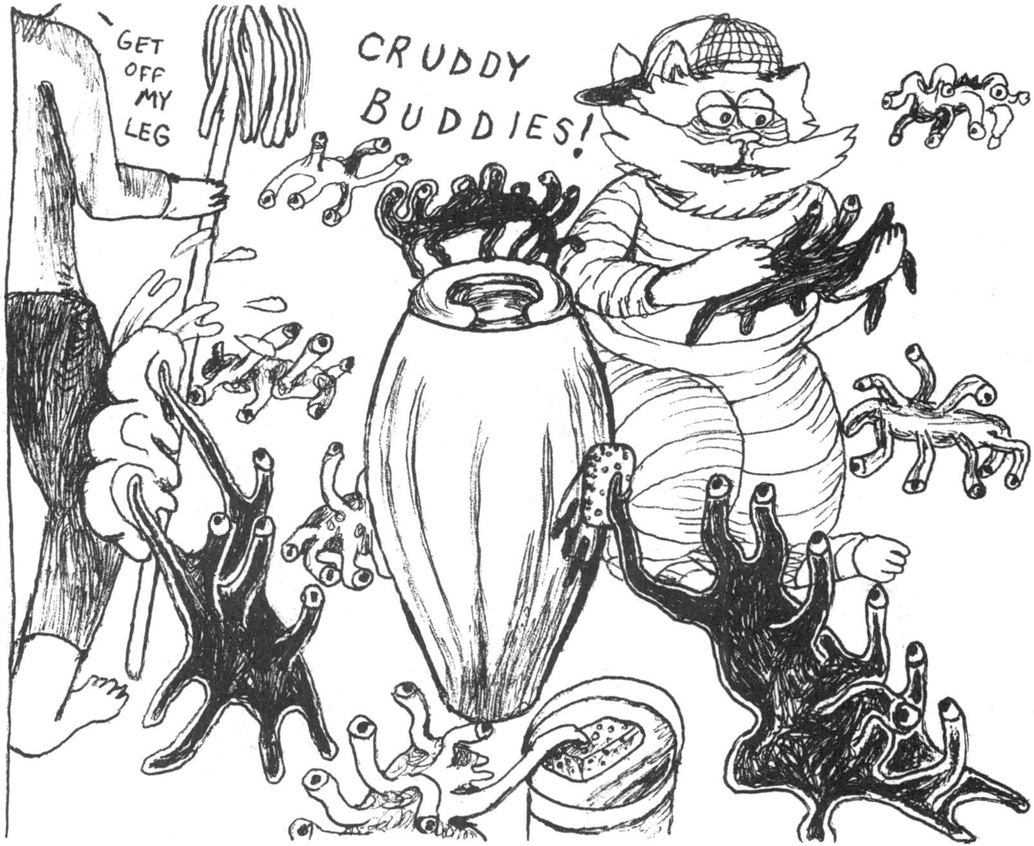

GET OFF MY LEG
CRUDDY BUDDIES!

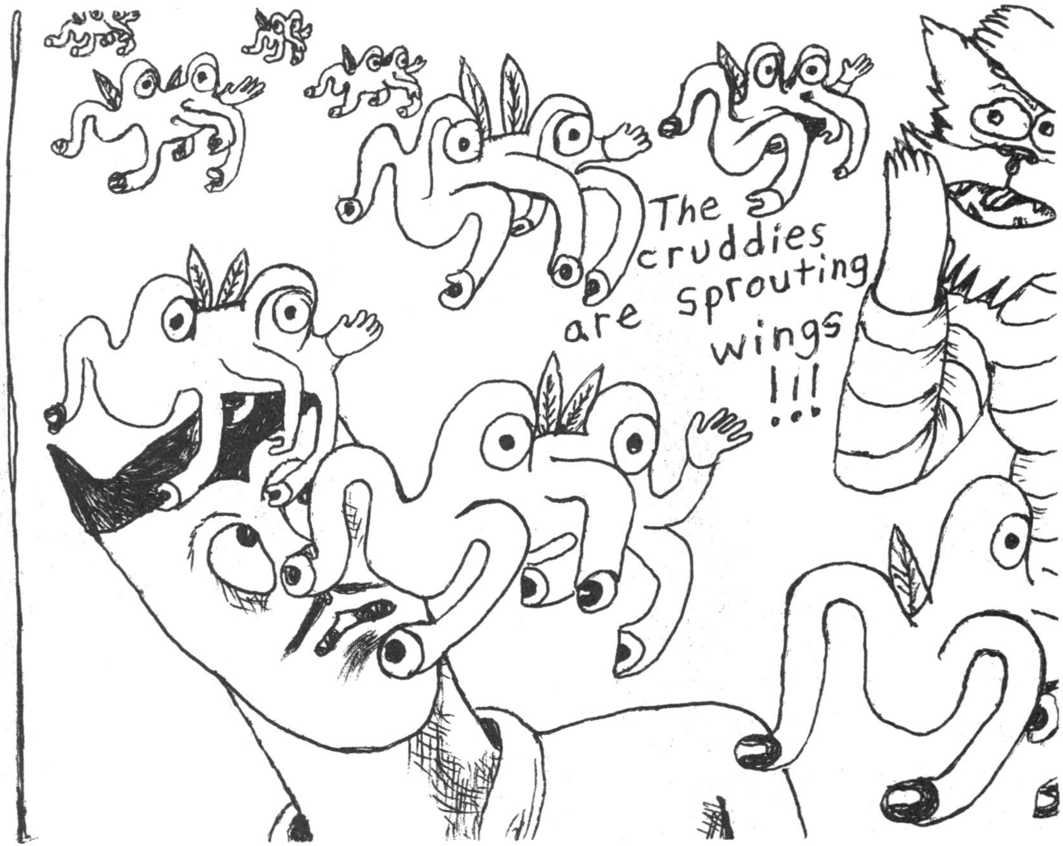
The cruddies are sprouting wings !!!

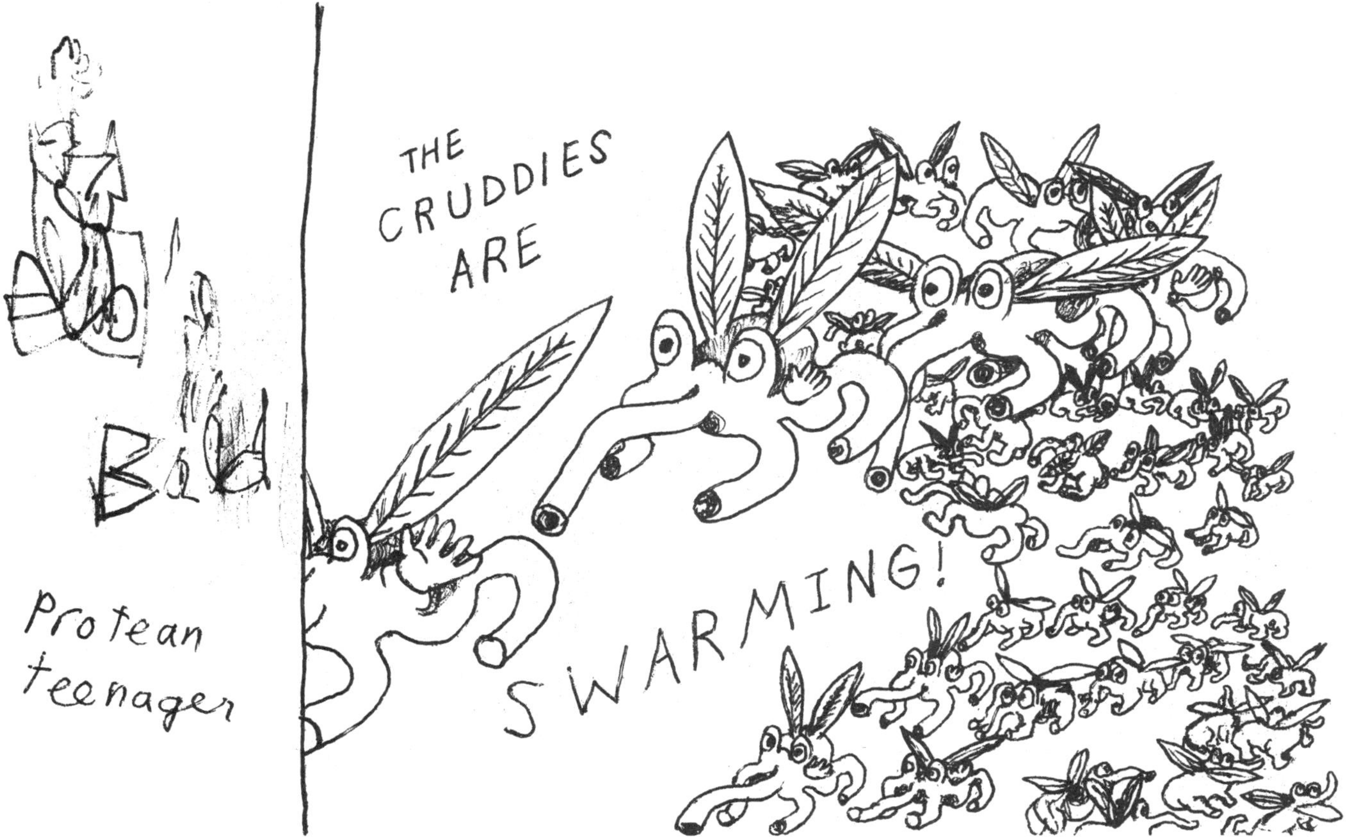
Bad
Protean teenager
THE CRUDDIES ARE SWARMING!

come in
demons,
stay for
tea

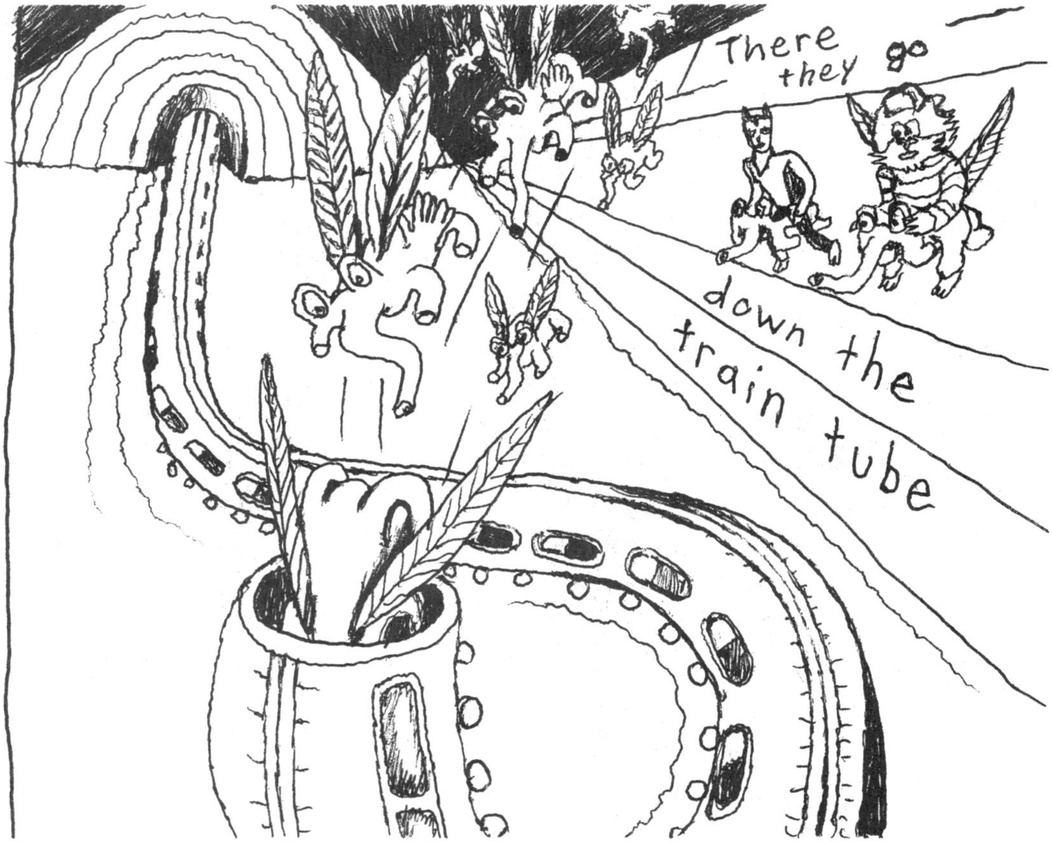
There go
they go
down the
train tube

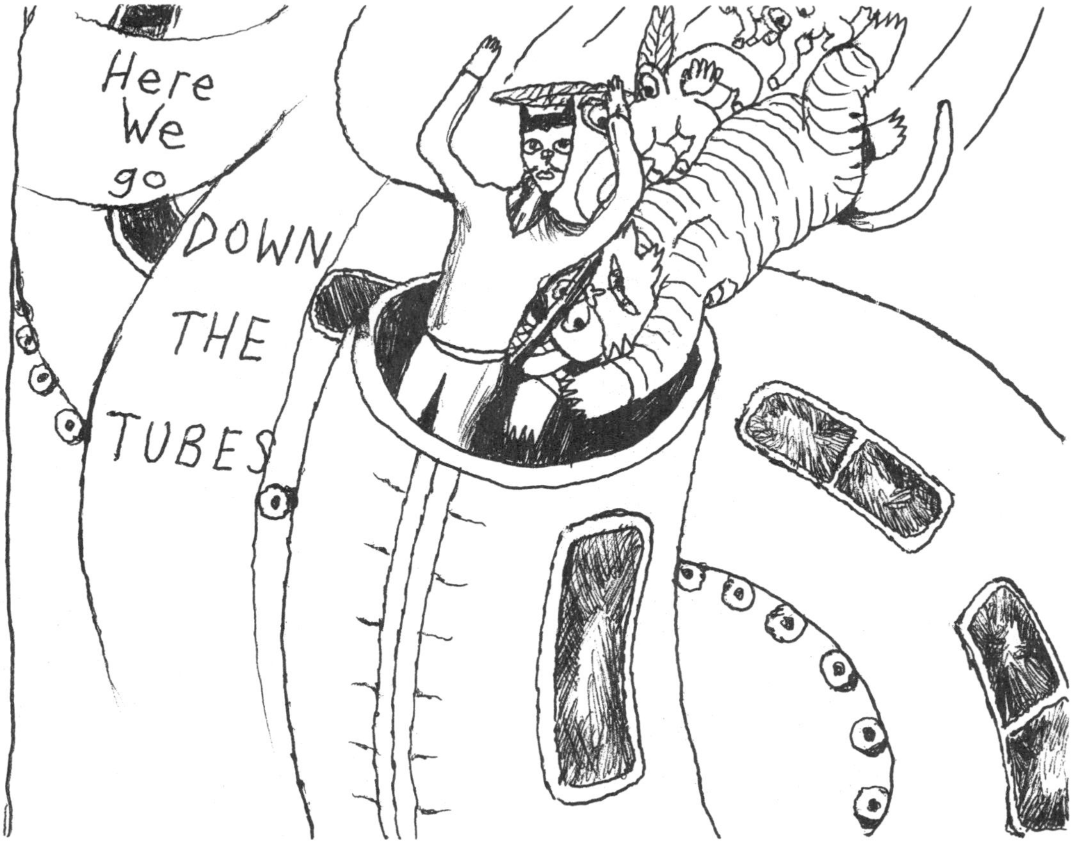
Here We go
DOWN THE TUBES

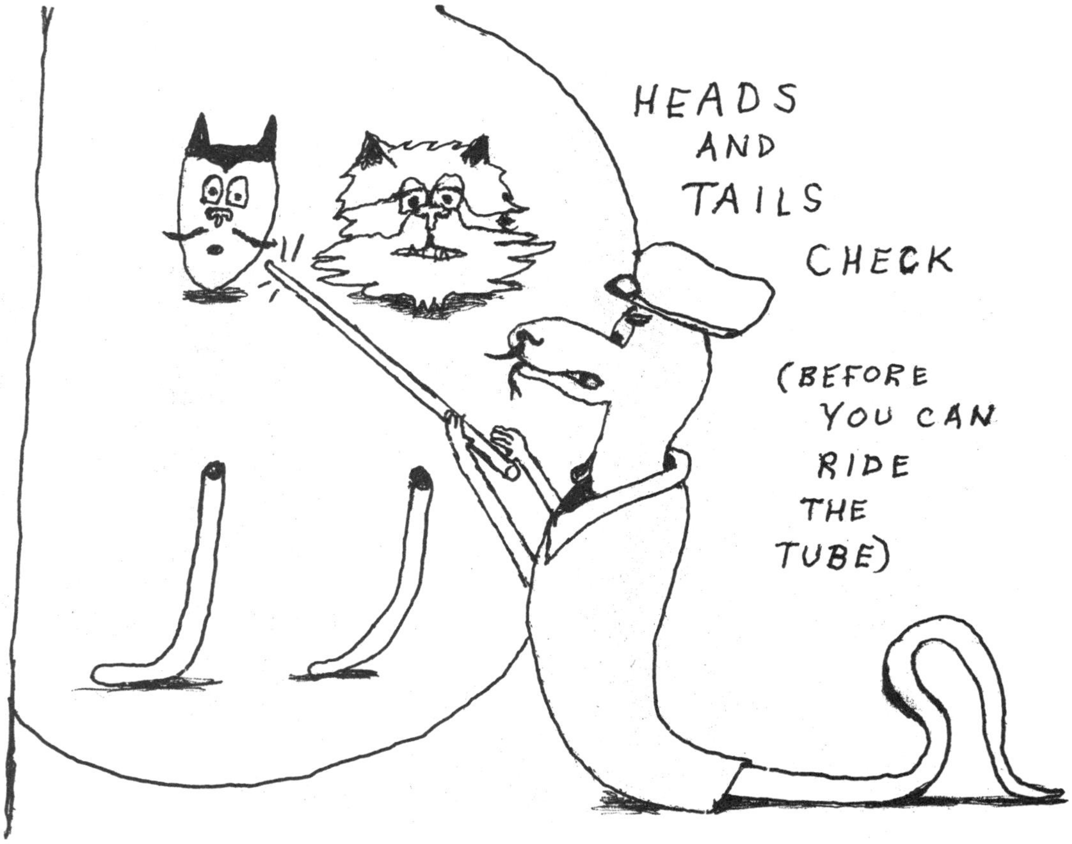
HEADS AND TAILS CHECK
(BEFORE YOU CAN RIDE THE TUBE)

ANY BOOK CAN BE PRINTED WITH AN EXCUSE

—

"EXCUSE ME IF I LET ONE"

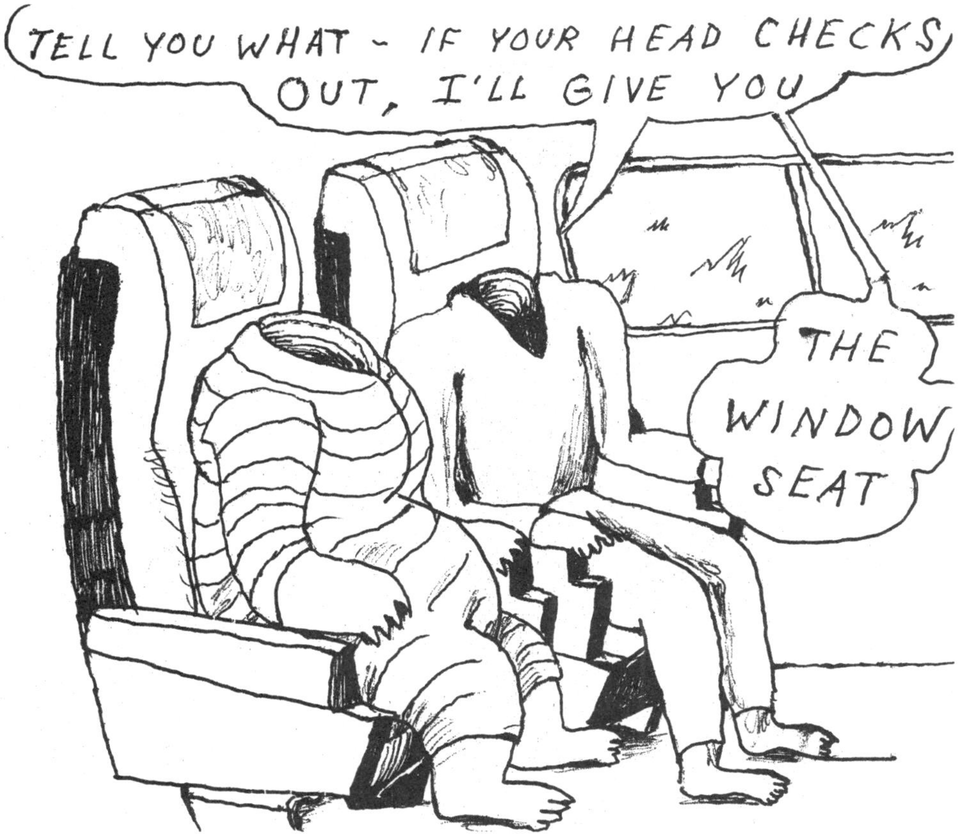
TELL YOU WHAT - IF YOUR HEAD CHECKS OUT, I'LL GIVE YOU
THE WINDOW SEAT

ALL WASTE

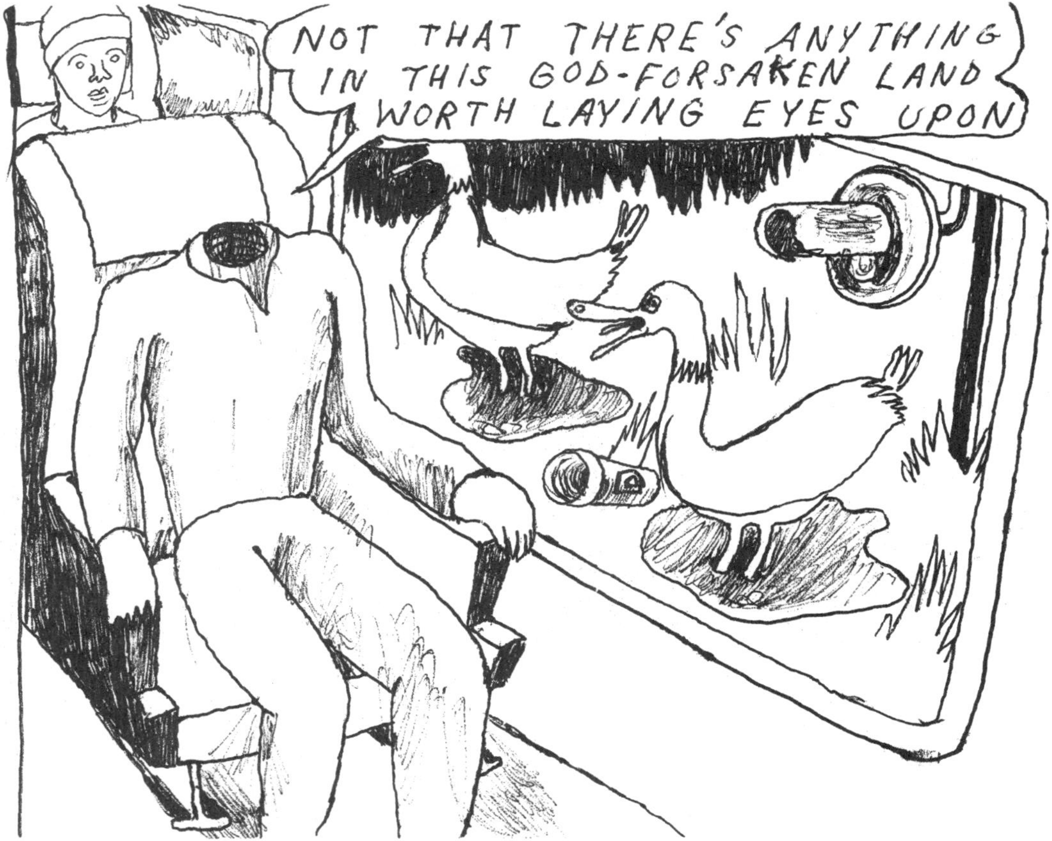
NOT THAT THERE'S ANYTHING IN THIS GOD-FORSAKEN LAND WORTH LAYING EYES UPON

hand
over
hand
over
hand
over
the
tail

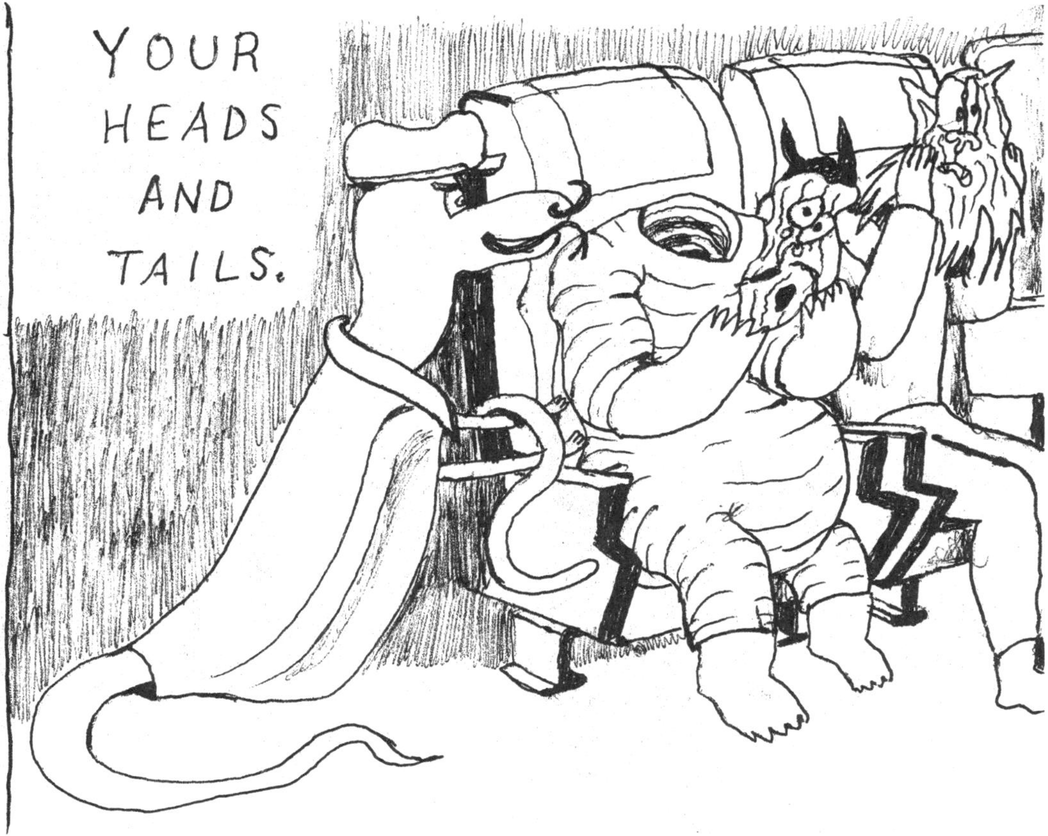
YOUR HEADS AND TAILS.

DUSTIN Yellin' AT RANDOM people on the bus...

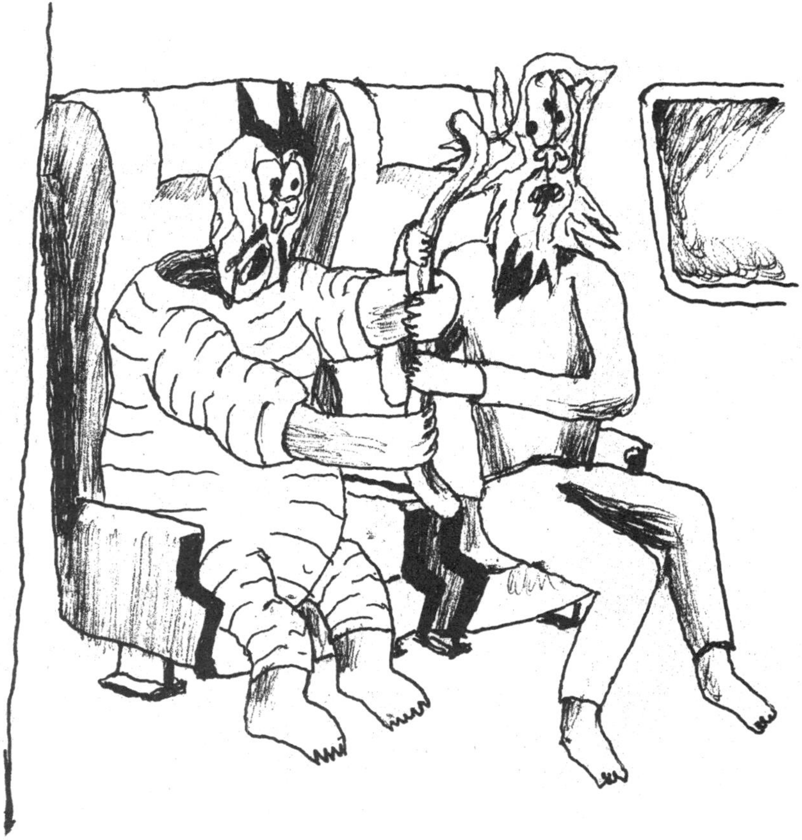

hand over hand over hand over hand over the tail.

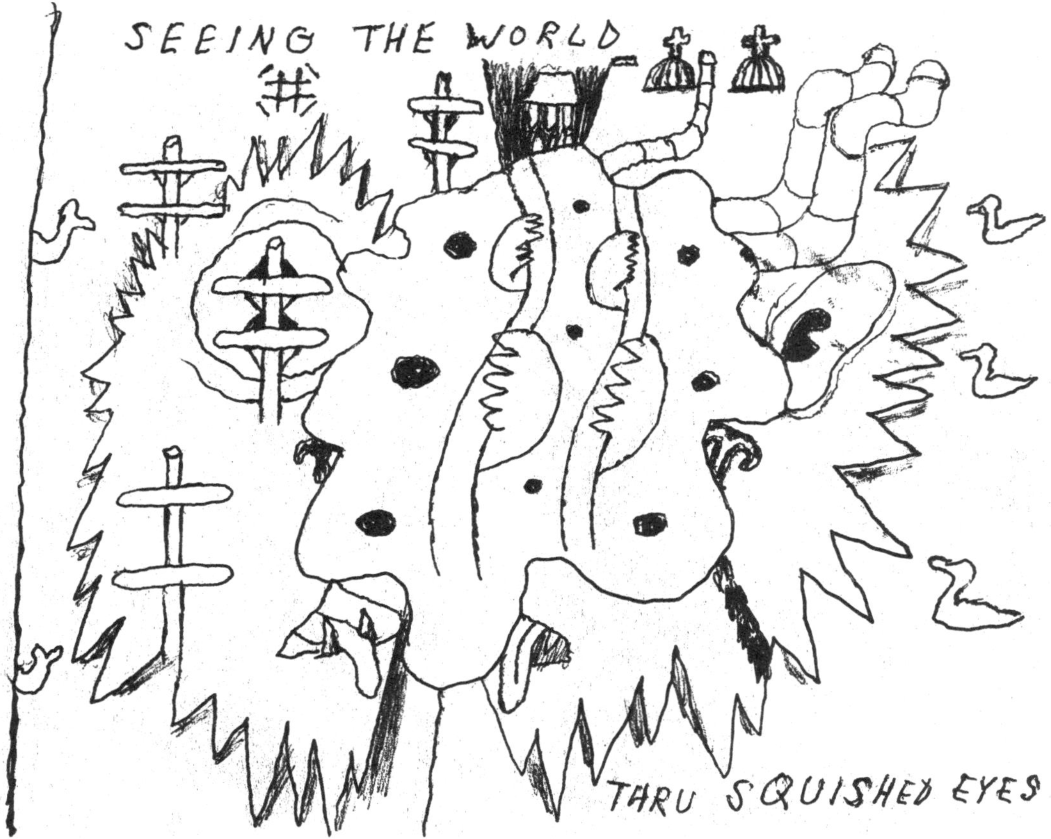
SEEING THE WORLD
THRU SQUISHED EYES

The New Yucker

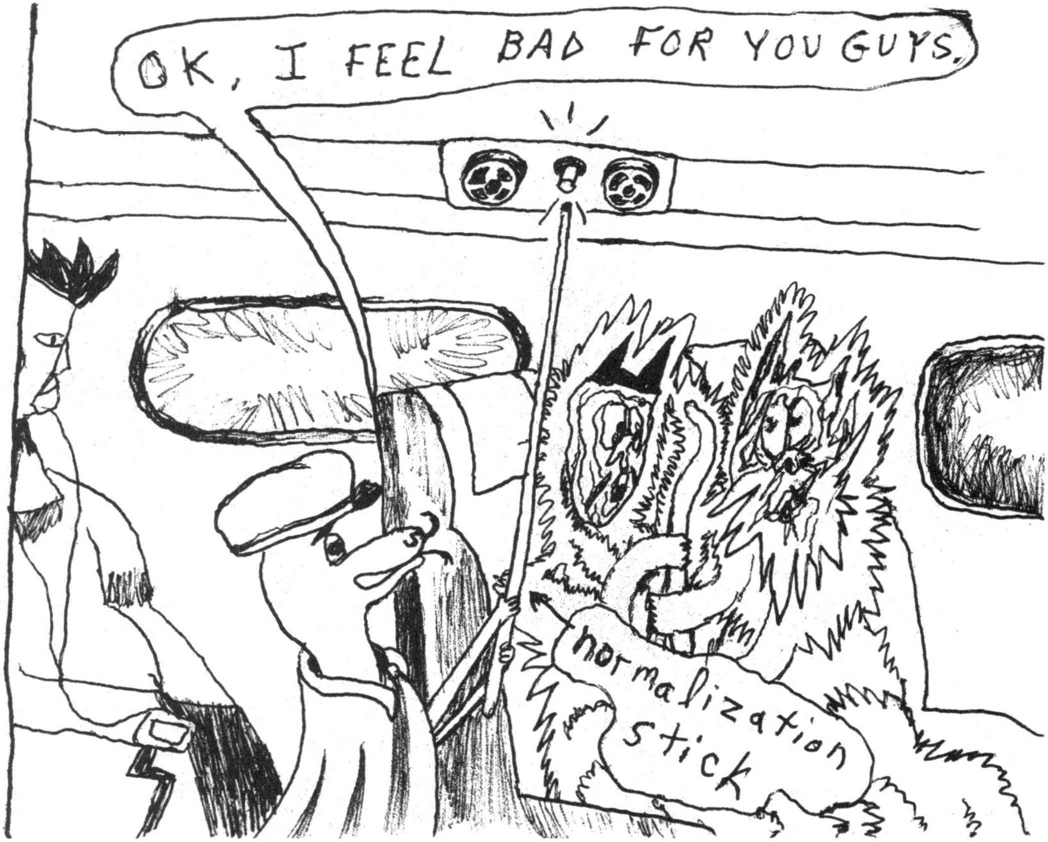
OK, I FEEL BAD FOR YOU GUYS.
normalization stick

Water from the source

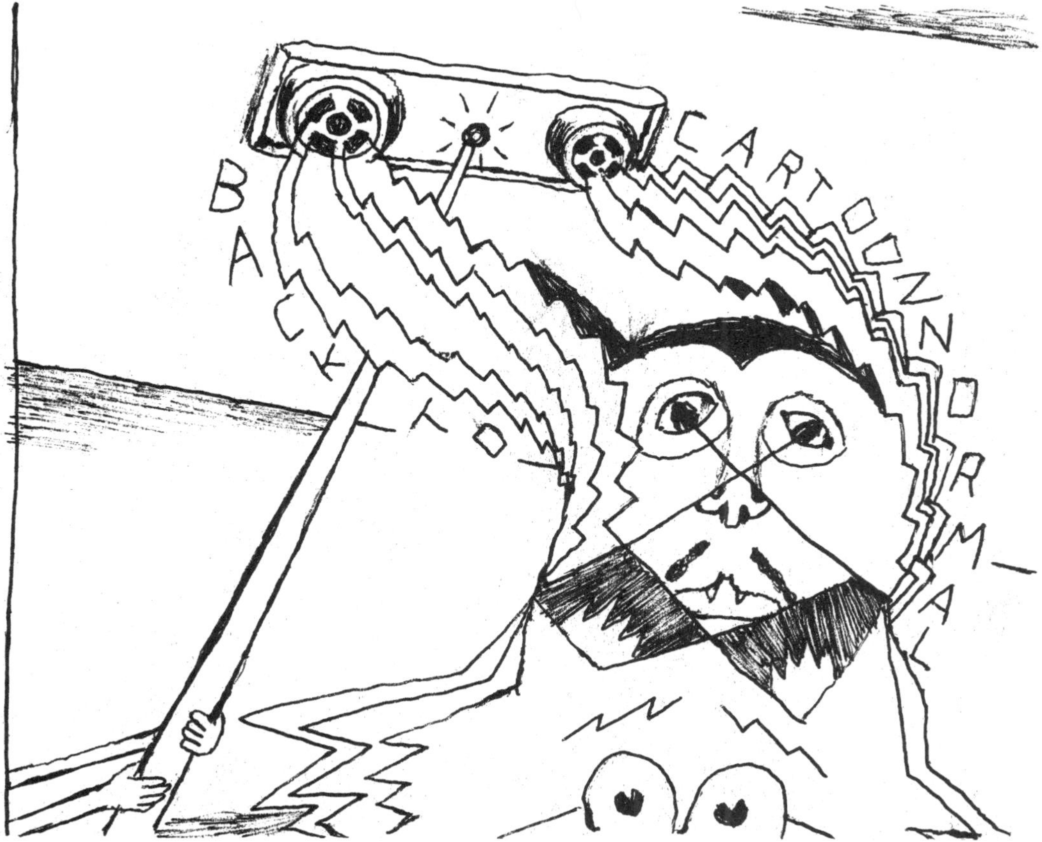

BACK TO
CARTOON NORM-AL

* except where otherwise noted

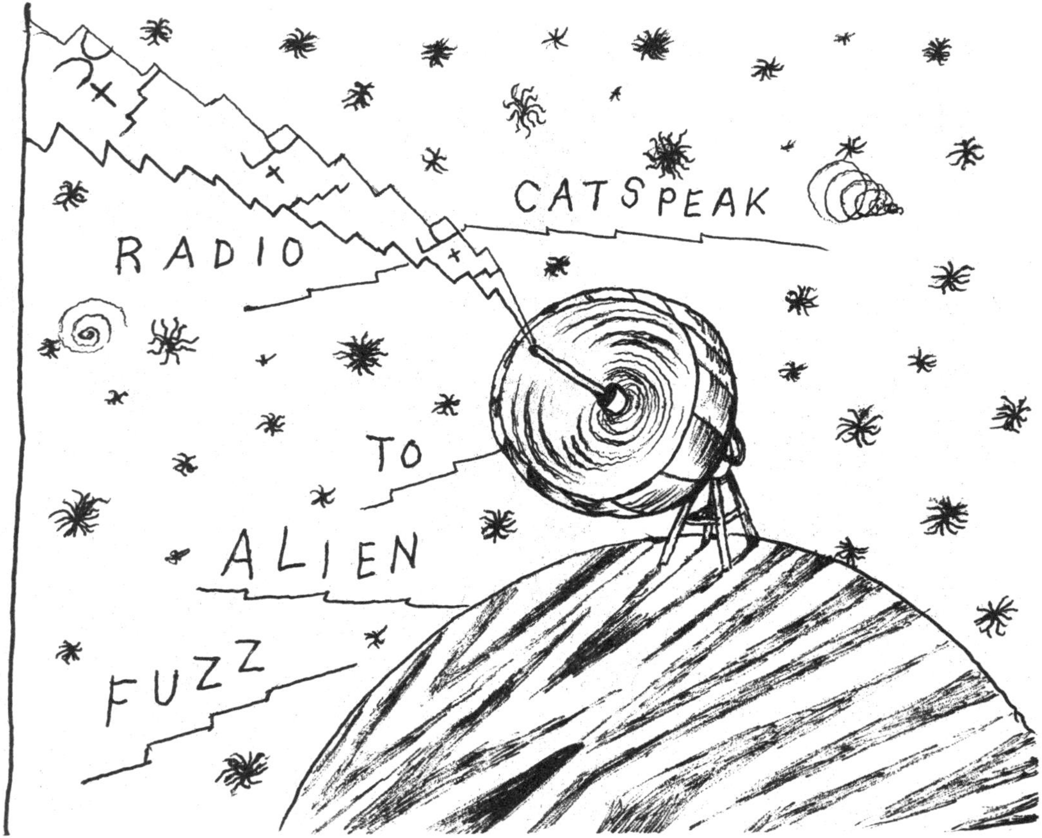
CATSPEAK
RADIO
TO
ALIEN
FUZZ

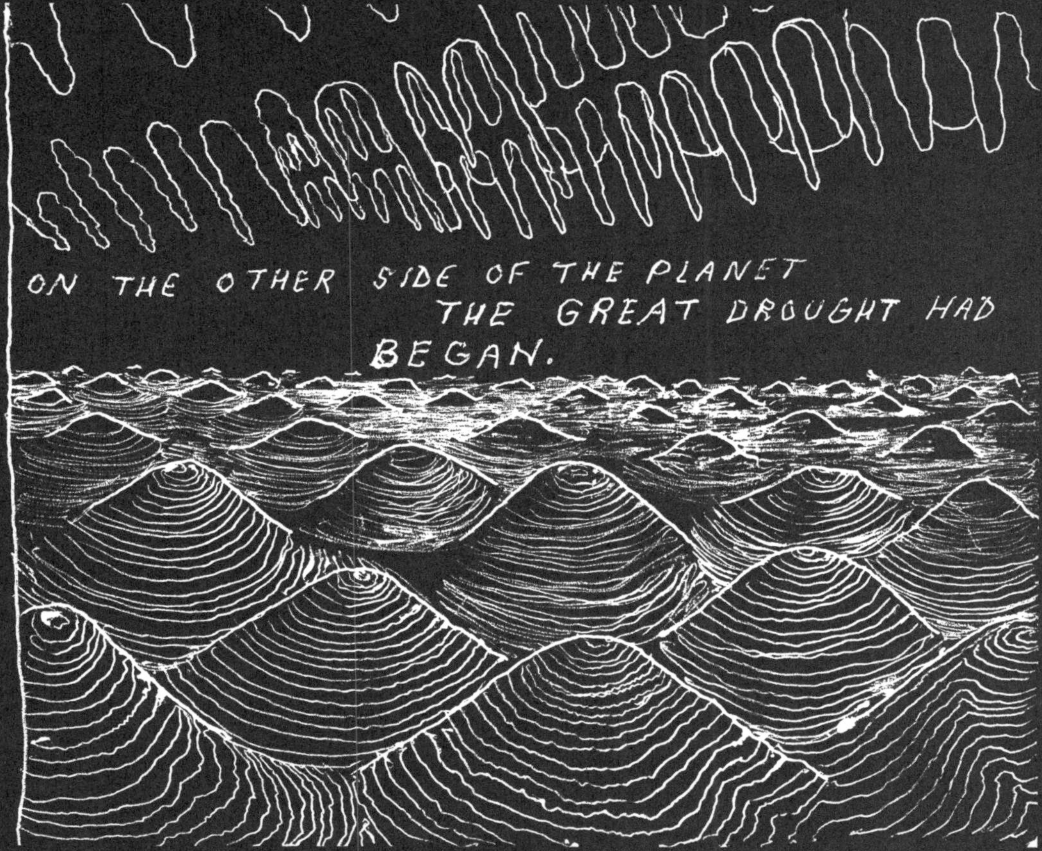
ON THE OTHER SIDE OF THE PLANET
THE GREAT DROUGHT HAD
BEGAN.

time to
hide myself
off in
the
corner

TO DRAW
THIS DIRTY
picture

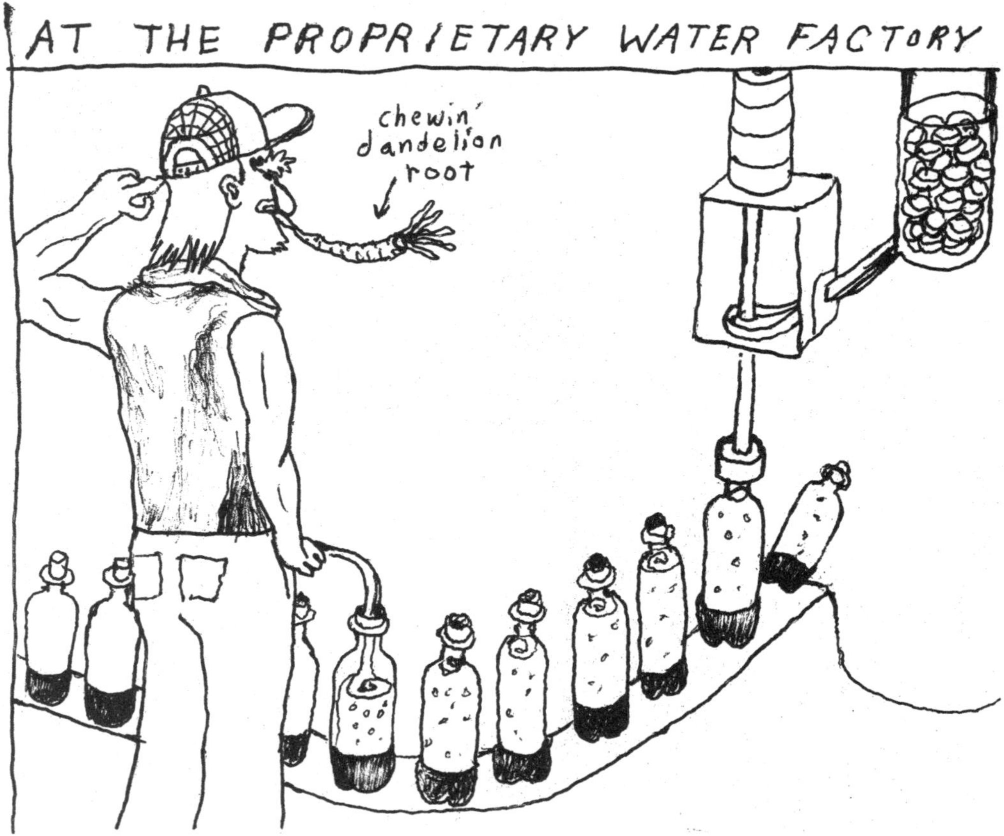
AT THE PROPRIETARY WATER FACTORY
chewin' dandelion root

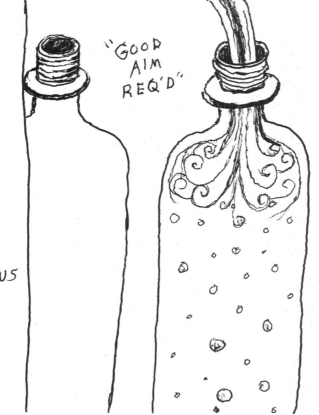

Why Buy This Book?

you know
the
subconscious
matters

"GOOD AIM REQ'D"

Direct WATER from the SOURCE

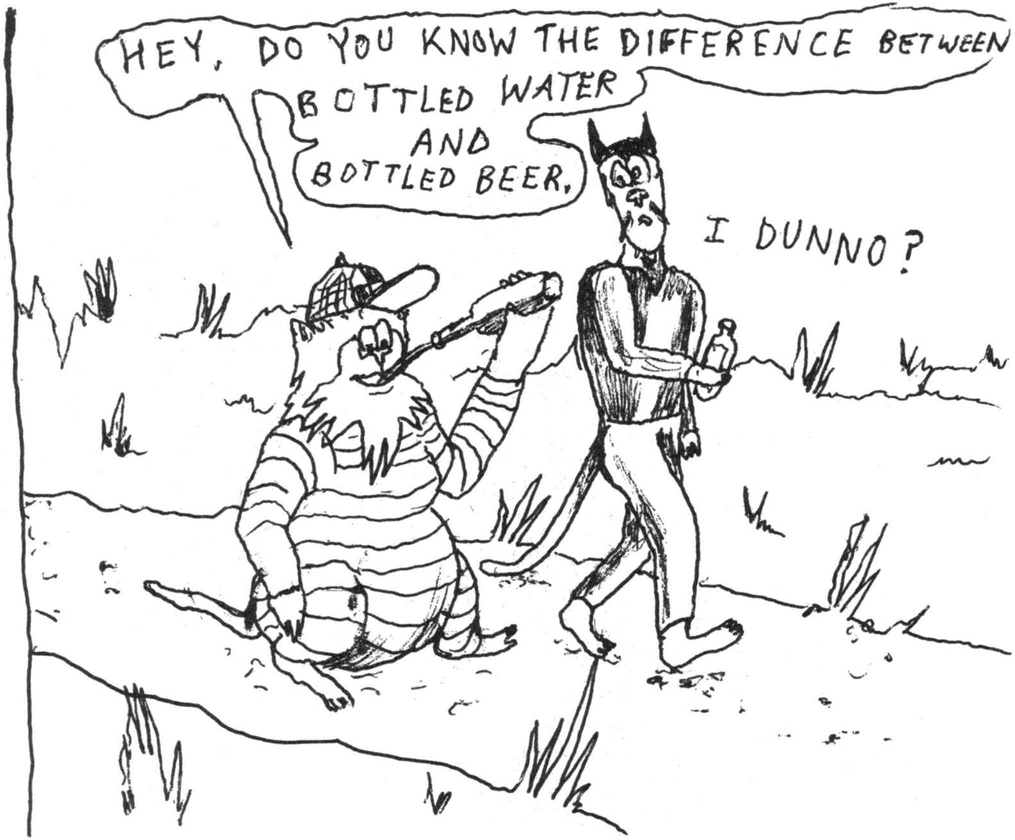
HEY, DO YOU KNOW THE DIFFERENCE BETWEEN BOTTLED WATER AND BOTTLED BEER.
I DUNNO?

X-country
A-musings

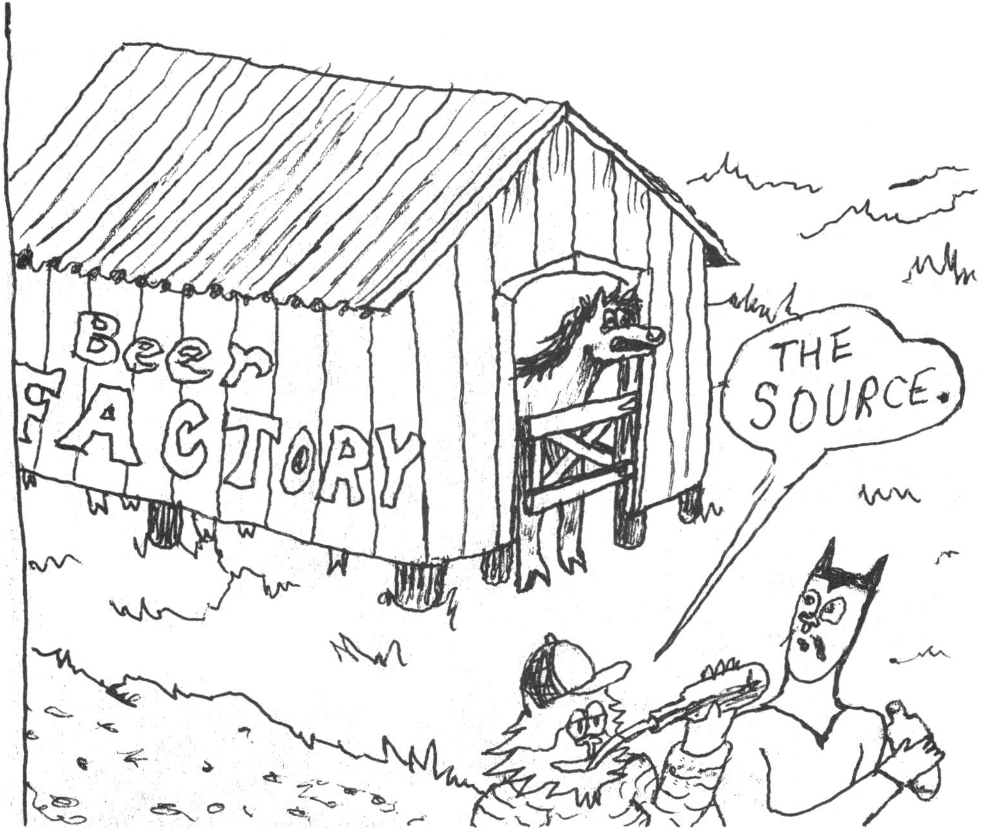

Beer
FACTORY
THE SOURCE.

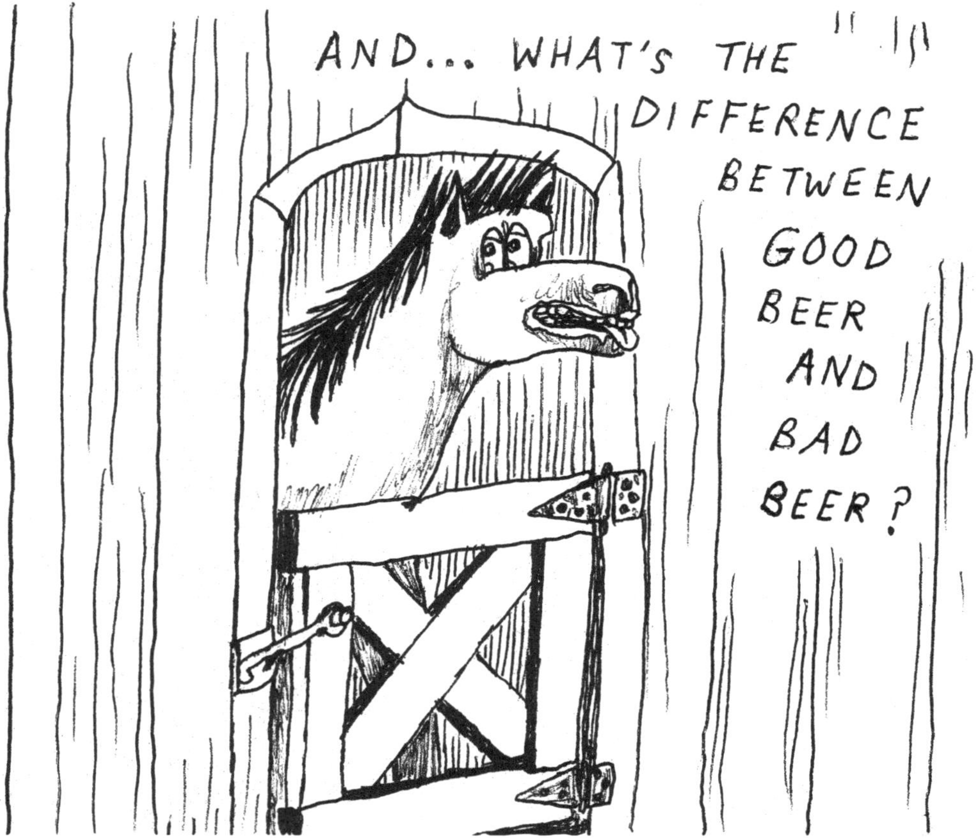
AND... WHAT'S THE DIFFERENCE BETWEEN GOOD BEER AND BAD BEER?

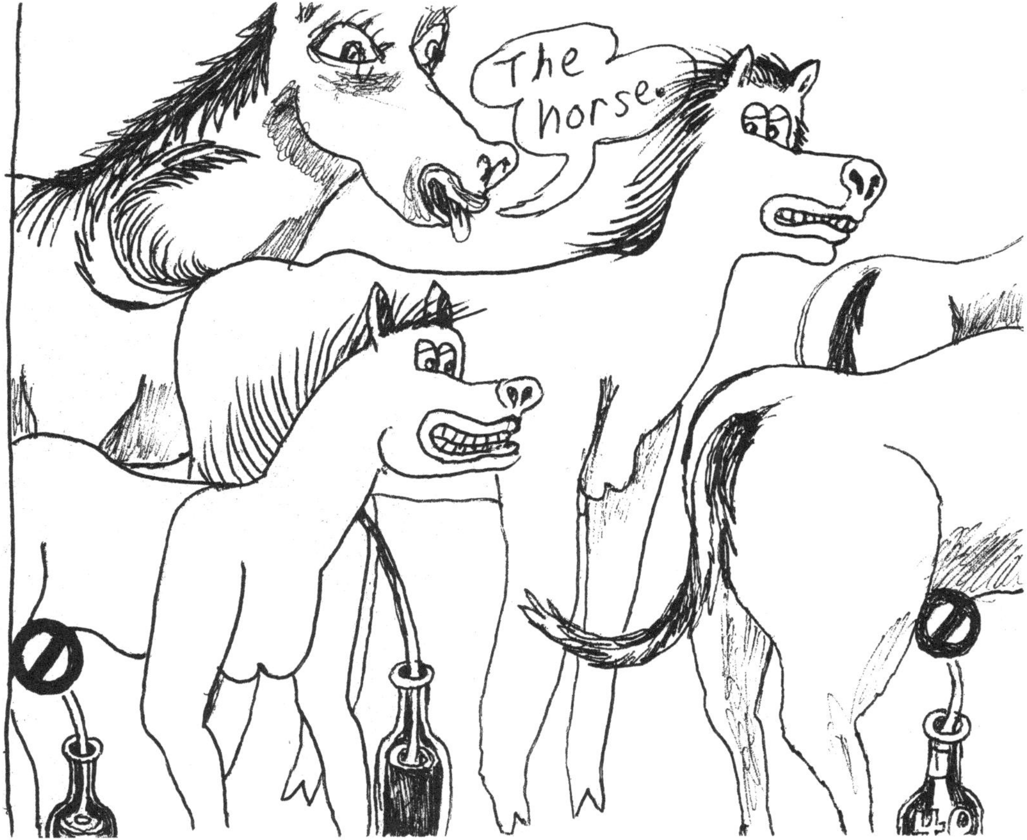
The horse.

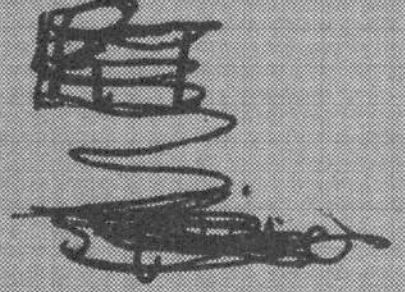

~~RI SQUIRREL~~

RI SQUIRREL REMOVAL

Hello, Dear Reader,

this is YOUR Ecological cartoonist here. Every page of this cartoon filth is dedicated to saving a plant or animal of YOUR choice. The first thing *you* can do for the environment is to zip your LID. If you don't ZIP your lid, all of that CRUD will fall out, get everywhere, and stick to my shoe. Also, I must note, that I have conserved energy (the world over) by not redrawing a single bad drawing. Everything is left as nature intended it: scribbled, stained, and misspelled.

Yours truly,

back of
the
throught
throat
&
eirs
piercing

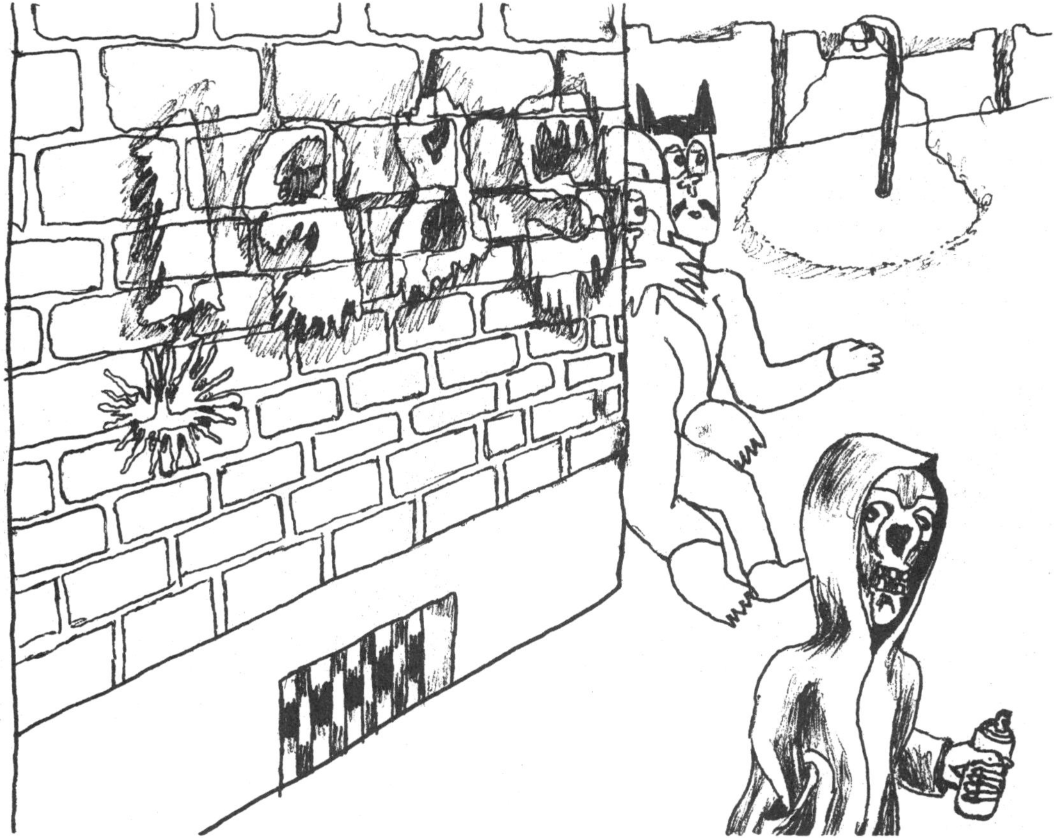

Rick's Bedbugs

@

~~Wino~~

World of Winos

Rock Crusher

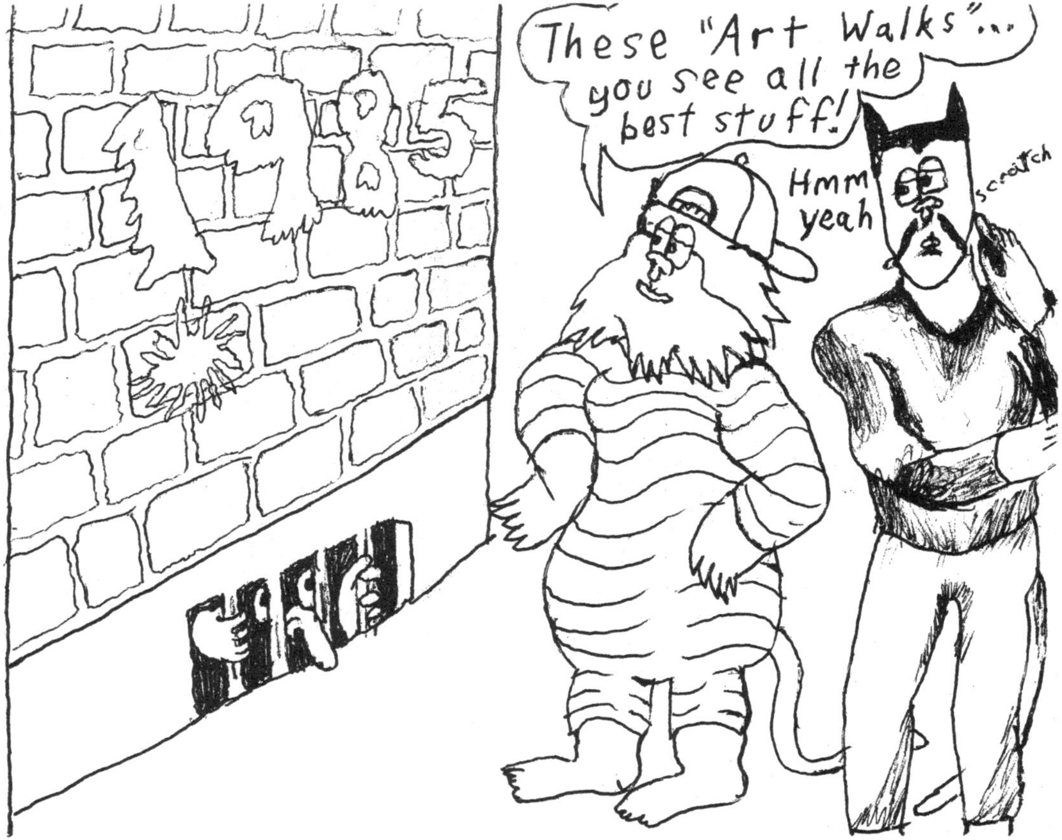

1985
These "Art Walks"... you see all the best stuff!
Hmm yeah
scratch

WINO COUNTRY

SINK-HOLE GUY

1-800-STINK HOLE

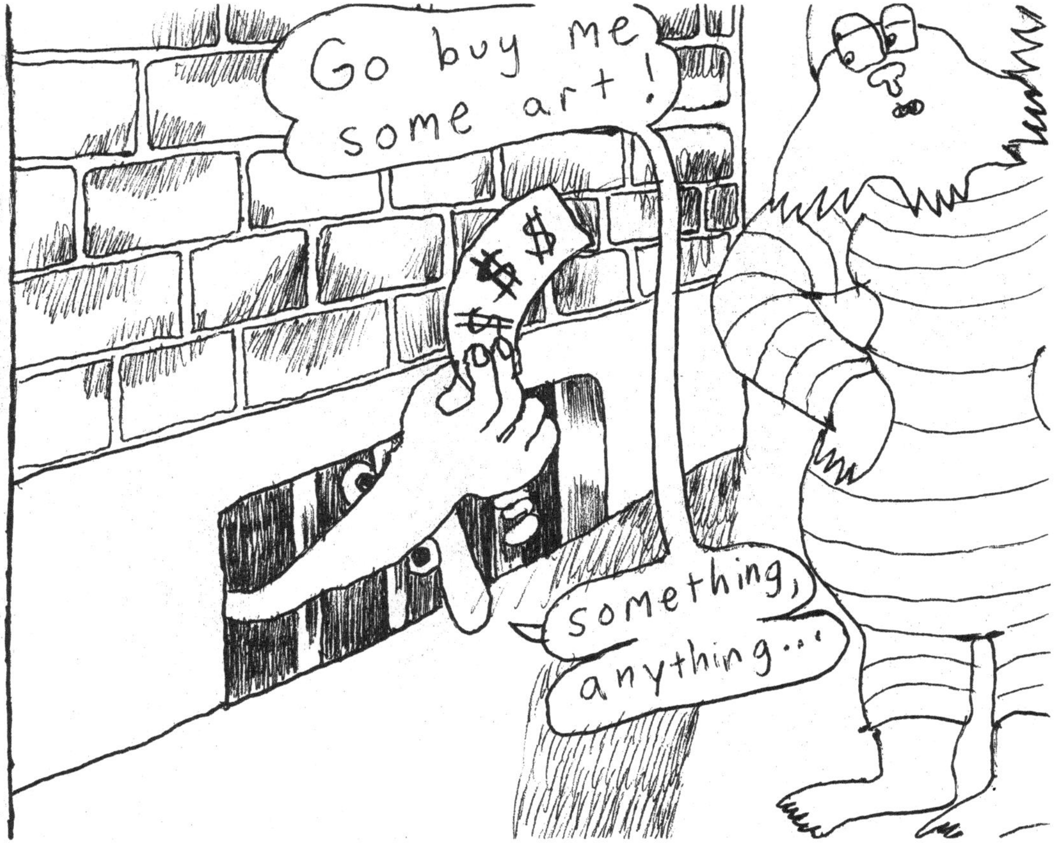

Go buy me some art!
something, anything...

My Great Aunt, She wanted to buy me a "Louis Fournious" shirt from Wal Mart

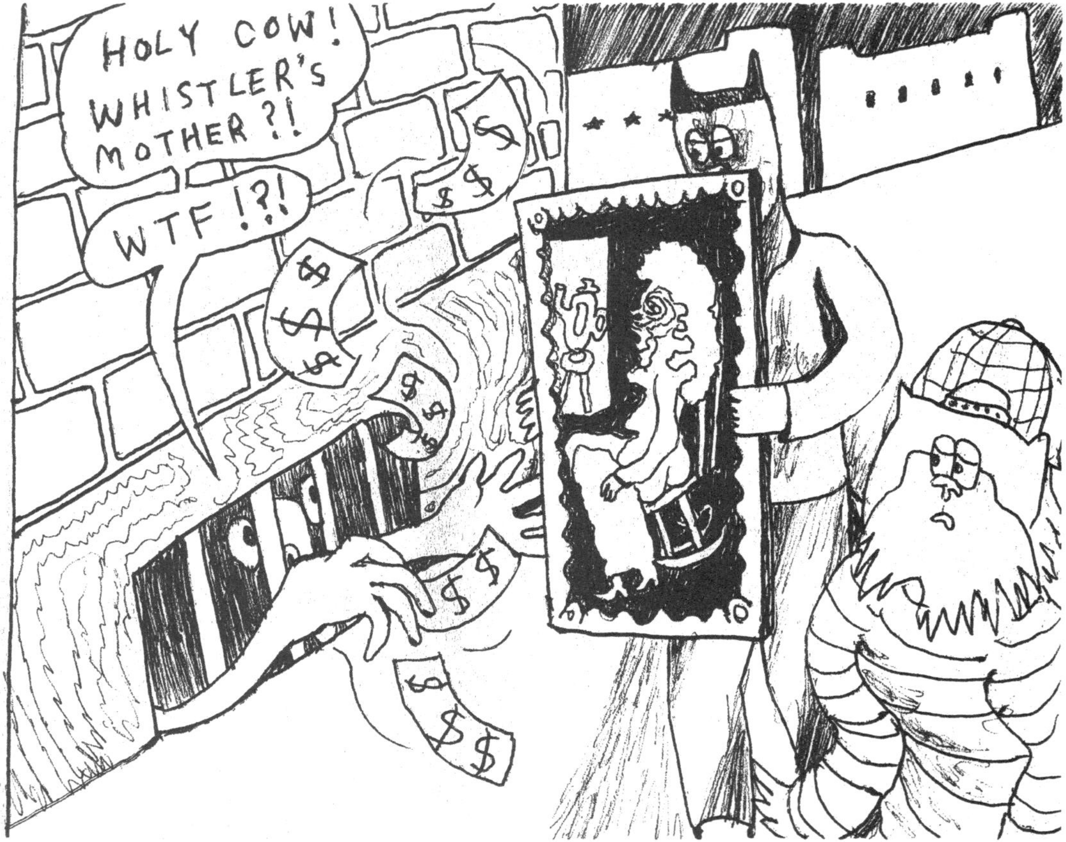
HOLY COW! WHISTLER'S MOTHER?!
WTF!?!

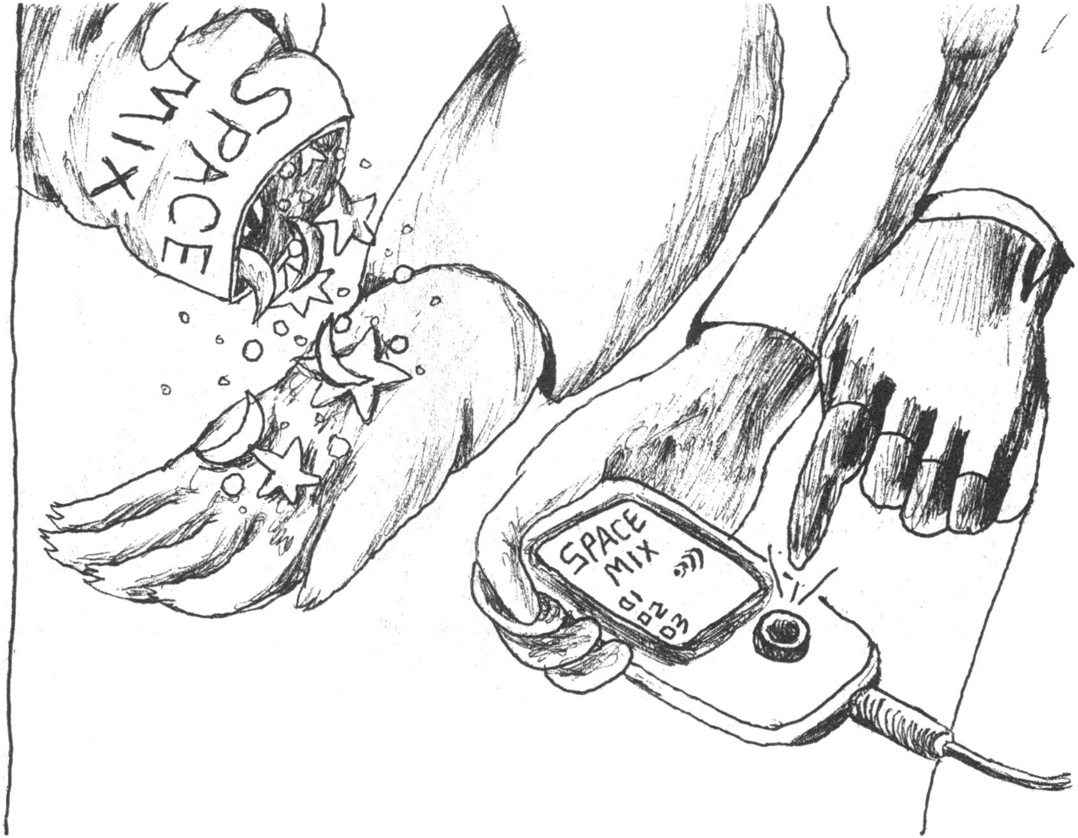
SPACE MIX
SPACE MIX

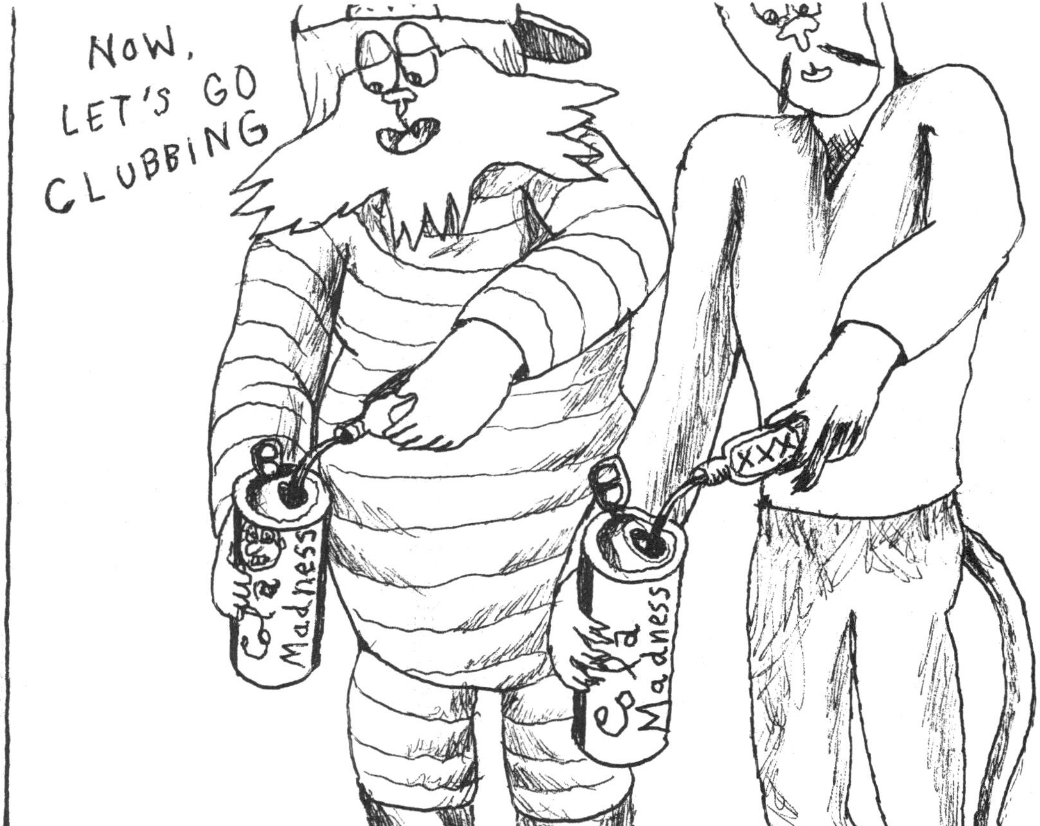
NOW, LET'S GO CLUBBING
Madness
XXX
Madness

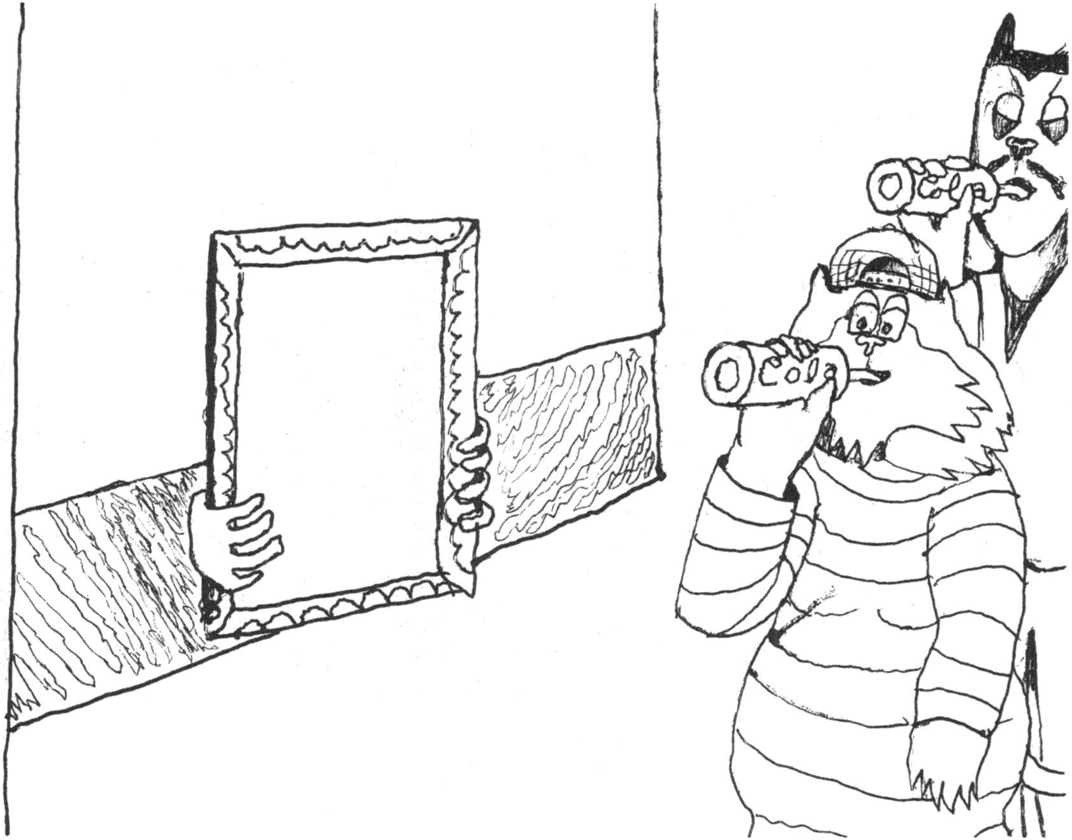
Cola
Cola

simplified
air flight

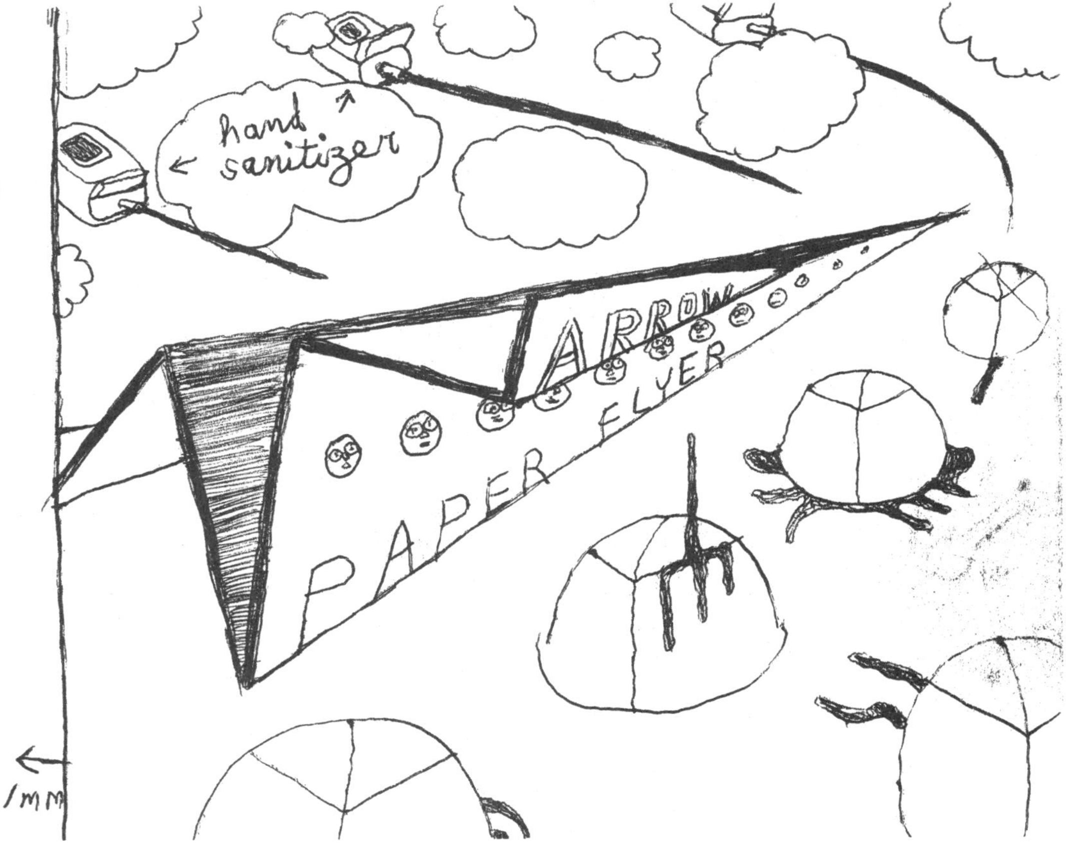

vintage
ball
point

Harveysboro

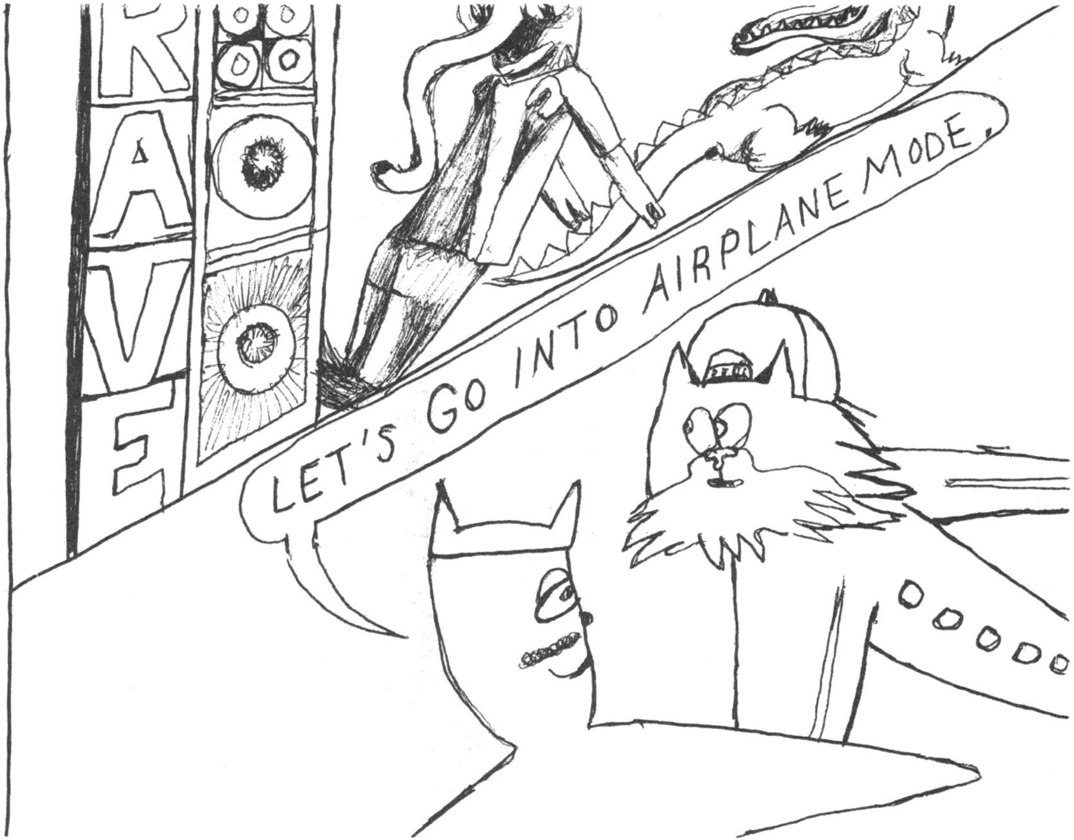

Pushing
the
Future
of
goofing
off

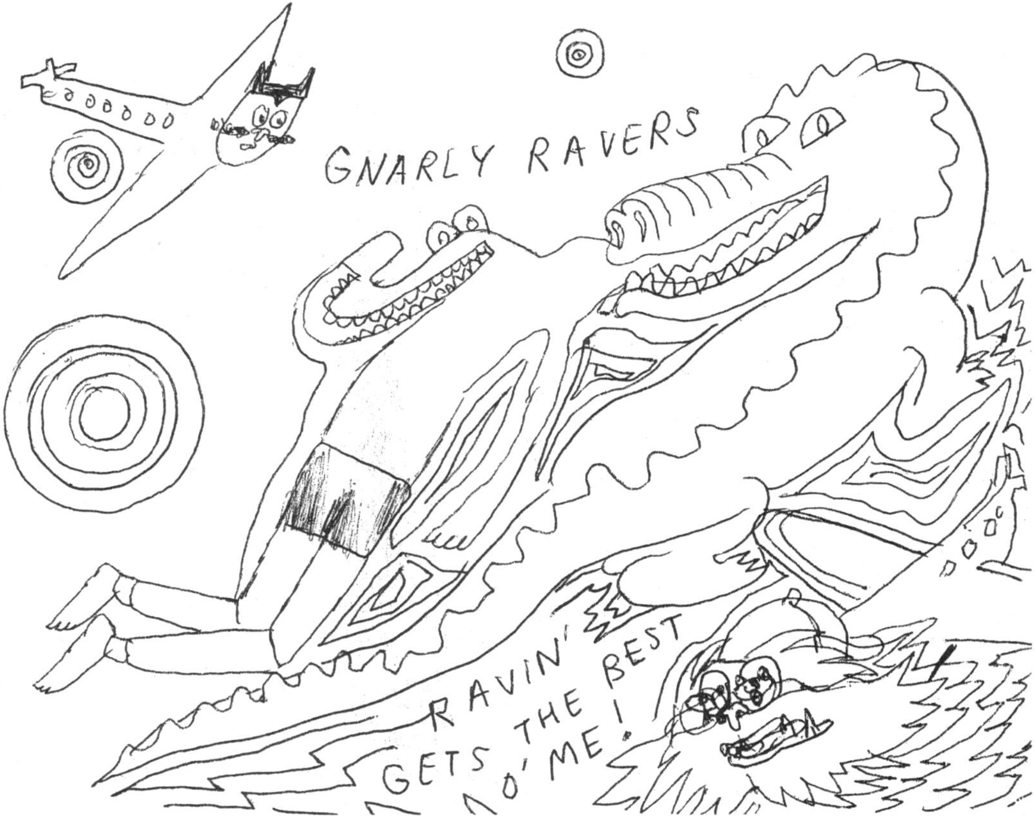
GNARLY RAVERS
RAVIN' GETS THE BEST O' ME!

Vintage
ball
shit

engagement
on
This
LEVEL
is
OK

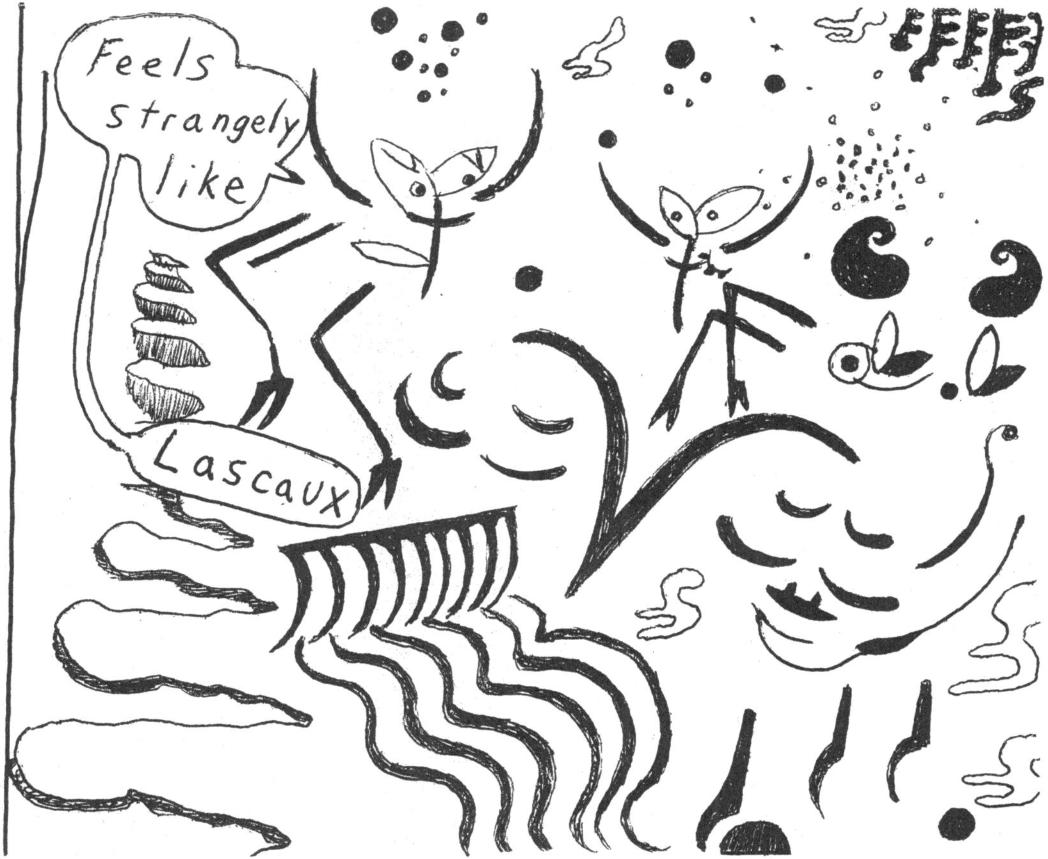

Feels strangely like
Lascaux

REVOLT

MORE SAVING,
MORE DOING
THAT'S THE
POWER OF
THE
HOME
DEPOT

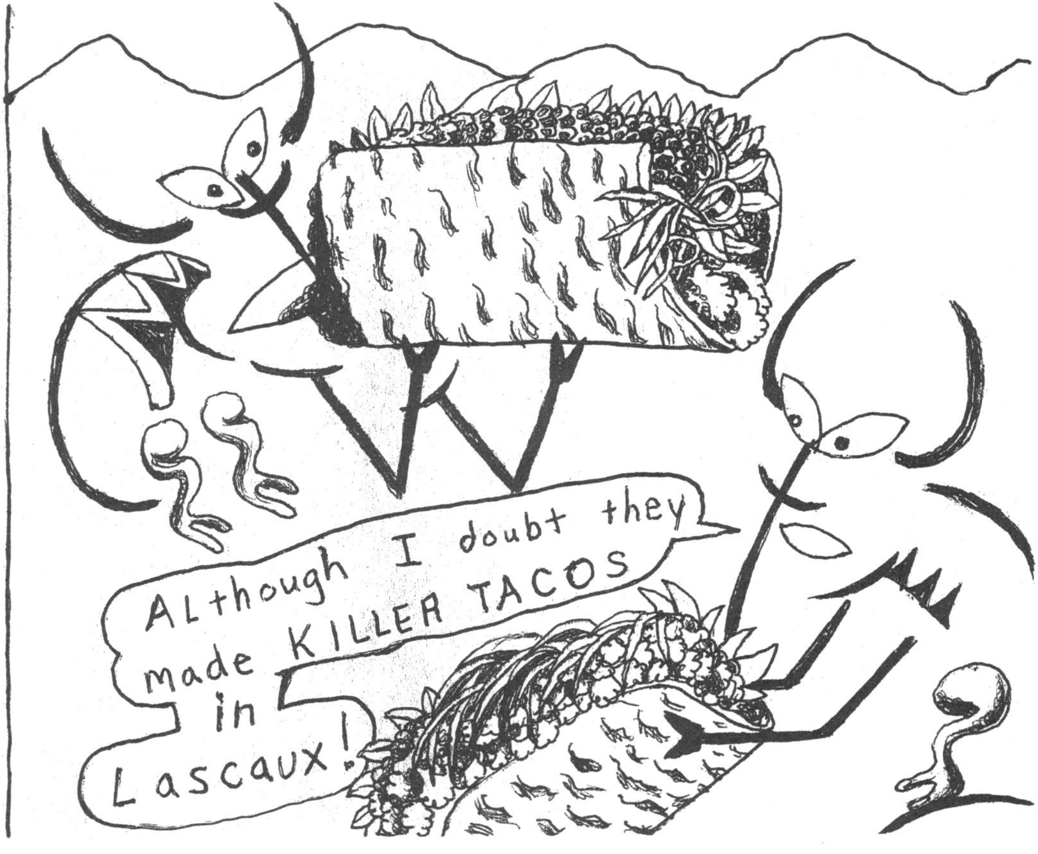
Although I doubt they made KILLER TACOS in Lascaux!

May is a time to make weird art that really can't be appreciated by anyone WHY BOTHER.

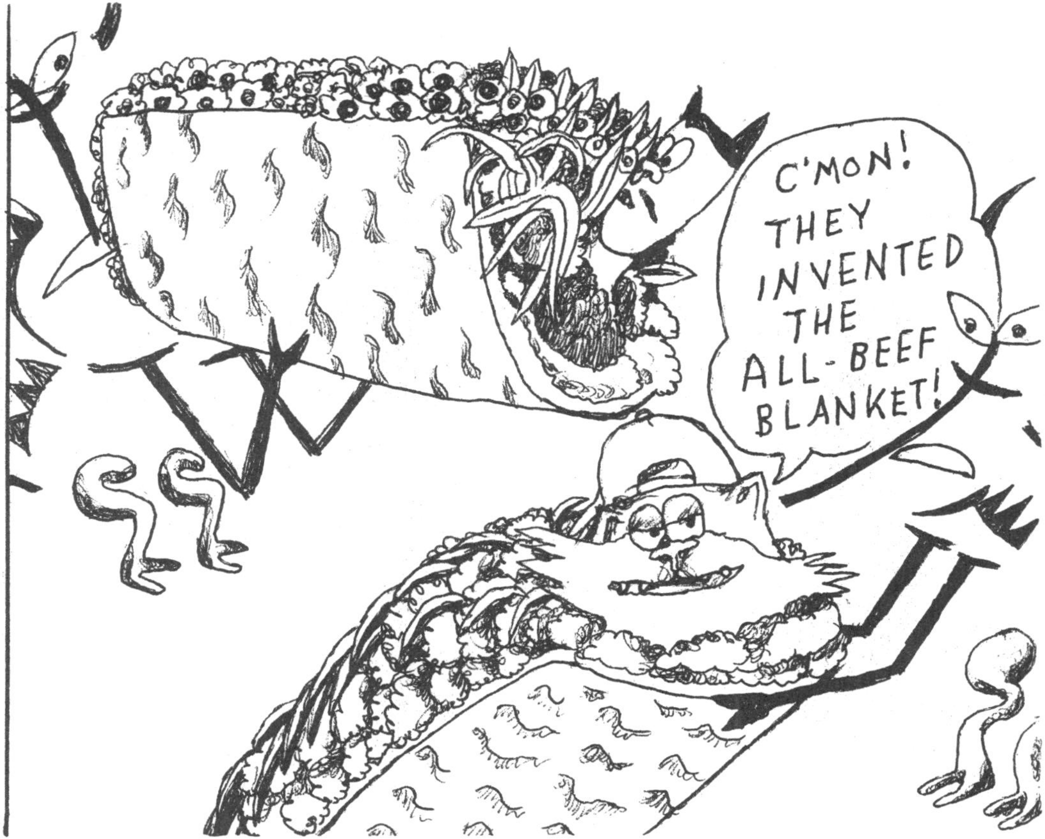
C'MON! THEY INVENTED THE ALL-BEEF BLANKET!

WORKING BETWEEN CARTOON AND FORMALIST ART IDEAS

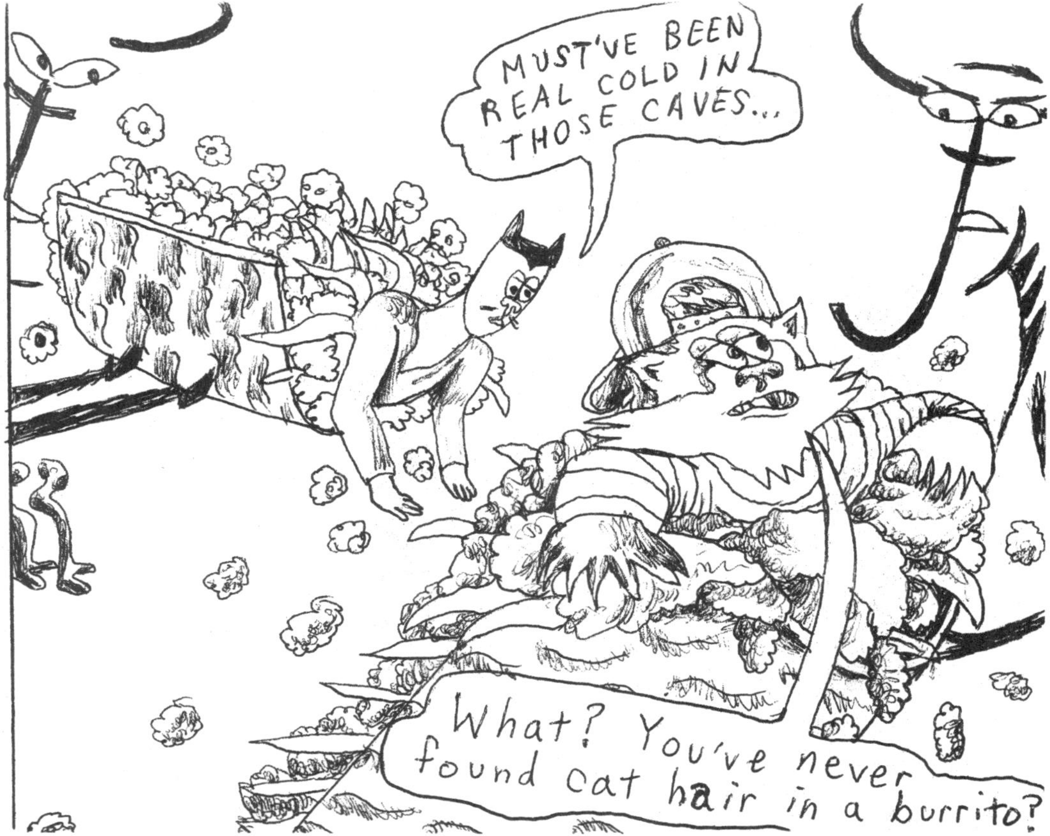
MUST'VE BEEN REAL COLD IN THOSE CAVES...
What? You've never found cat hair in a burrito?

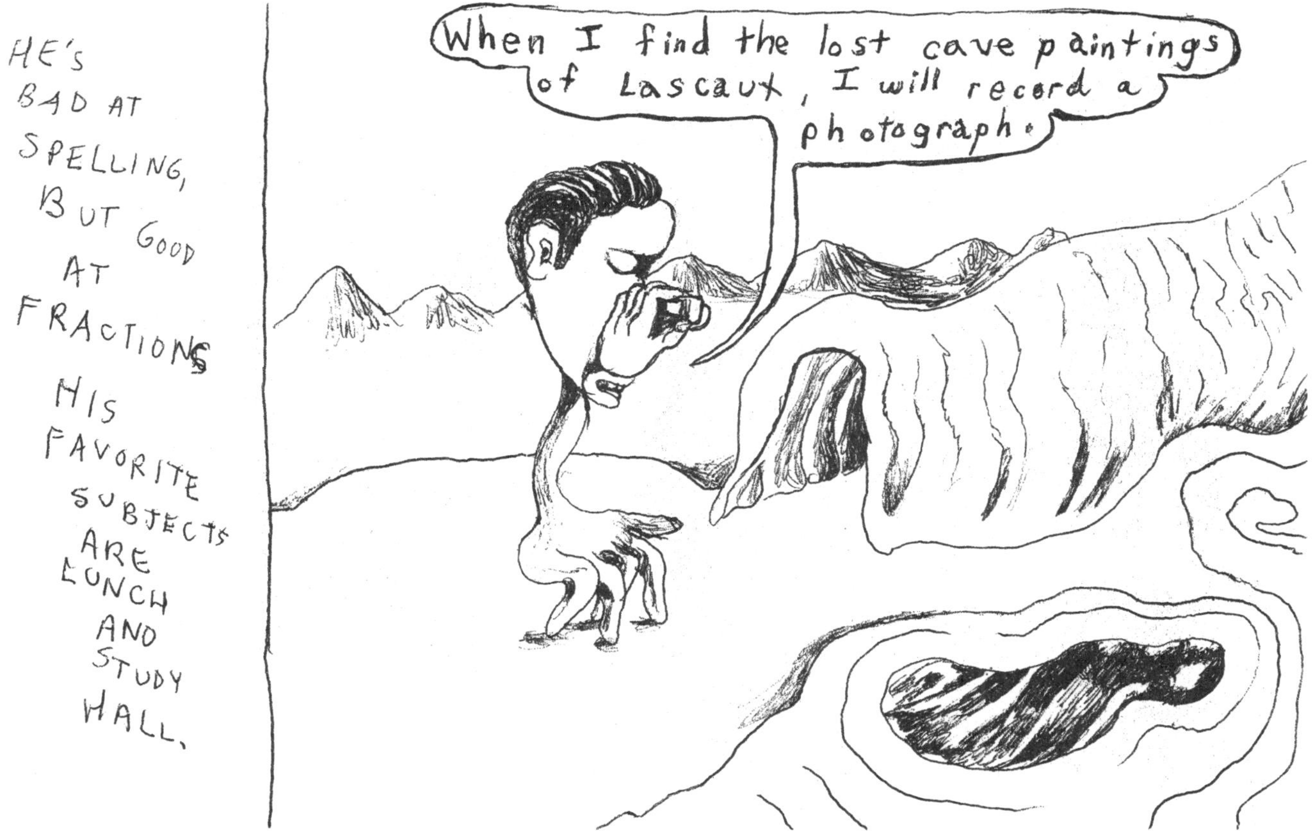
HE'S BAD AT SPELLING, BUT GOOD AT FRACTIONS
HIS FAVORITE SUBJECTS ARE LUNCH AND STUDY HALL.
When I find the lost cave paintings of Lascaux, I will record a photograph.

ACE
BANDAGES
<u>BOTH</u>
ARMS

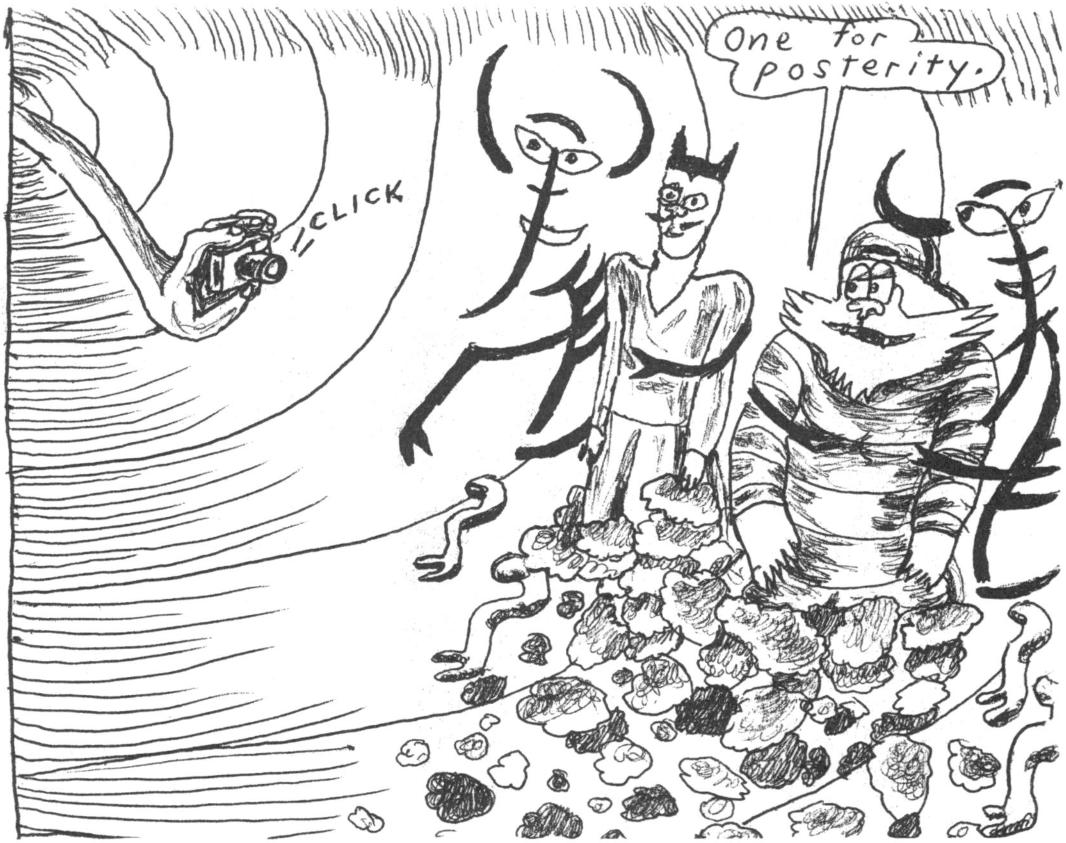

CLICK
One for posterity.

Ramantatic

Romantic Comics

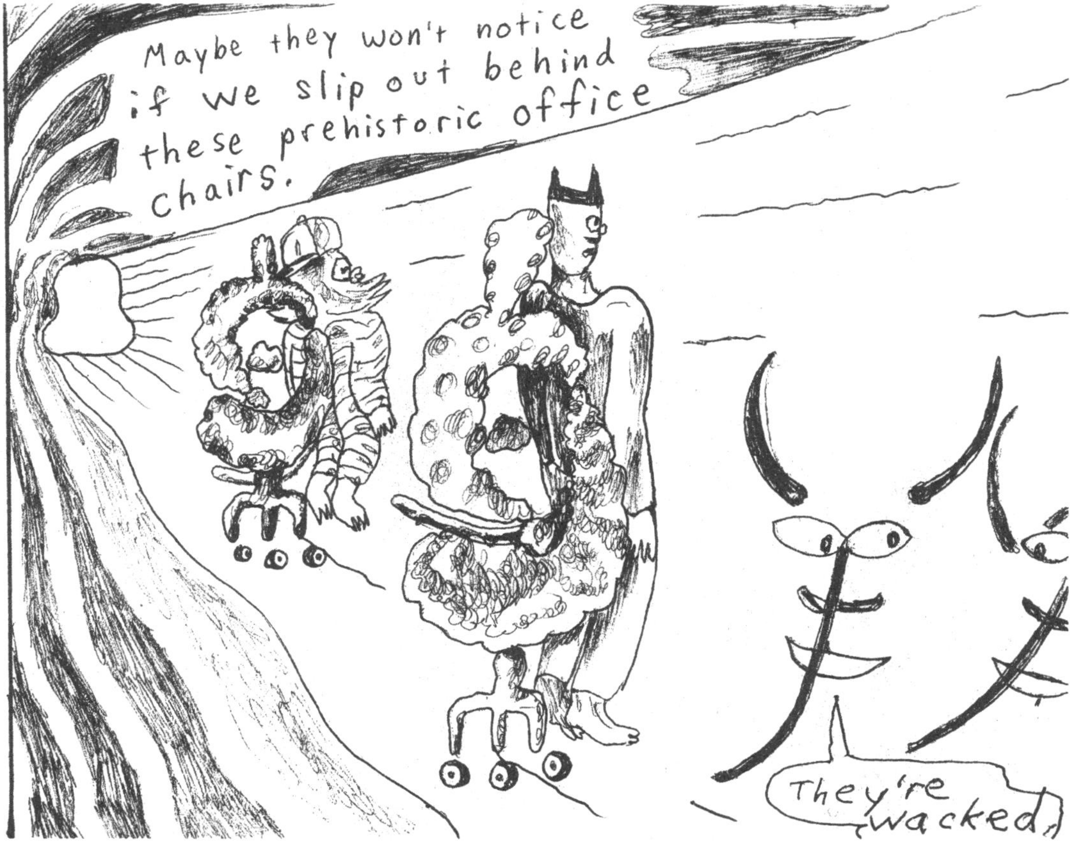

Maybe they won't notice if we slip out behind these prehistoric office chairs.
They're wacked.

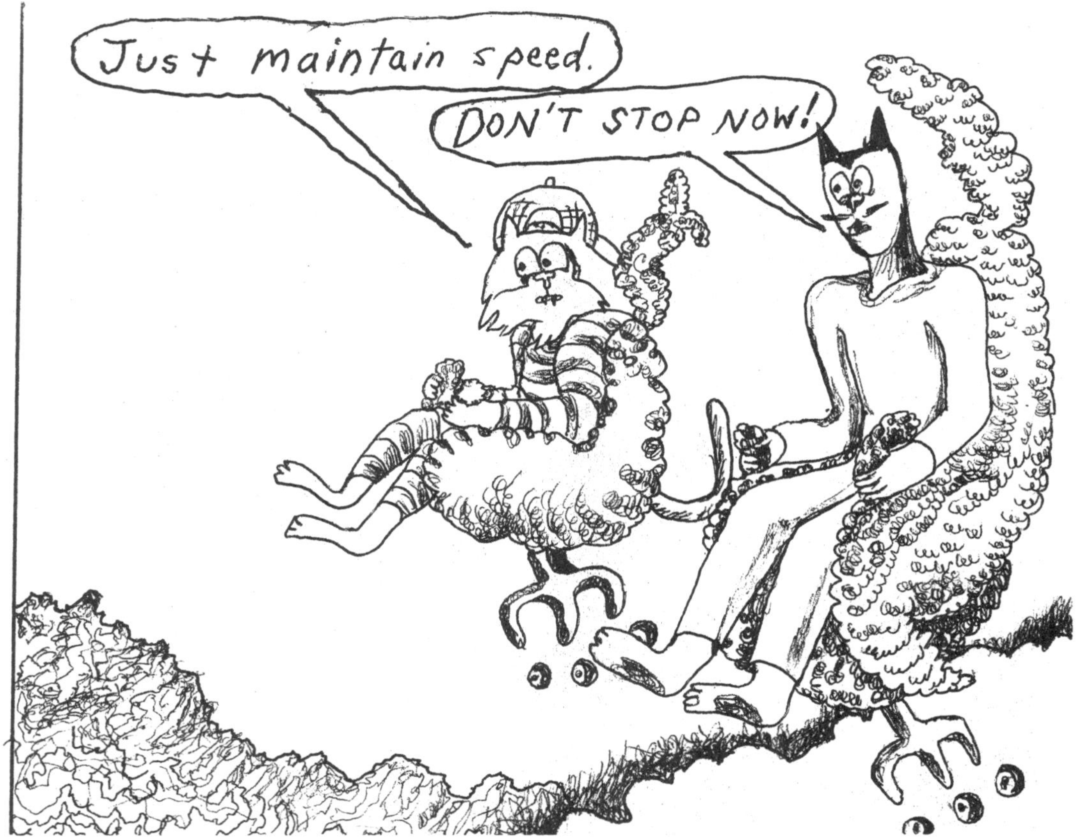
Just maintain speed.
DON'T STOP NOW!

unscheduled
protological
examination

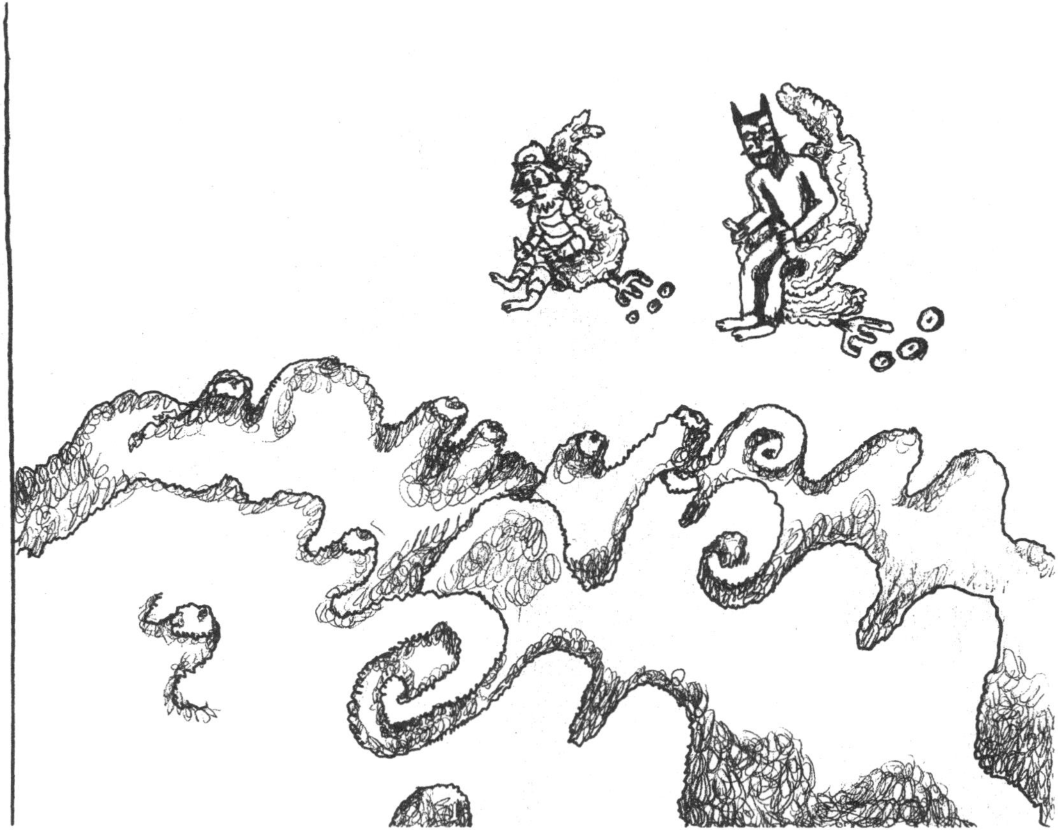

BLOBULES

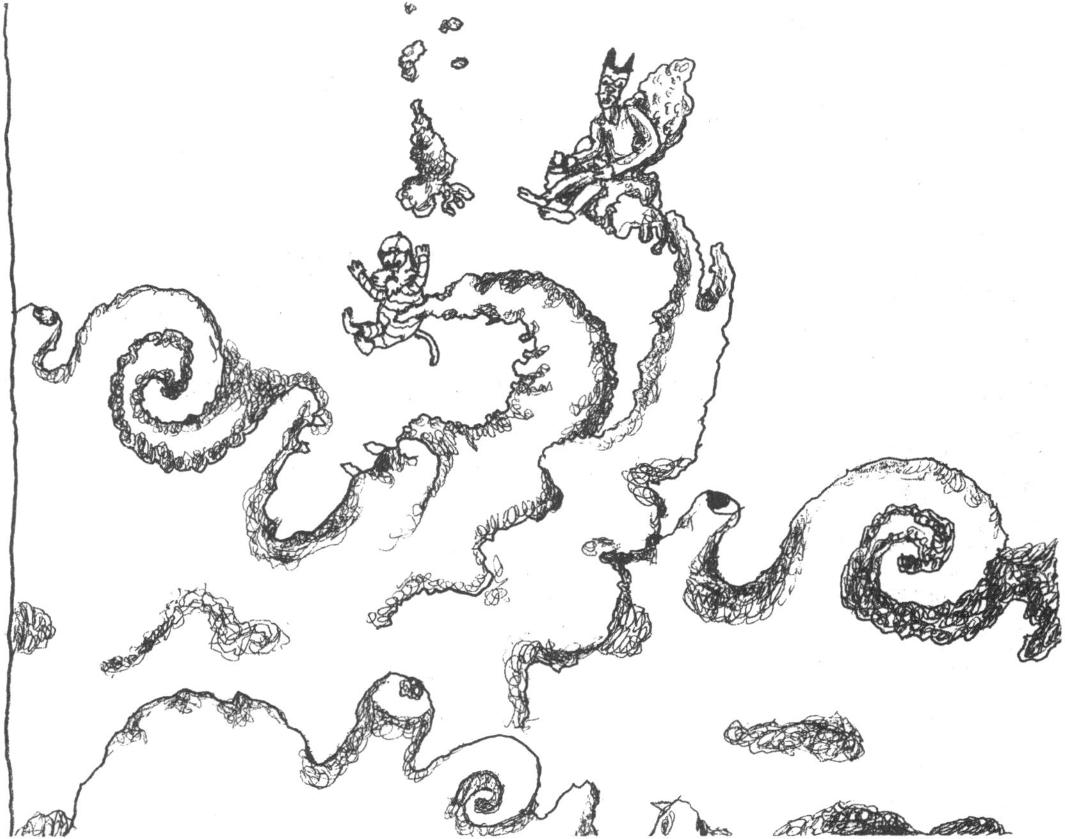

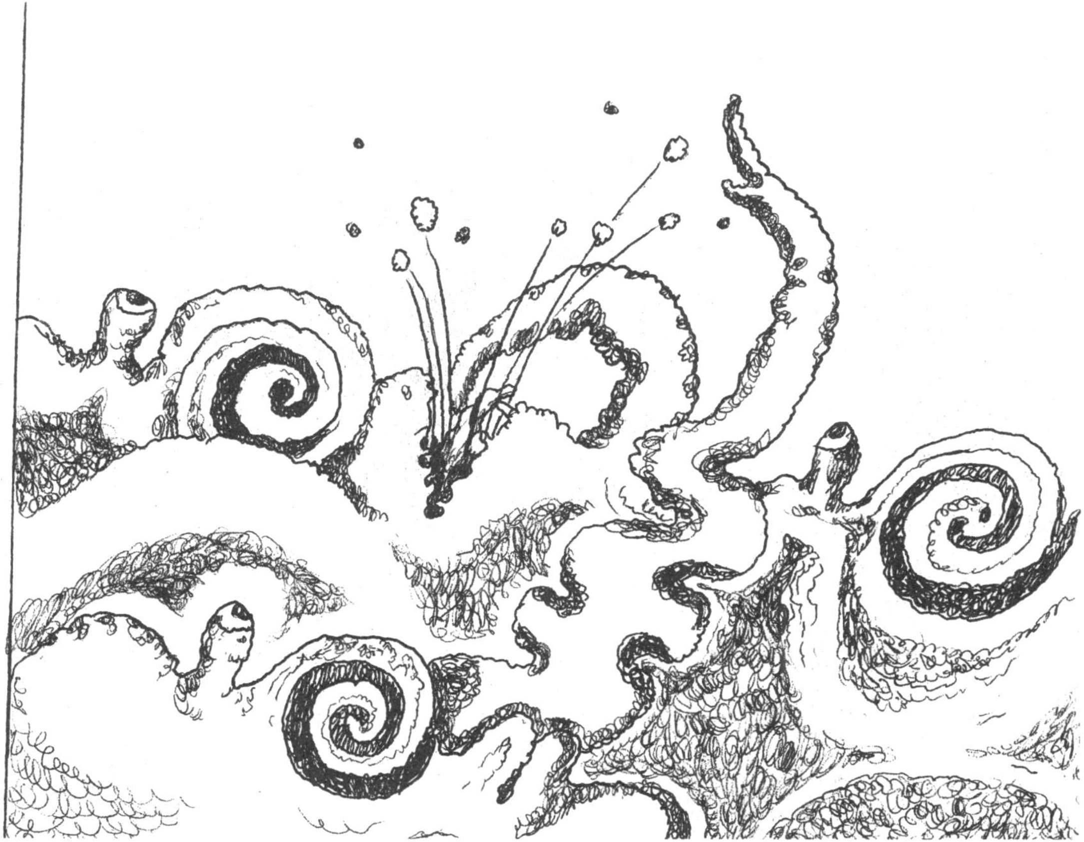

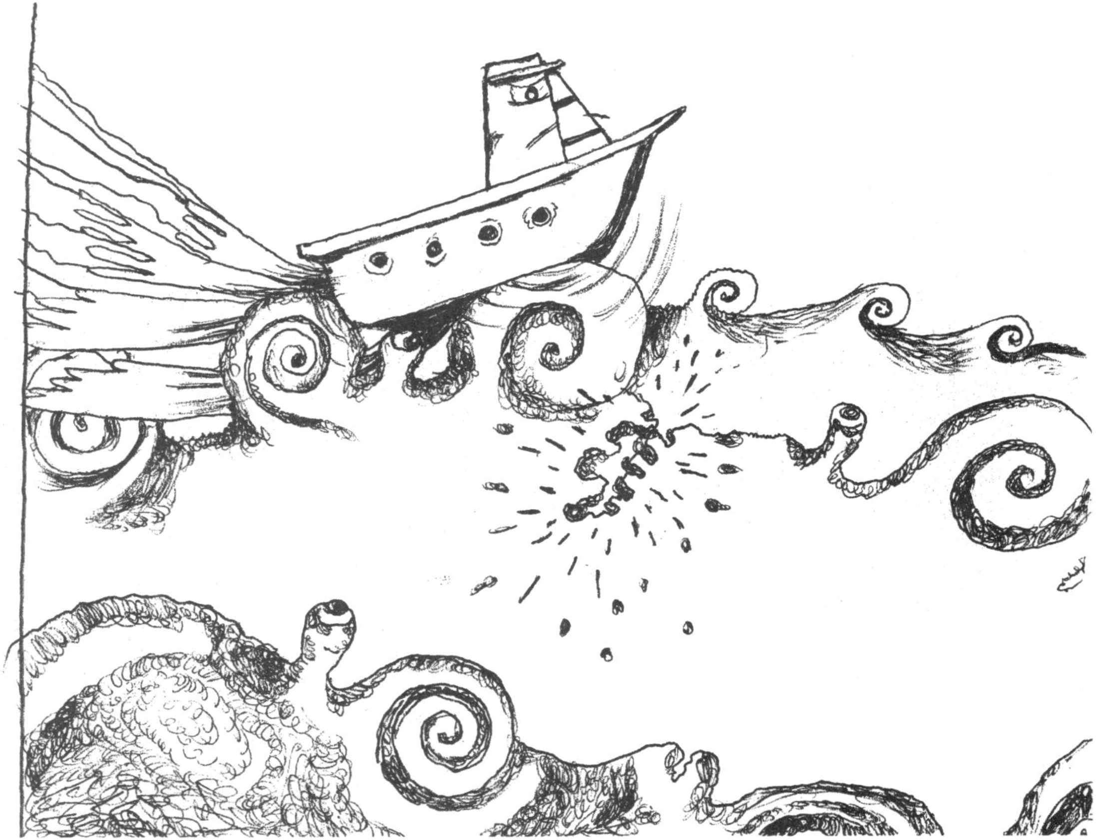

A A A
Grand
Day
Out
Wallrus

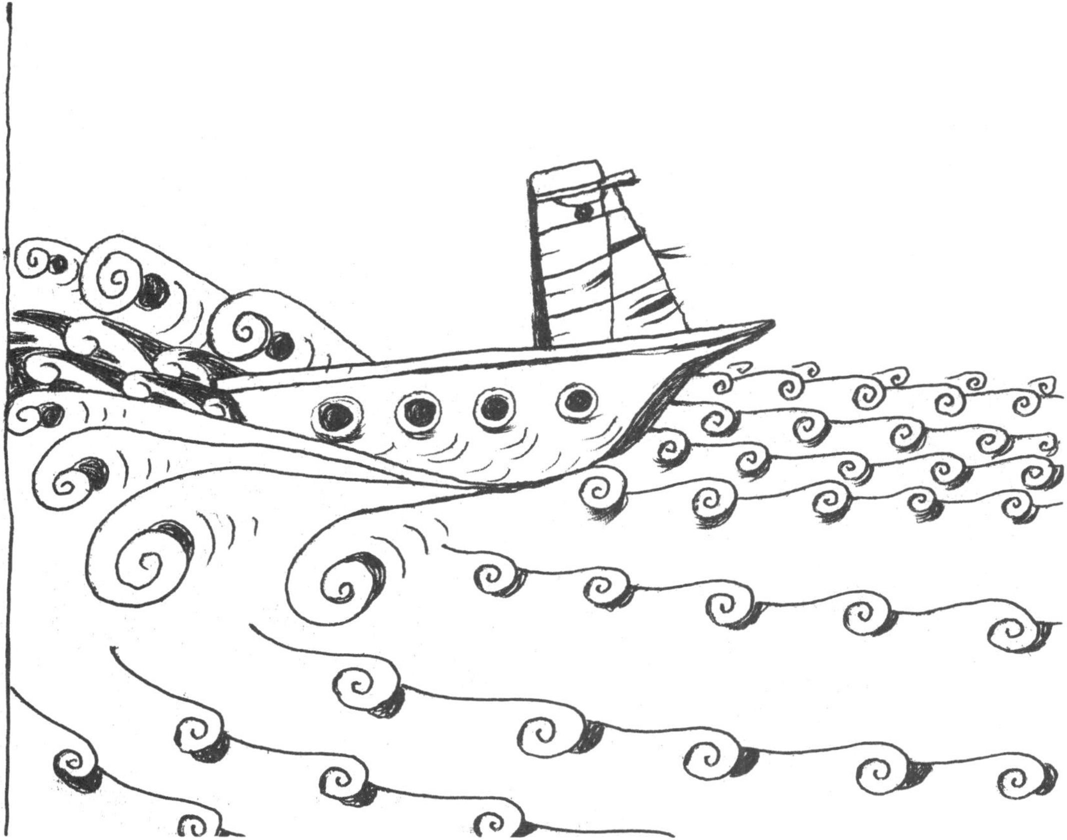

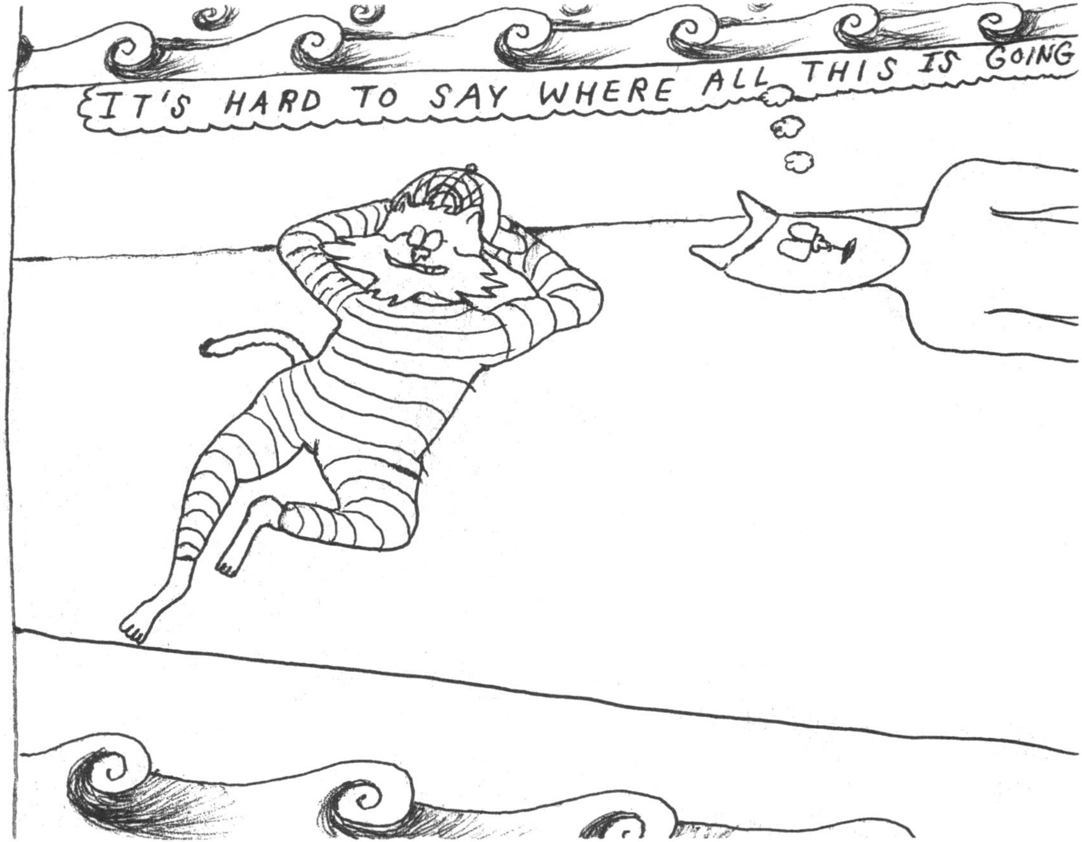
IT'S HARD TO SAY WHERE ALL THIS IS GOING

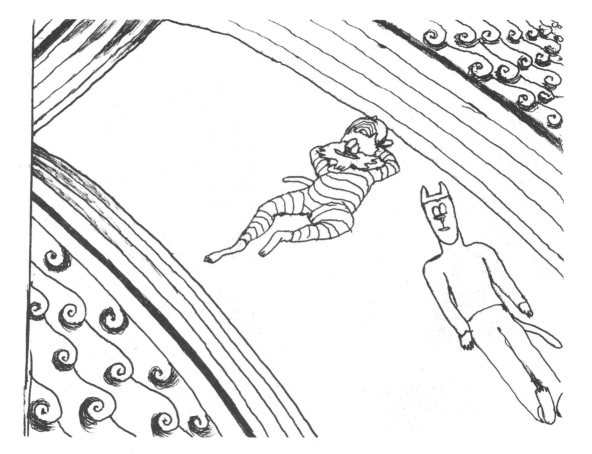

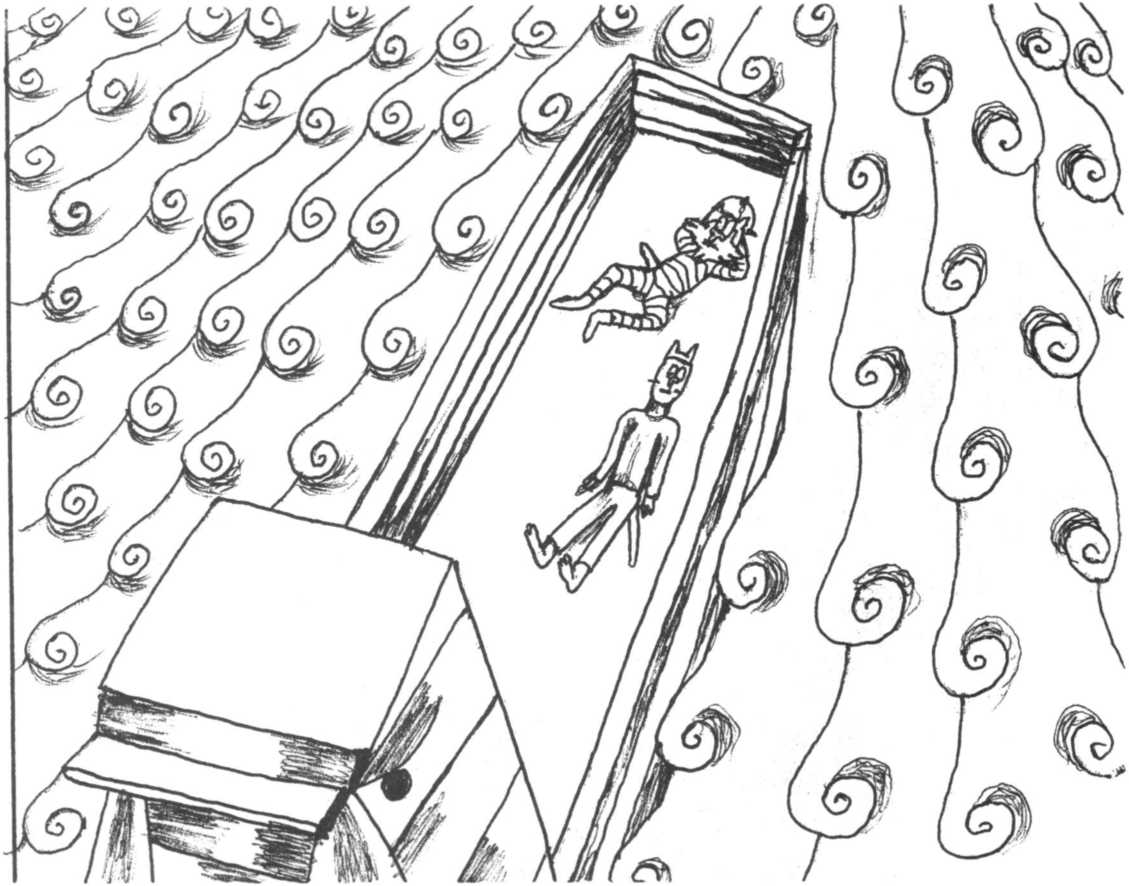

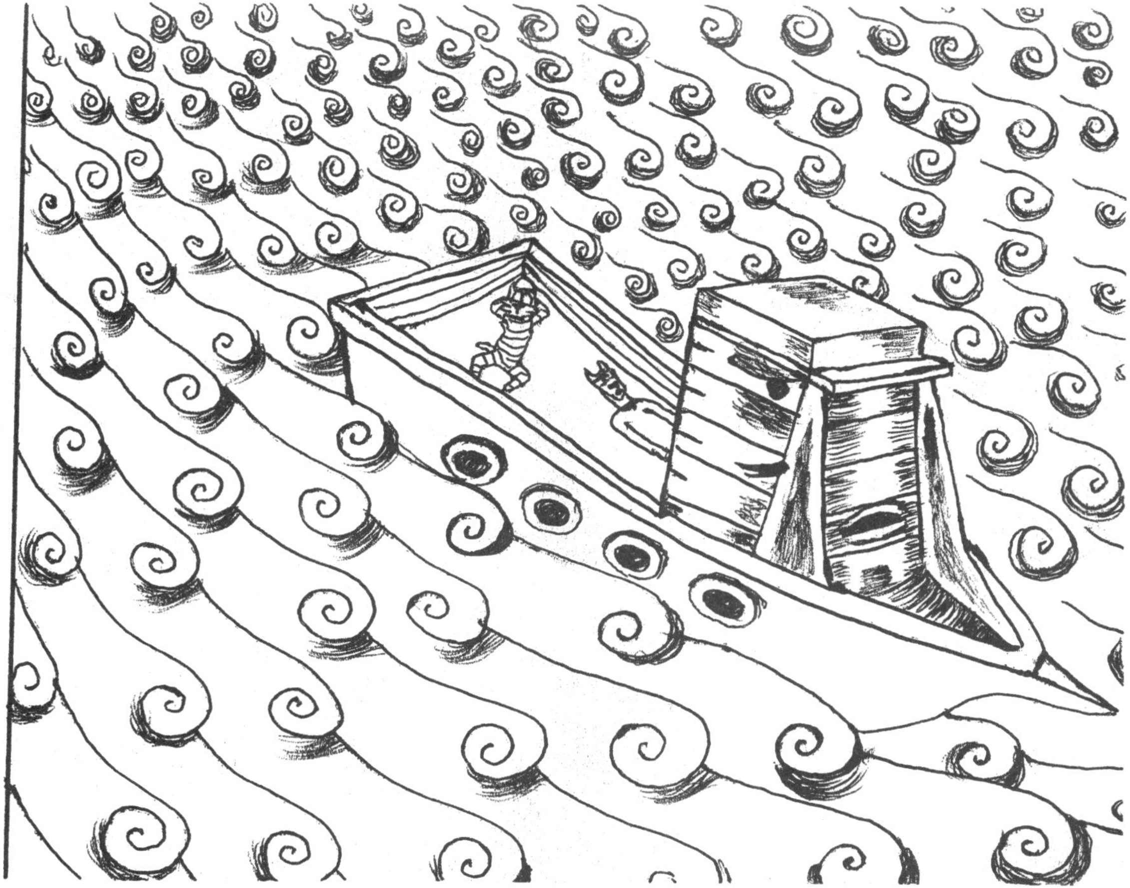

Y.R.Y.?

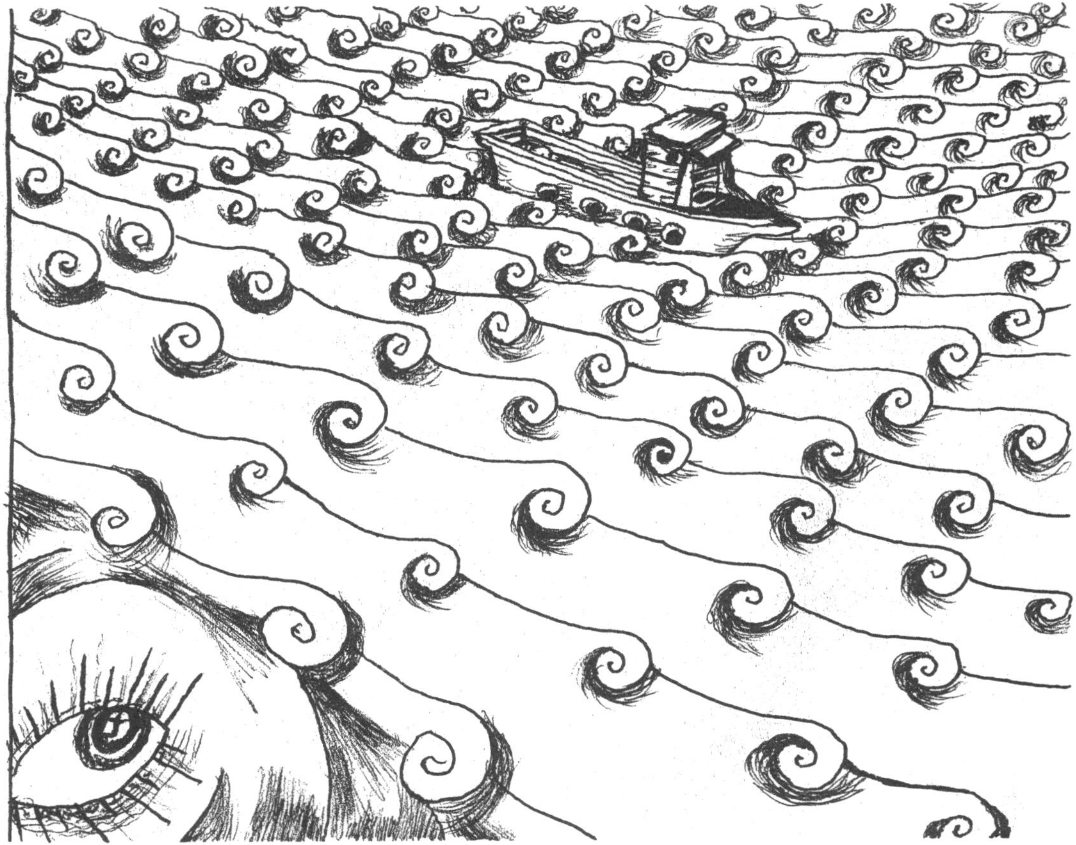

man
suit
mask
garbage

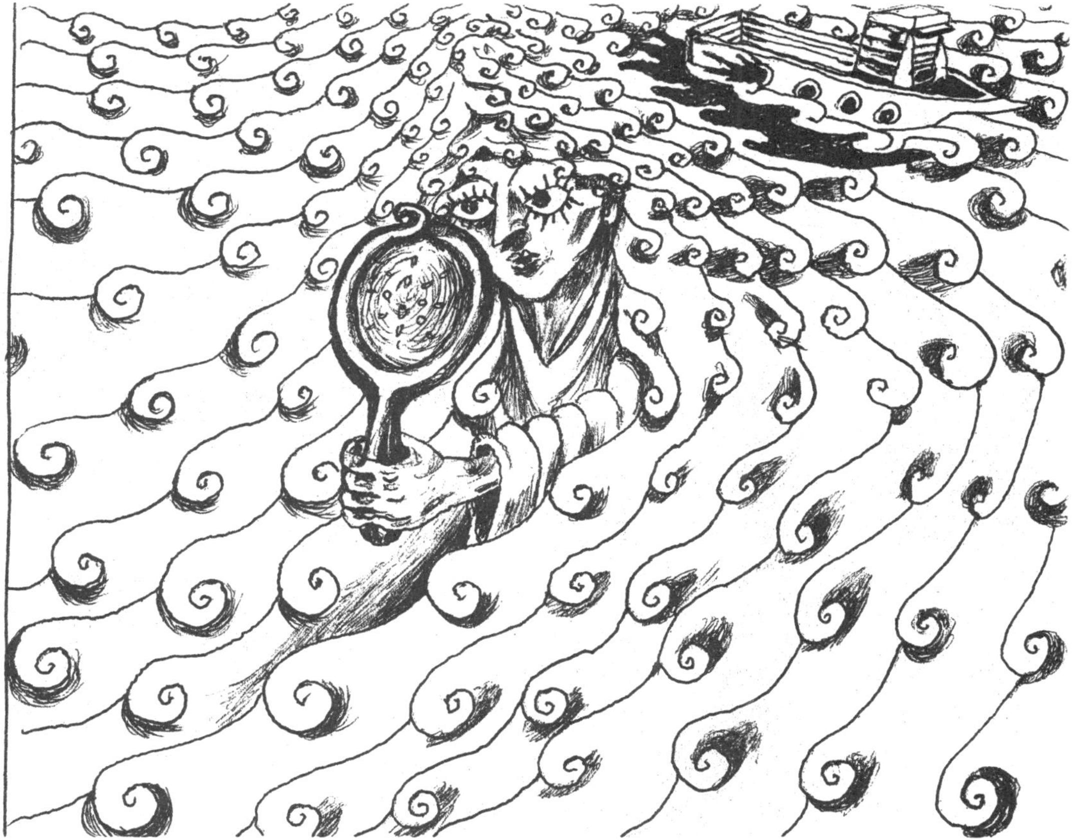

generic BLACK ANTS

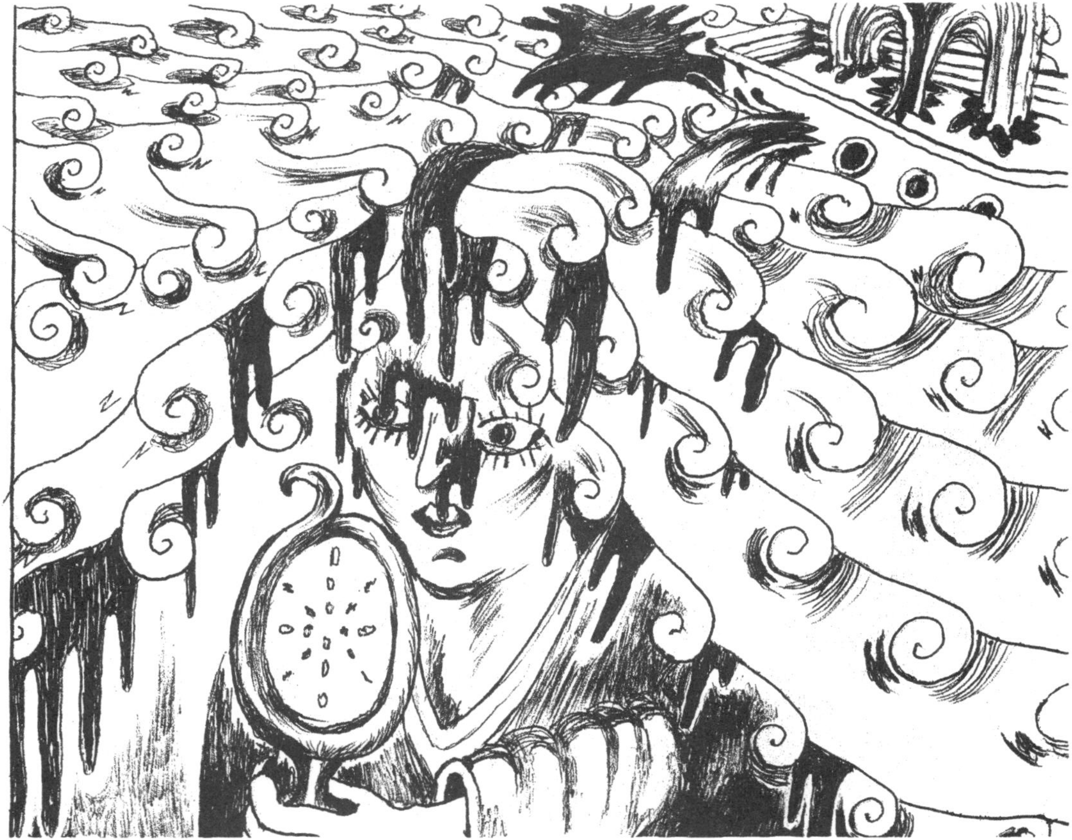

ego
maniacal
cartoon
(ist)

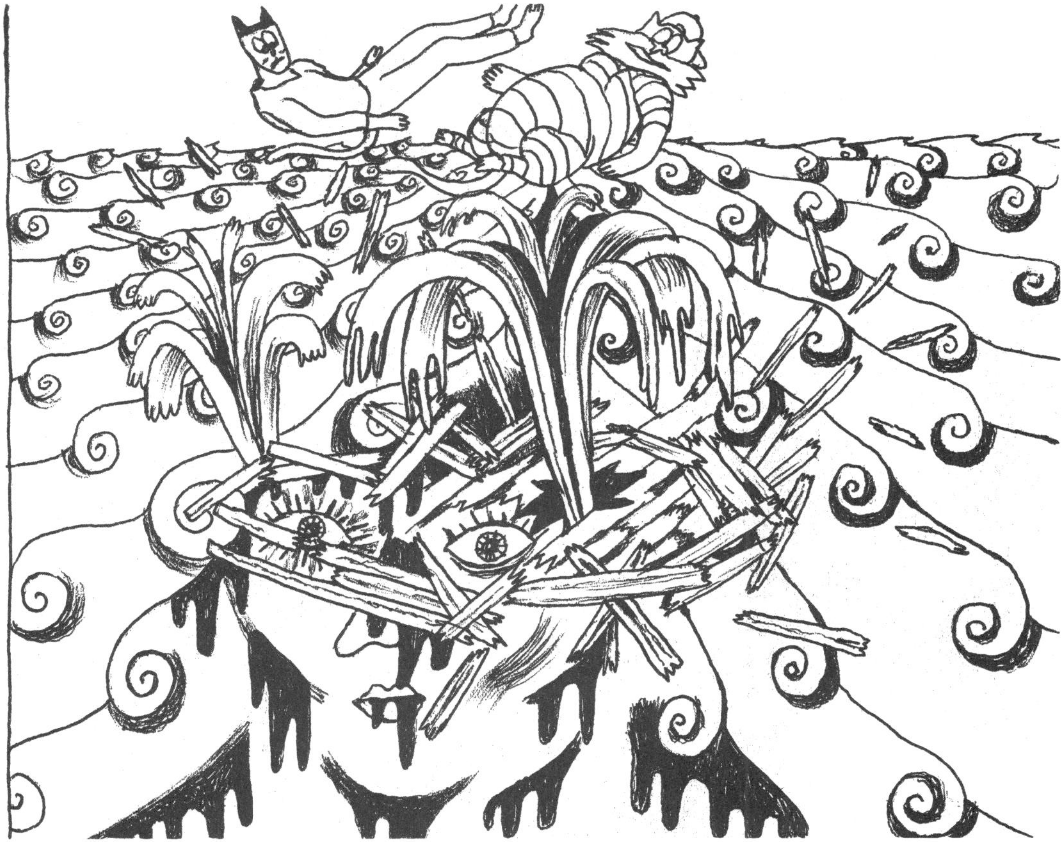

V for V for V

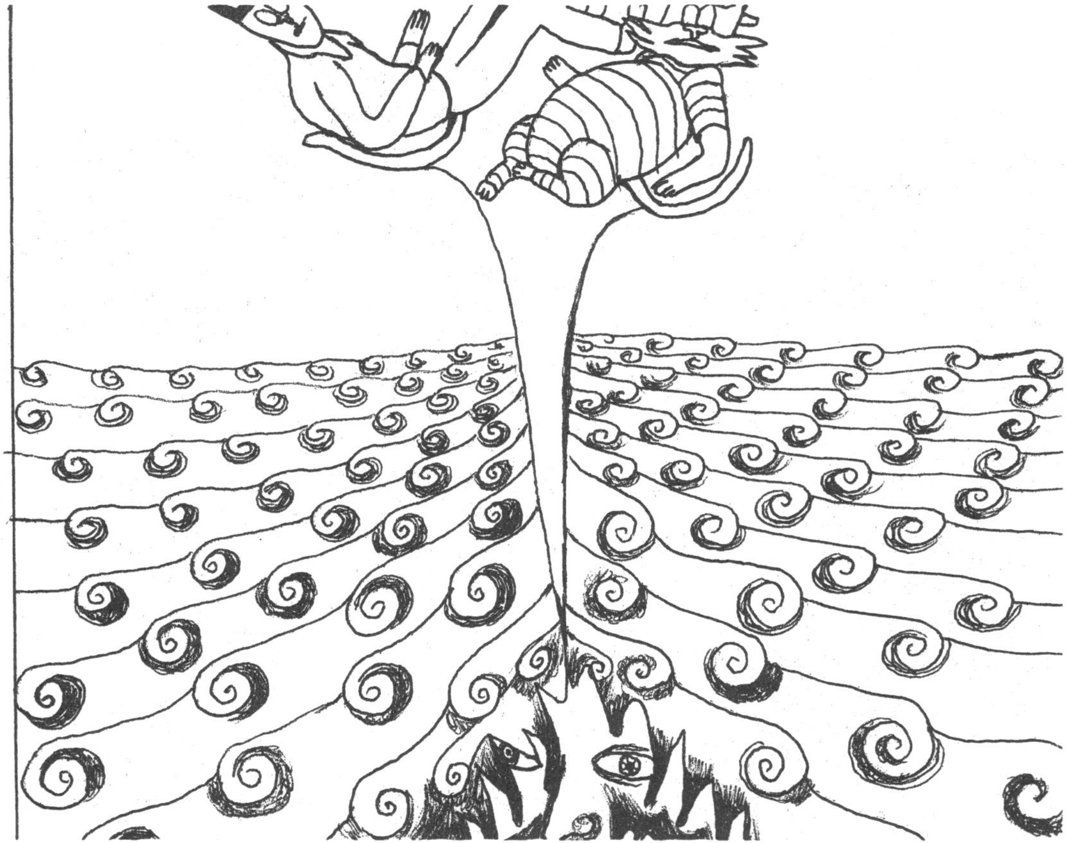

Full Moon is levitating my glandus

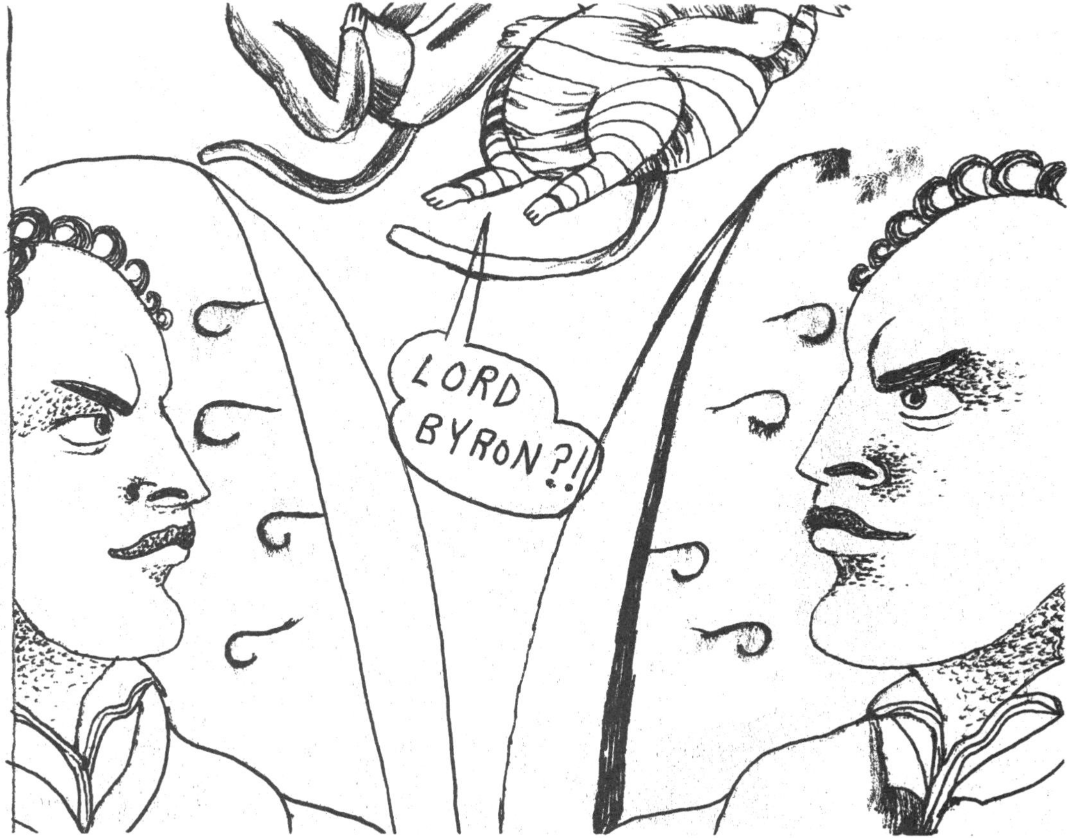
LORD BYRON?!

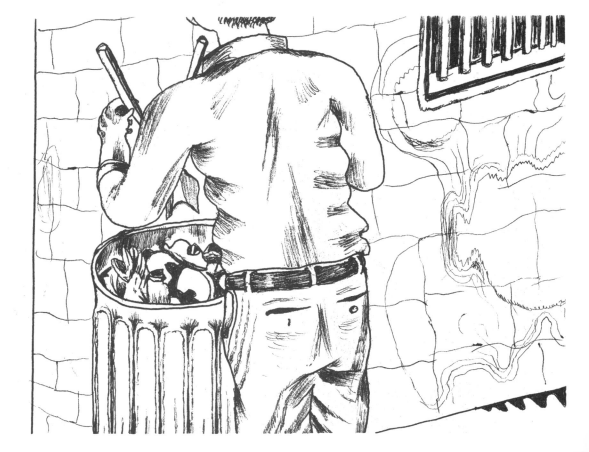

NICE PAINTING BRIAN

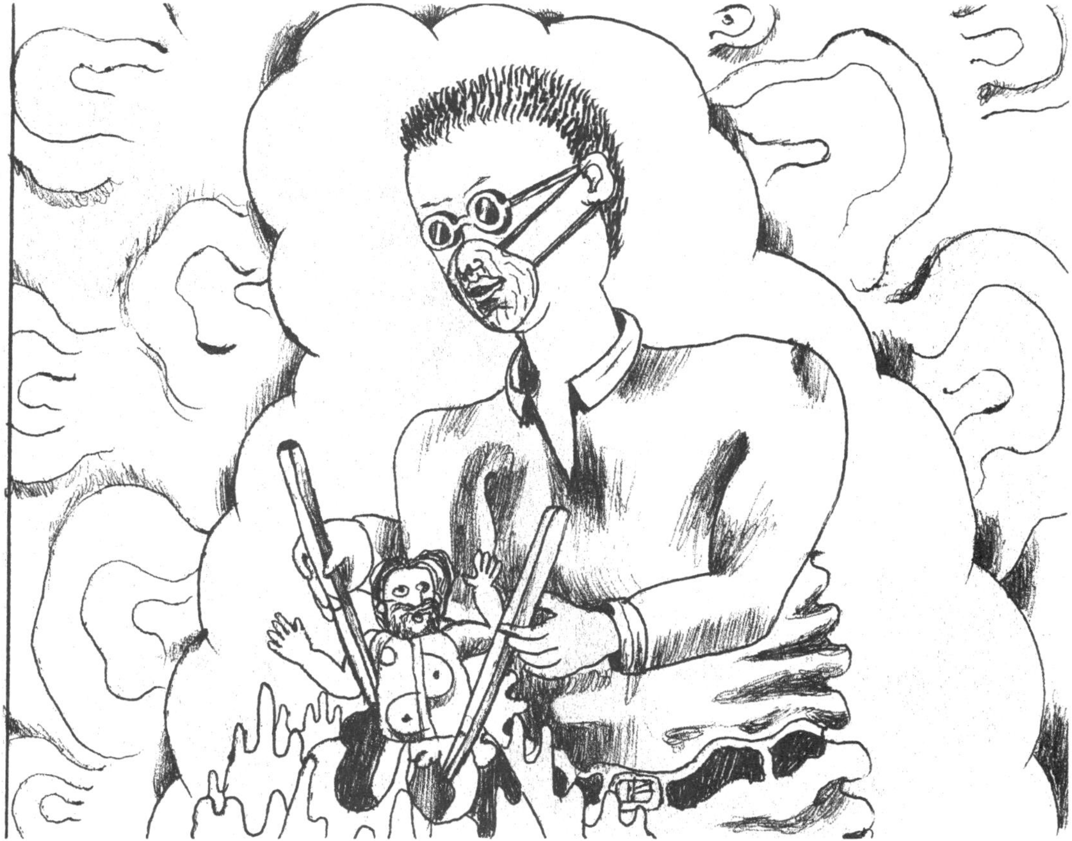

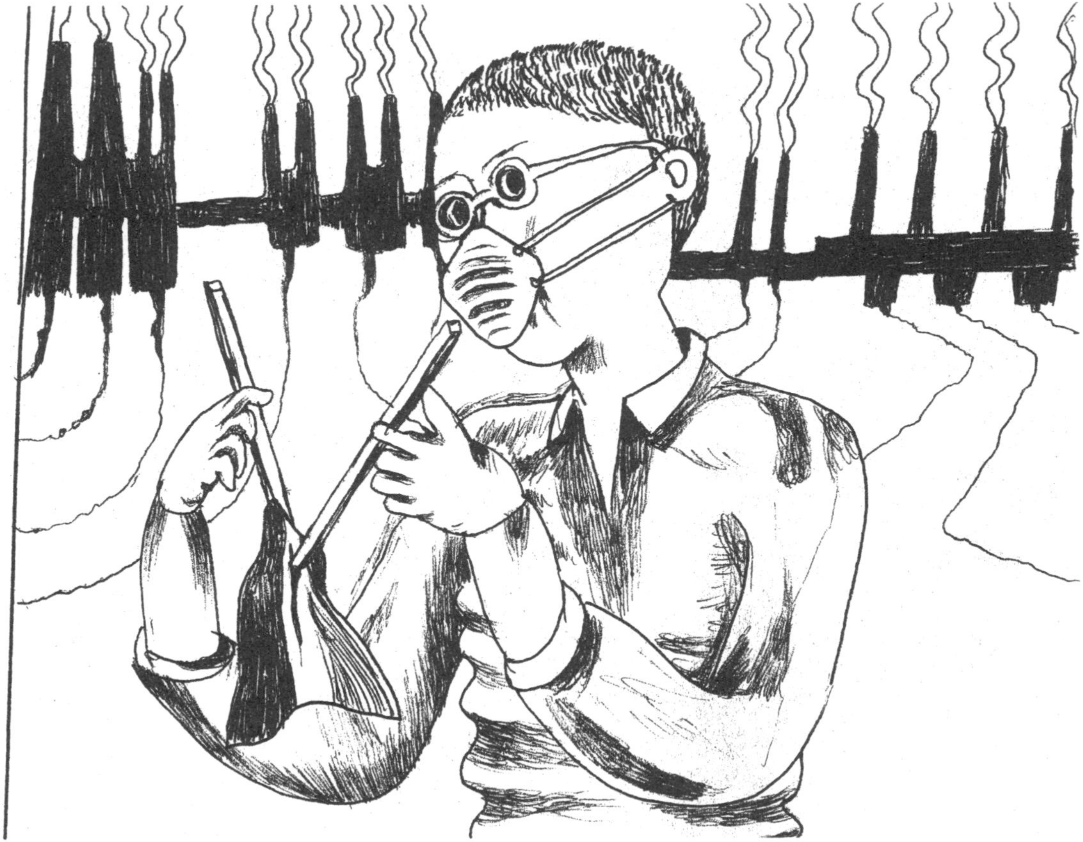

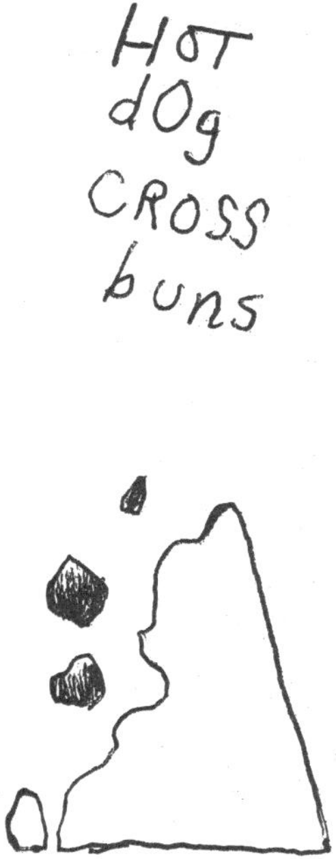
HoT dOg CROSS buns

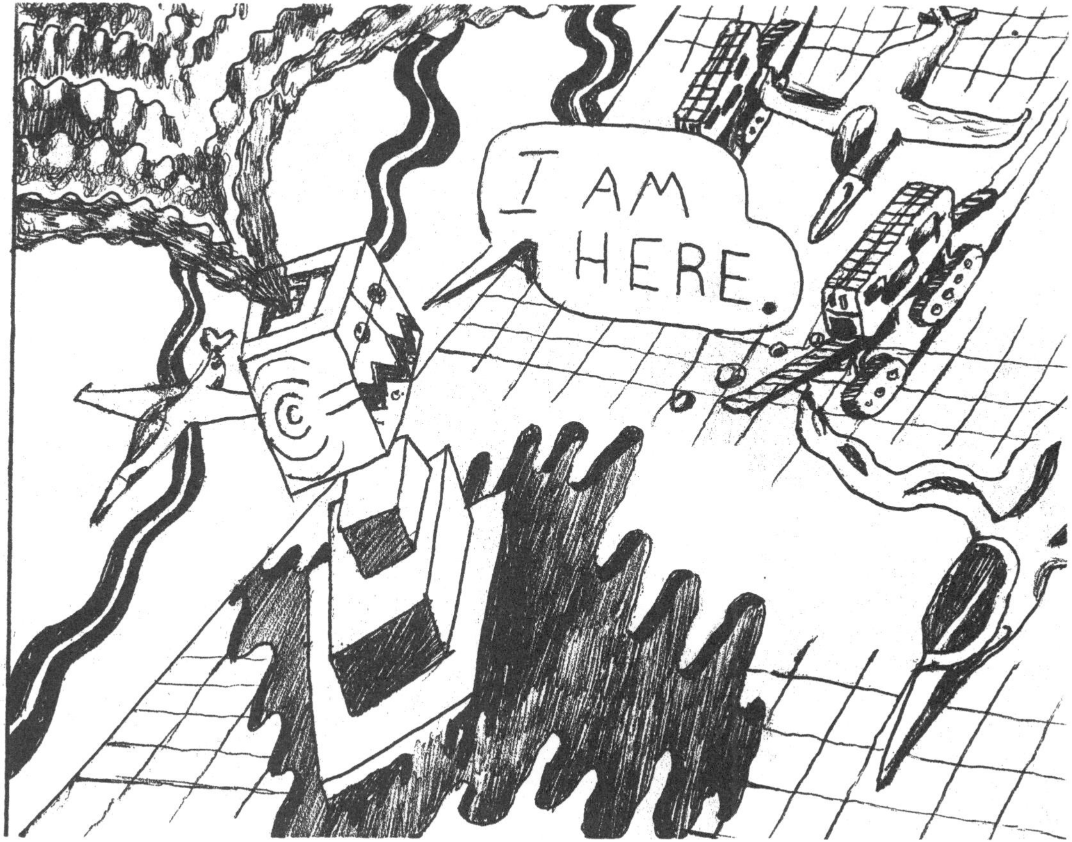
I AM HERE.

Put your blinders ON

"These are the Rebels? Who cares about Parlaimant

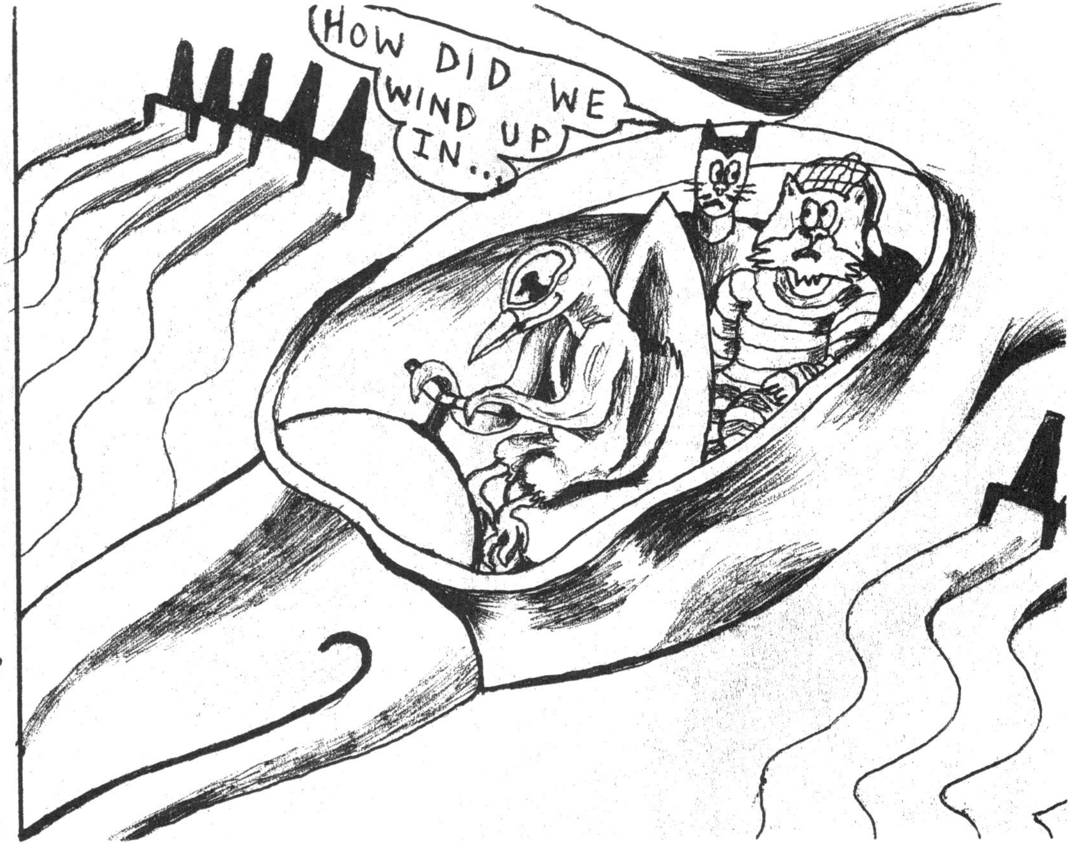
HOW DID WE WIND UP IN...

LIKE
KICKING
THE
CAN
DOWN
THE
ROAD

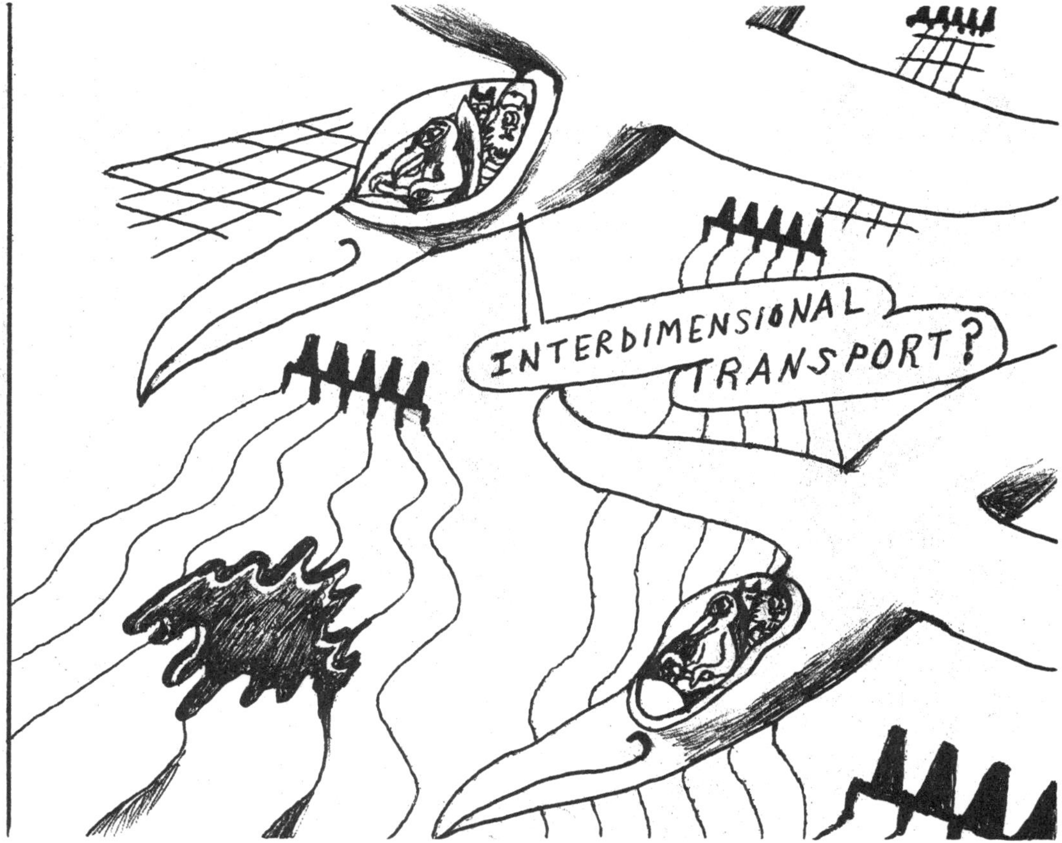
INTERDIMENSIONAL TRANSPORT?

laceration
ache
pain
S

swollen
hand
ER

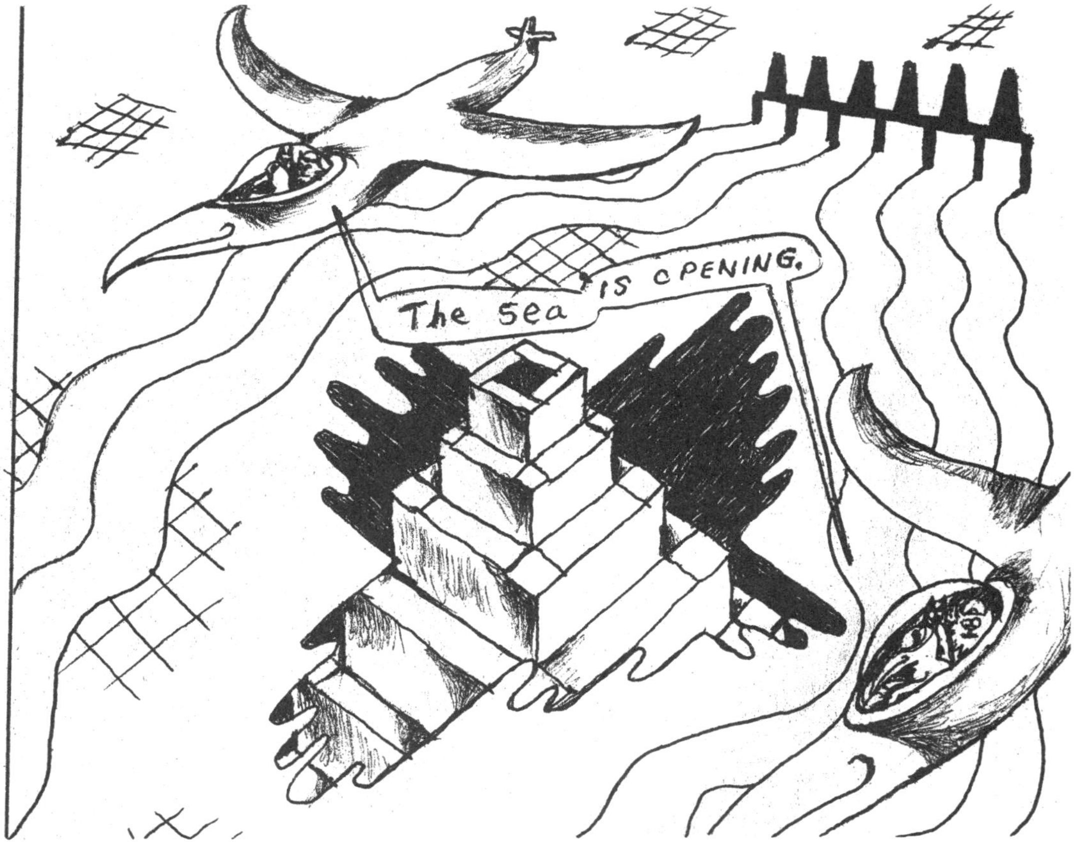
The sea IS OPENING.

sometimes
you
gotta
let
the
marbles
roll,

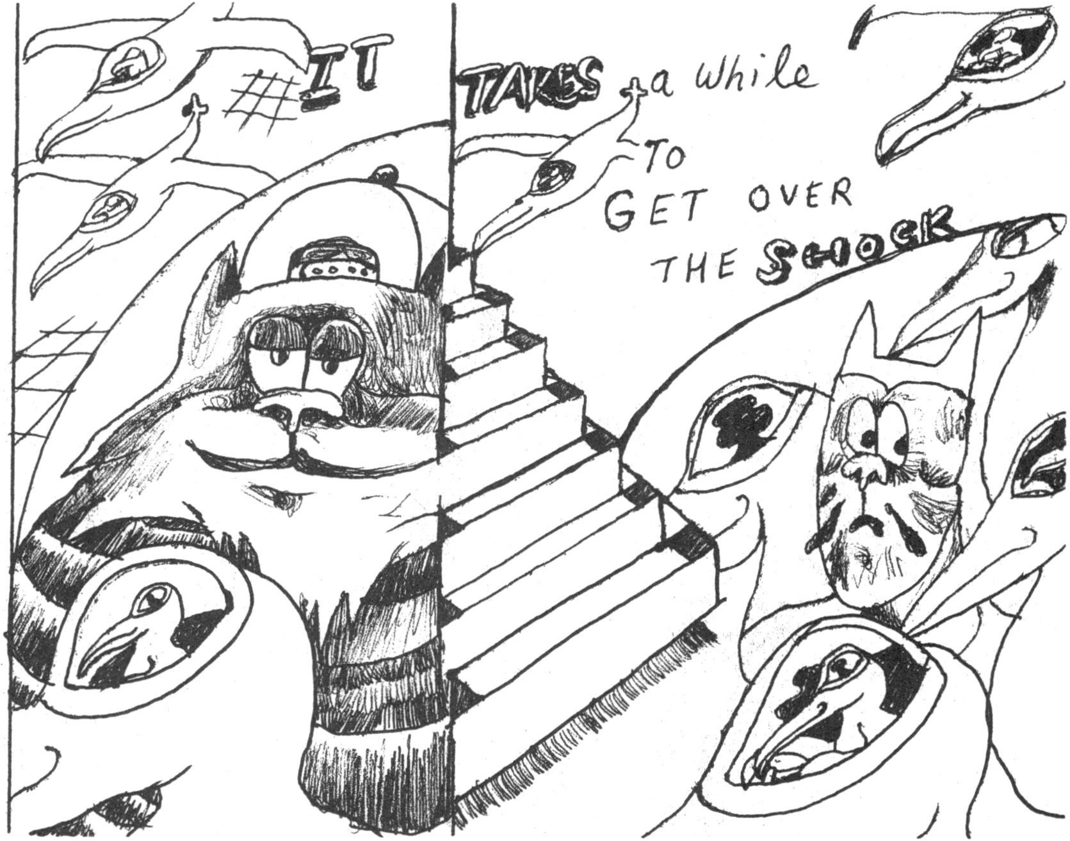
IT
TAKES a while
TO
GET OVER
THE SHOCK

just
be
sure
not
to
lose
'em

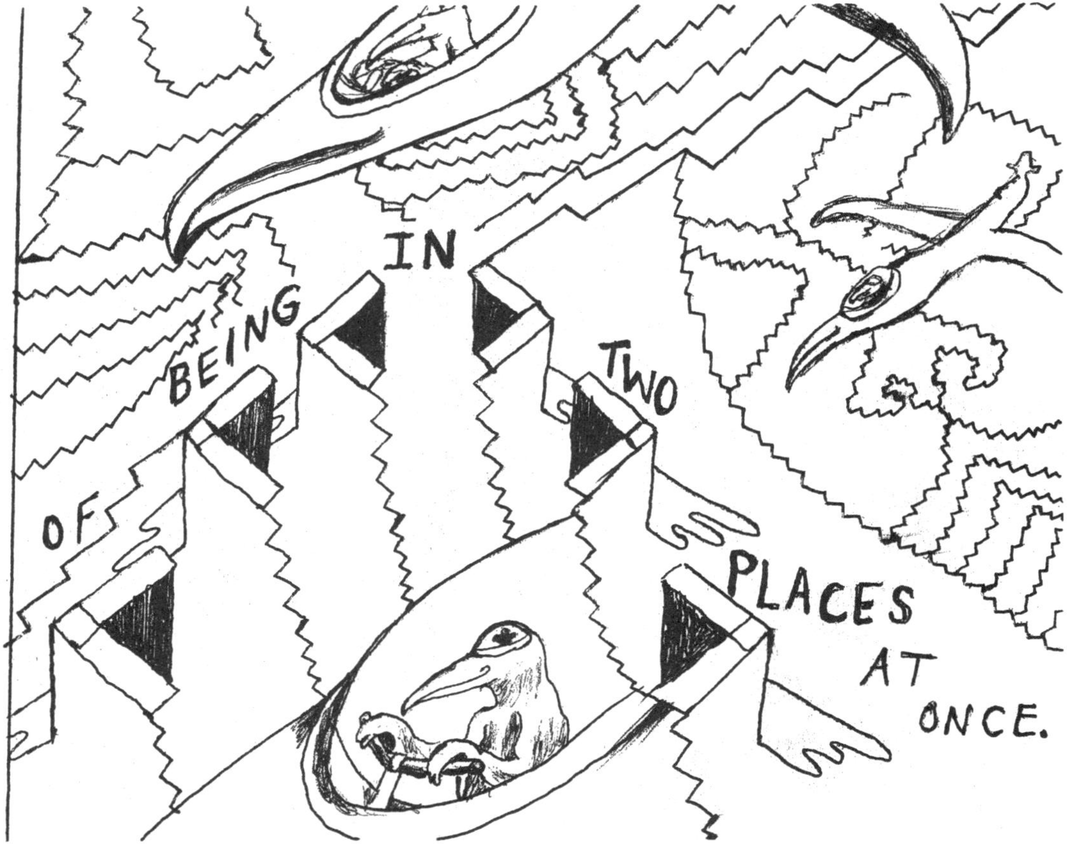
OF
BEING
IN
TWO
PLACES
AT
ONCE.

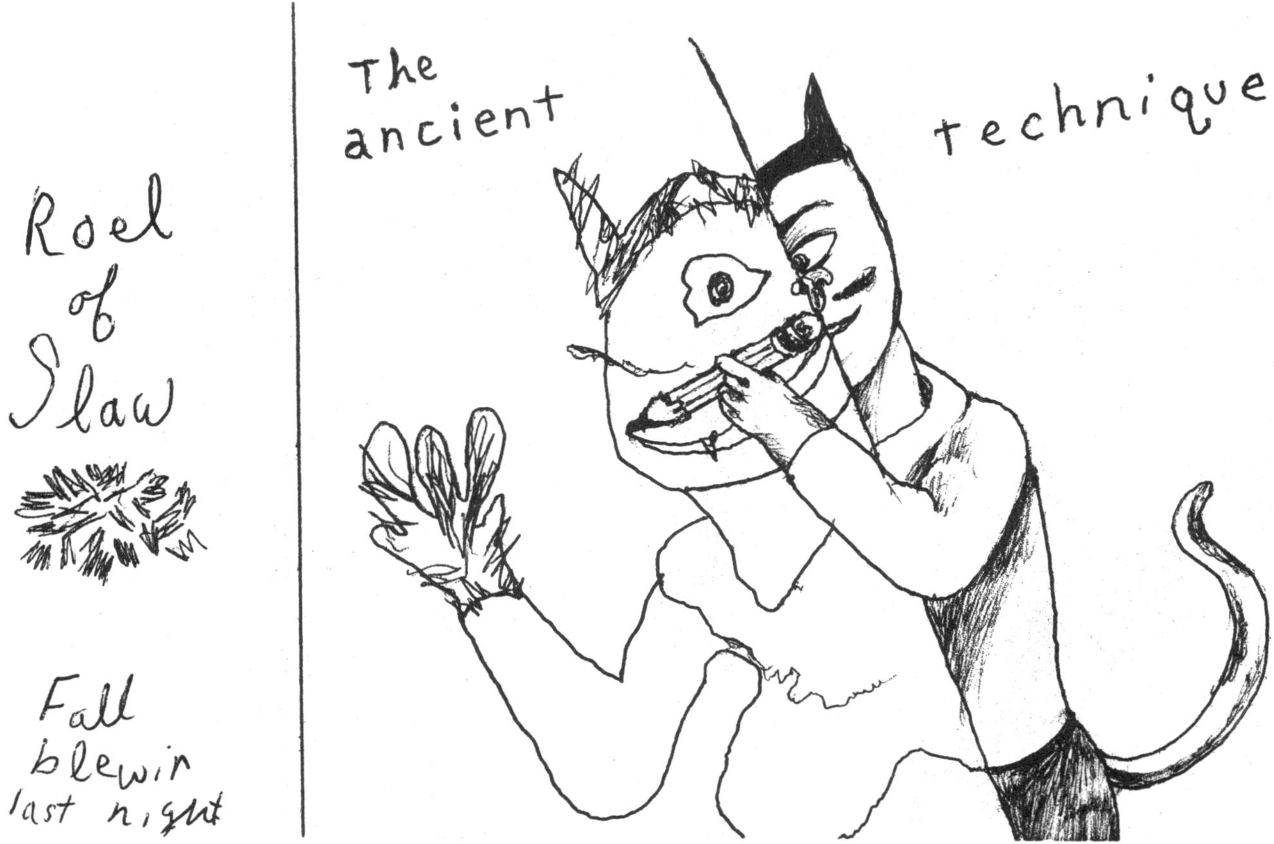
Roel of Slaw
Fall blewin last night
The ancient technique

heavy pettin'

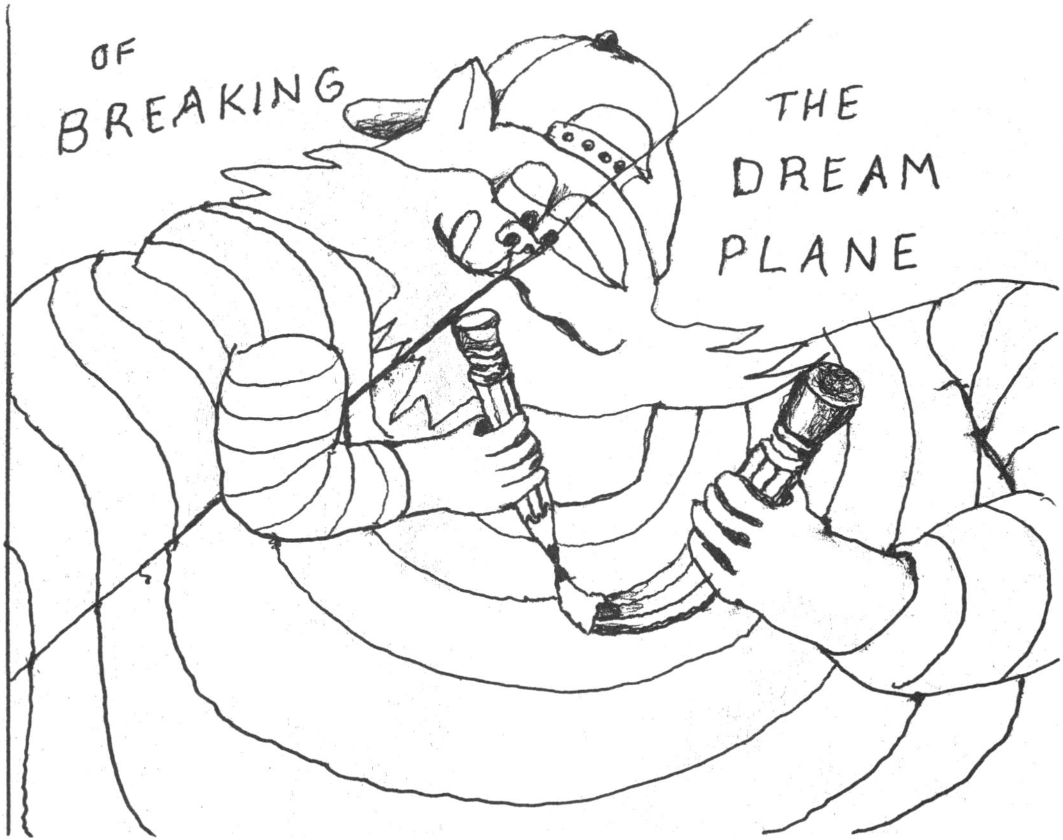

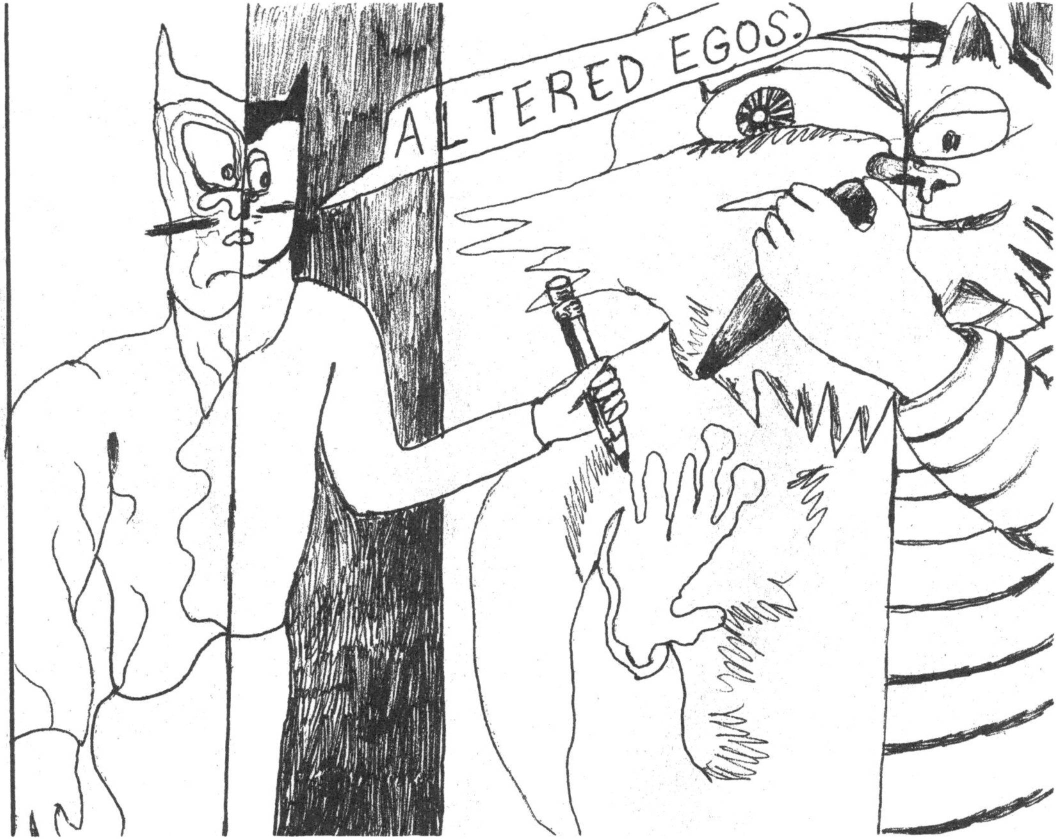
ALTERED EGOS.

romantacism of the banjo

diane cephalan

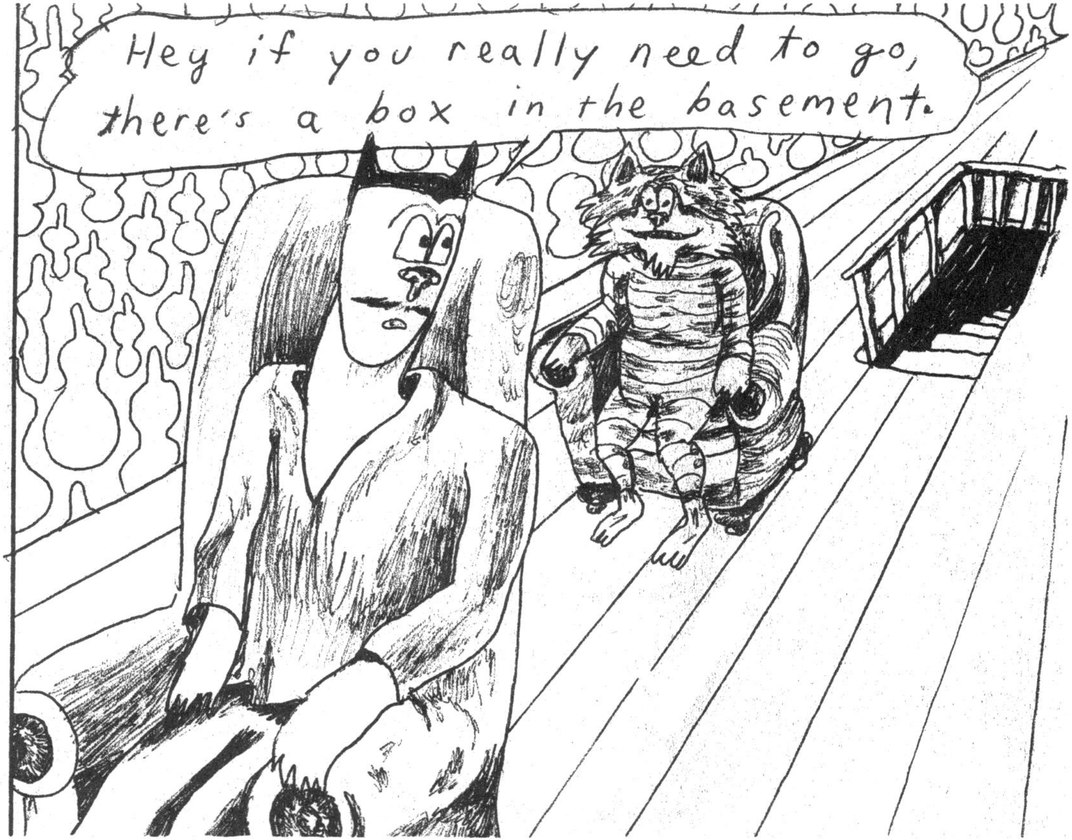
Hey if you really need to go, there's a box in the basement.

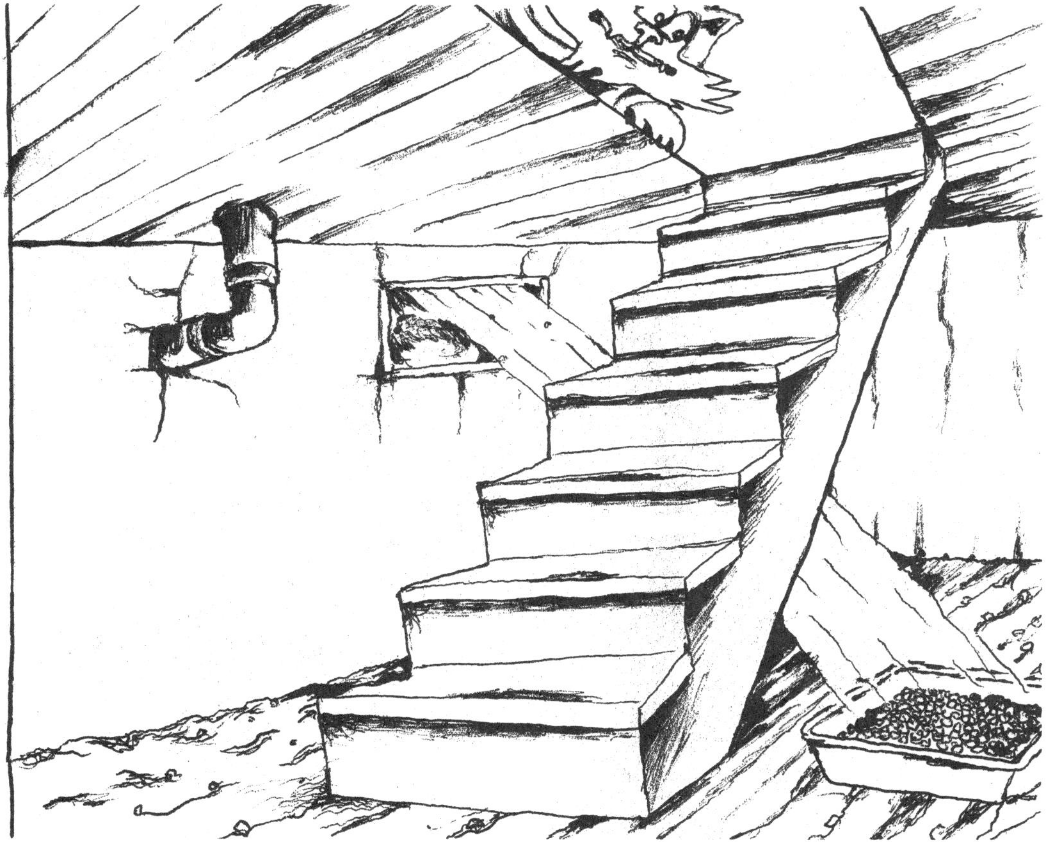

can do
more
with
this
PEN
than
that
IP
system

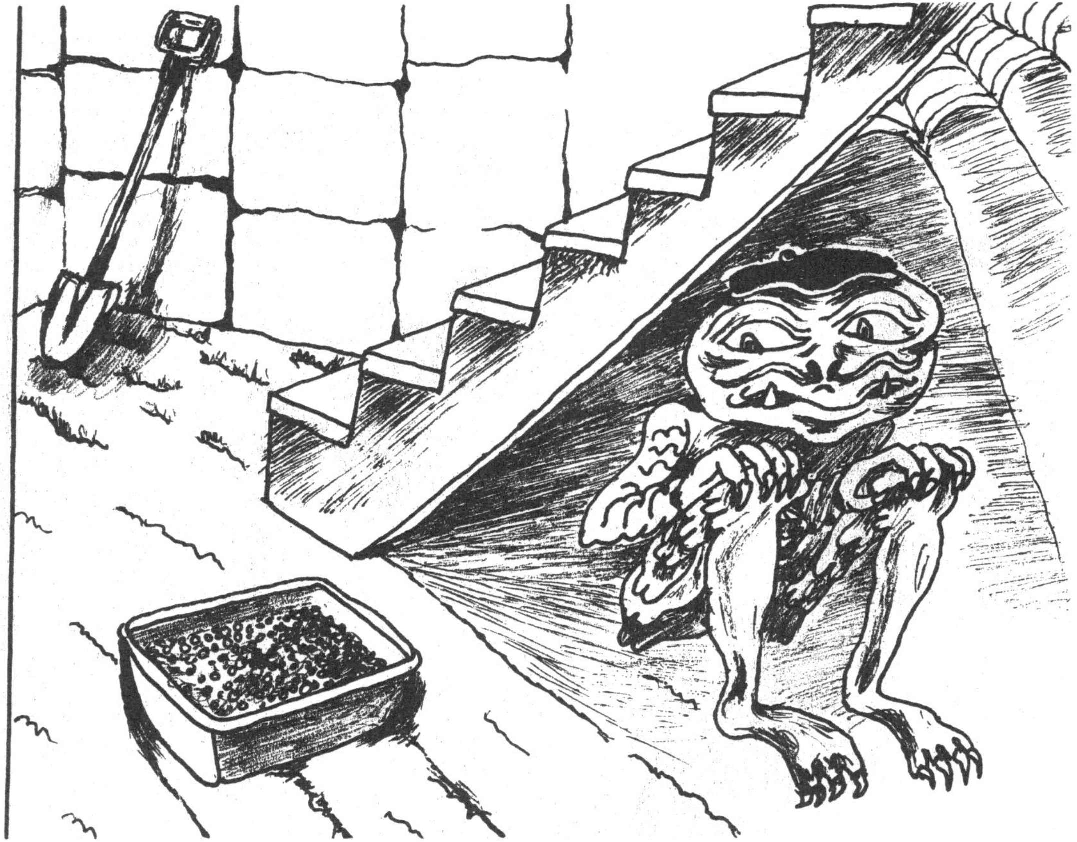

24 hr
LIVE
stream
Heavy
Metal
___
WORLD
WIDE
LIVE

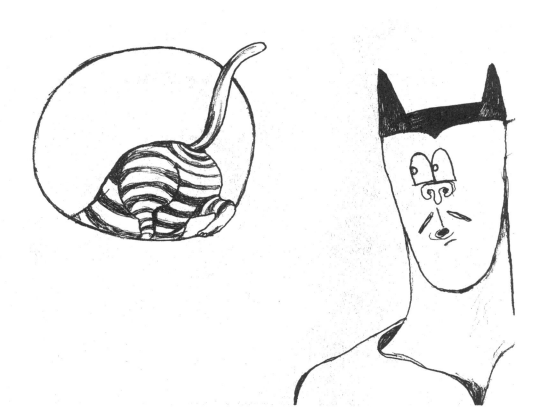

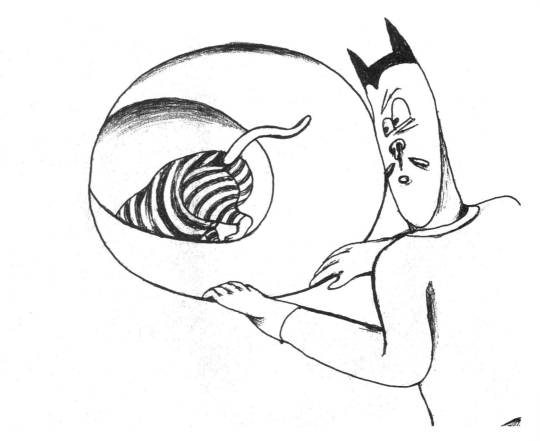

Peeping

Tom's

*

into
the
garbage

Down
the
shoot

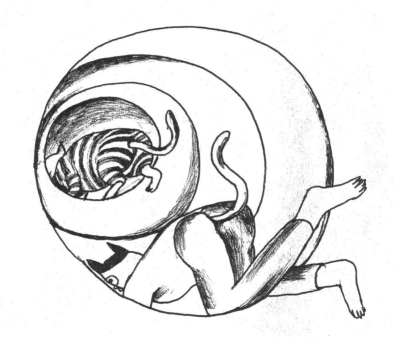

circular
flyer

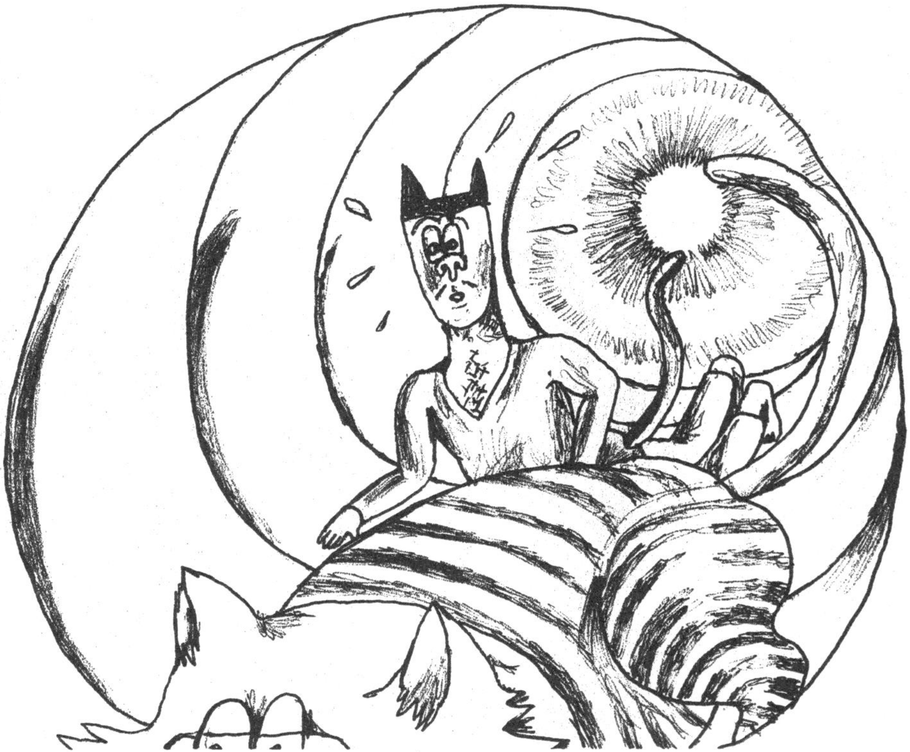

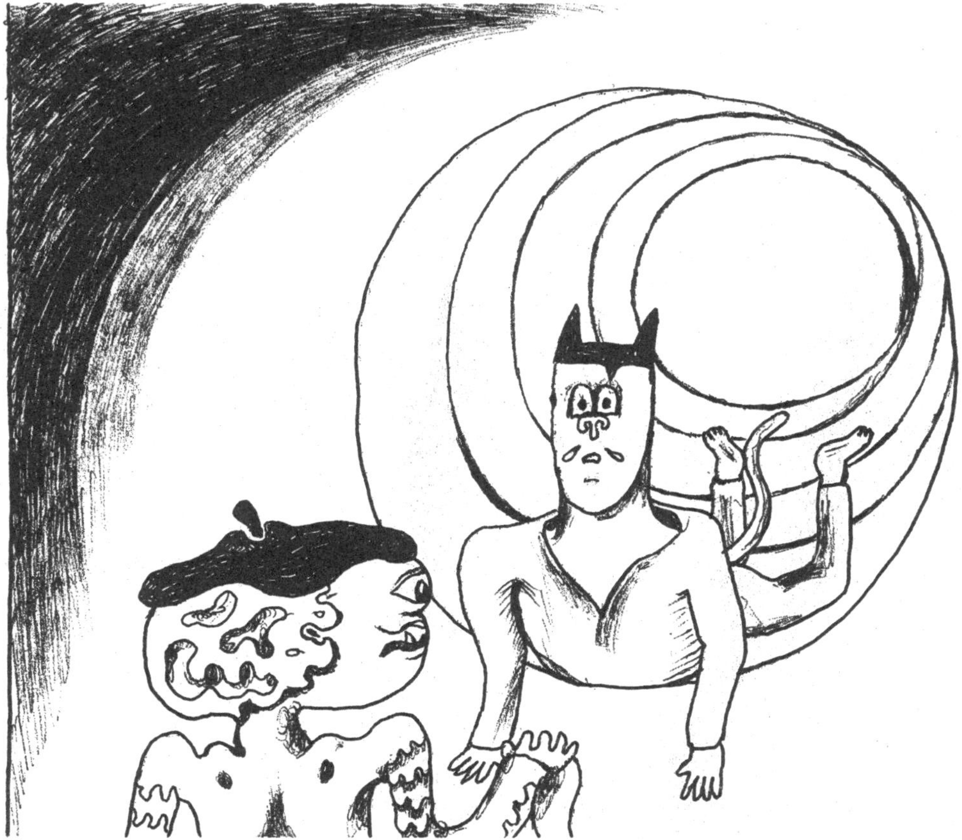

Fresh
MUD

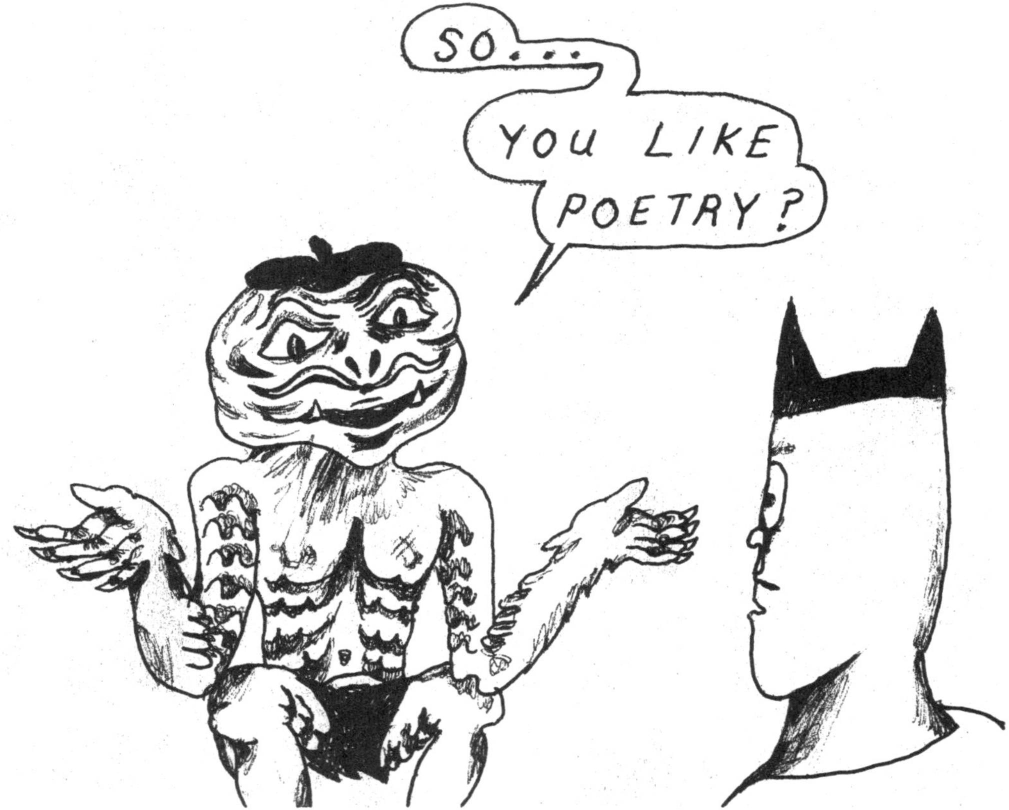
SO...
YOU LIKE POETRY?

common
"demon"
onator

dreams

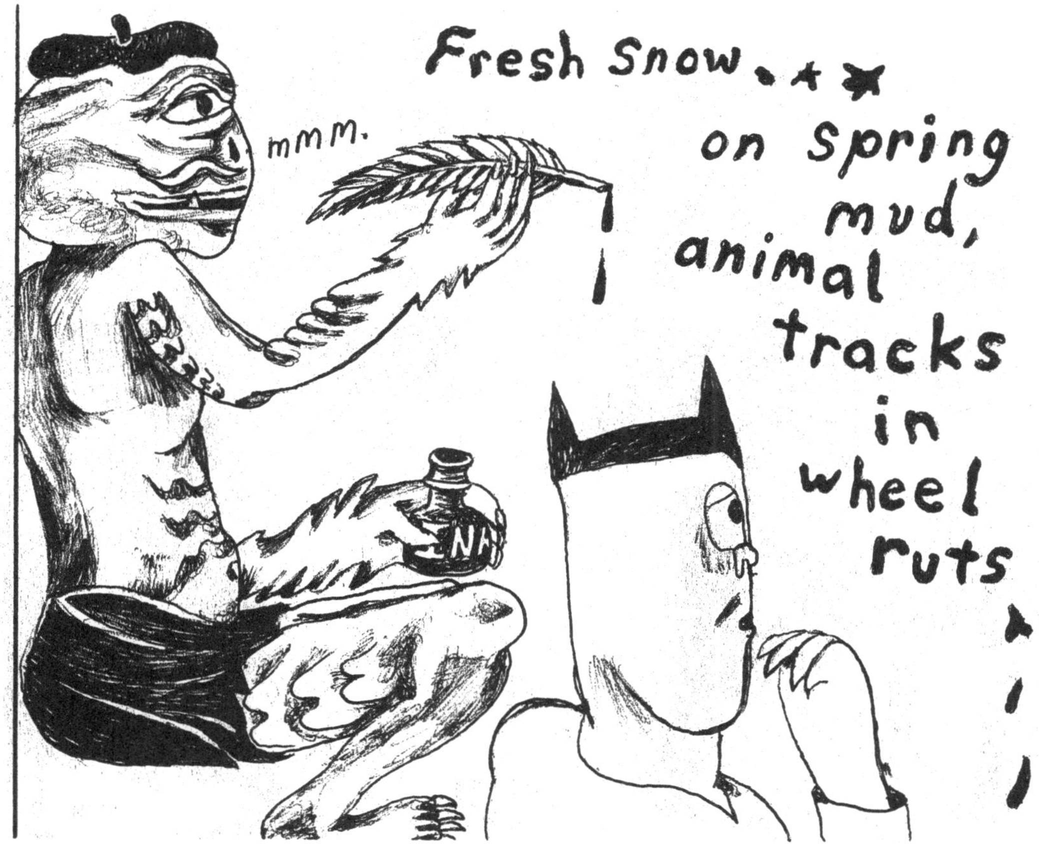
mmm.
Fresh Snow
on spring
mud,
animal
tracks
in
wheel
ruts

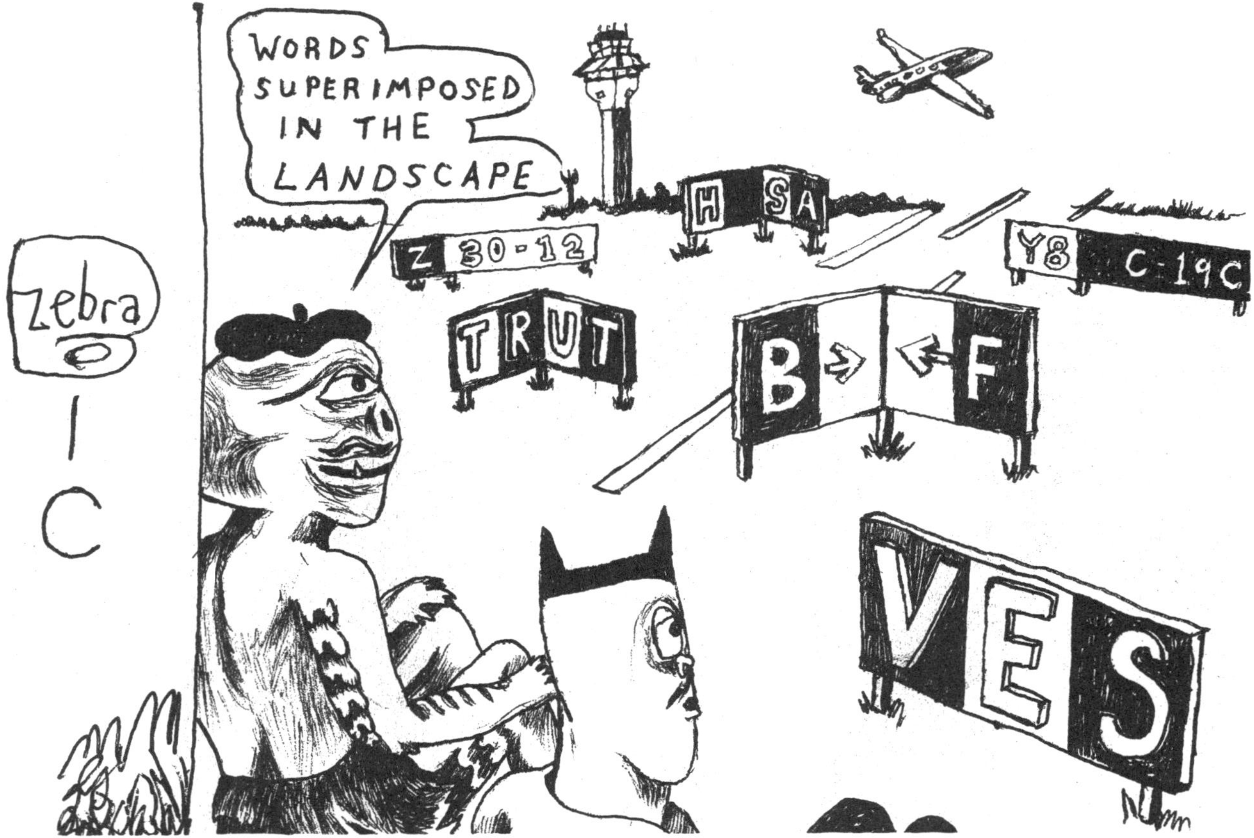
Zebra
WORDS SUPERIMPOSED IN THE LANDSCAPE
Z 30-12
H SA
Y8 C-19C
TRUT
B F
VES

Where
does
foolery
stop

EAST/WEST

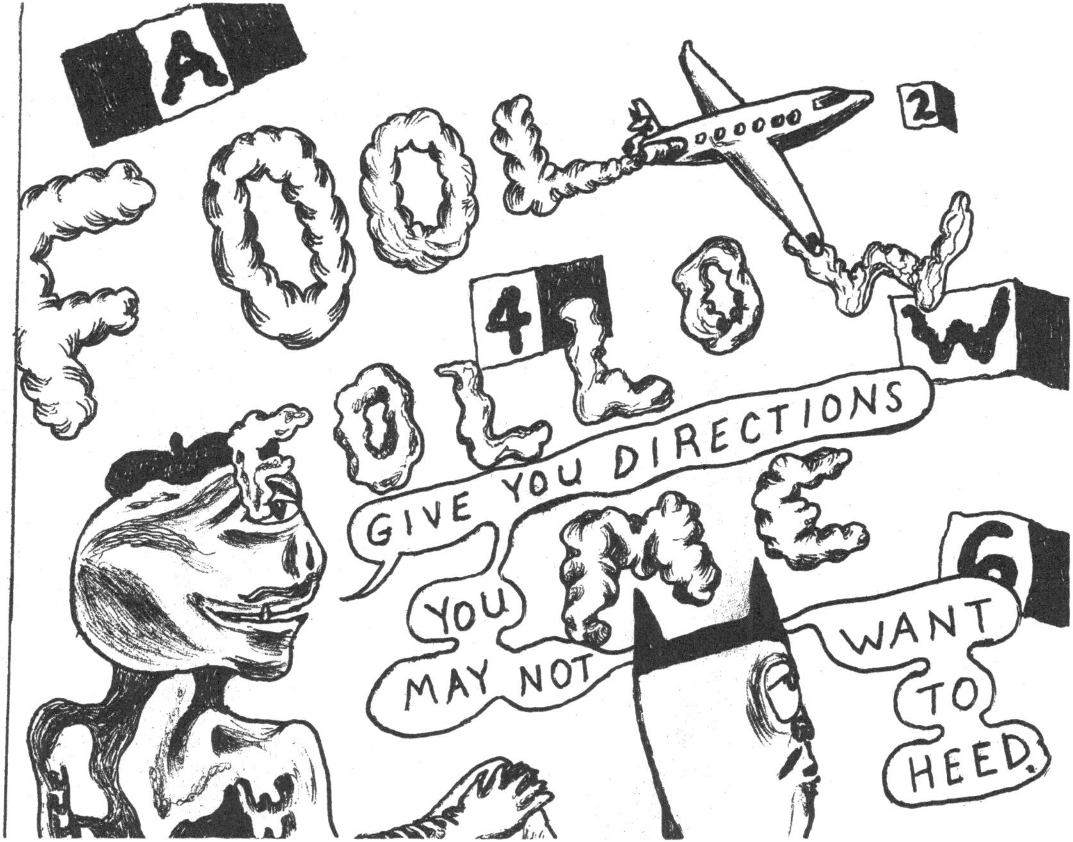
A
FOOL
2
4
FOLLOW
W
GIVE YOU DIRECTIONS
ME
6
YOU
MAY NOT
WANT
TO
HEED.

UNO
Pizzeria
Domino

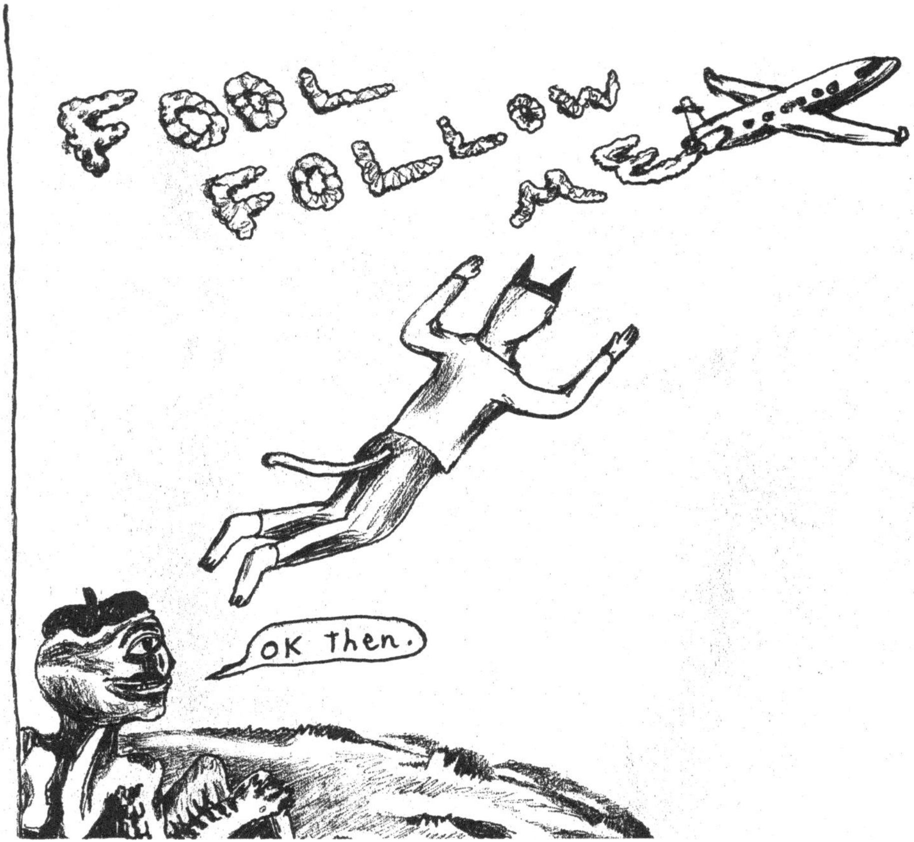
FOOL
FOLLOW ME
OK then.

First Class Lip-Service

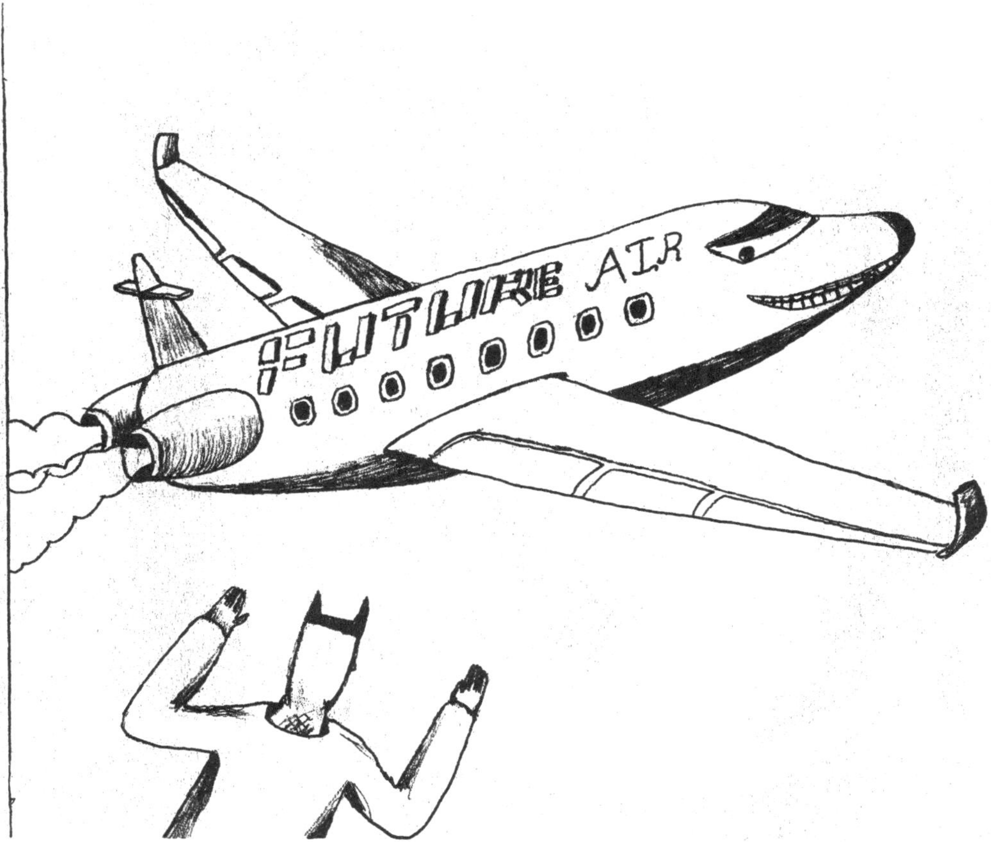
FUTURE AIR

This pen has travelled to Seattle and Back

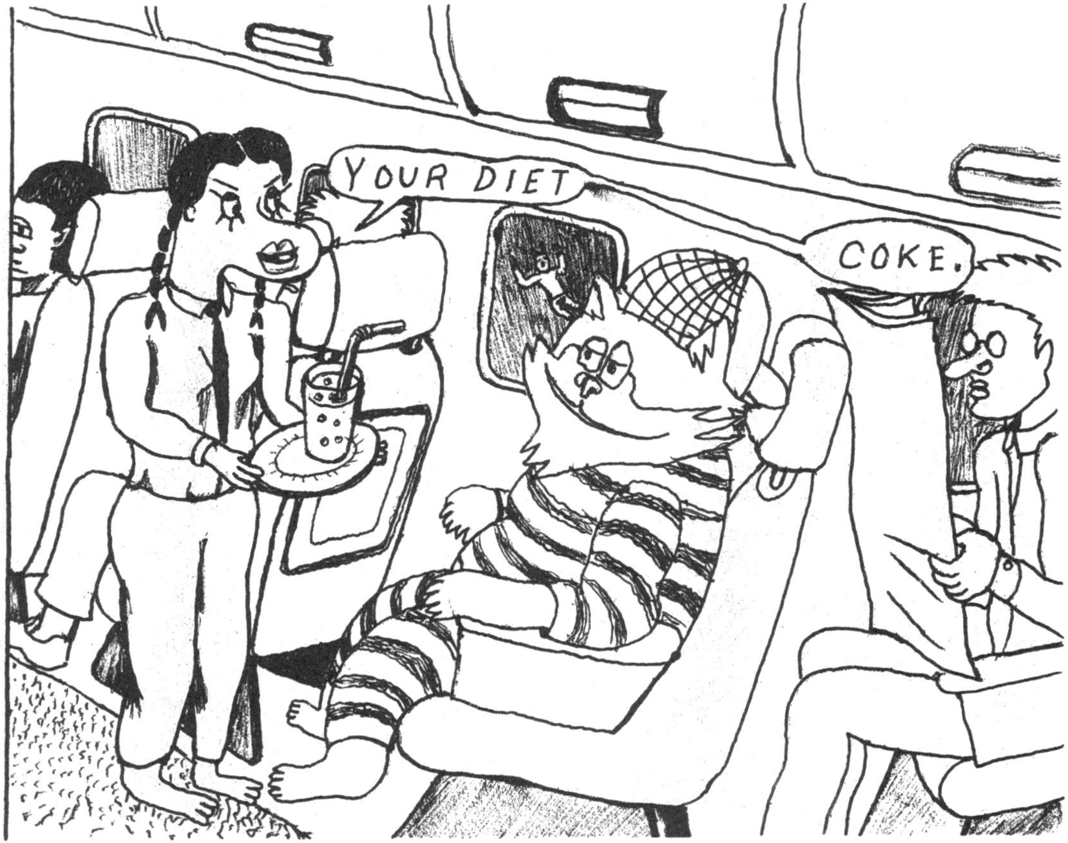
YOUR DIET
COKE.

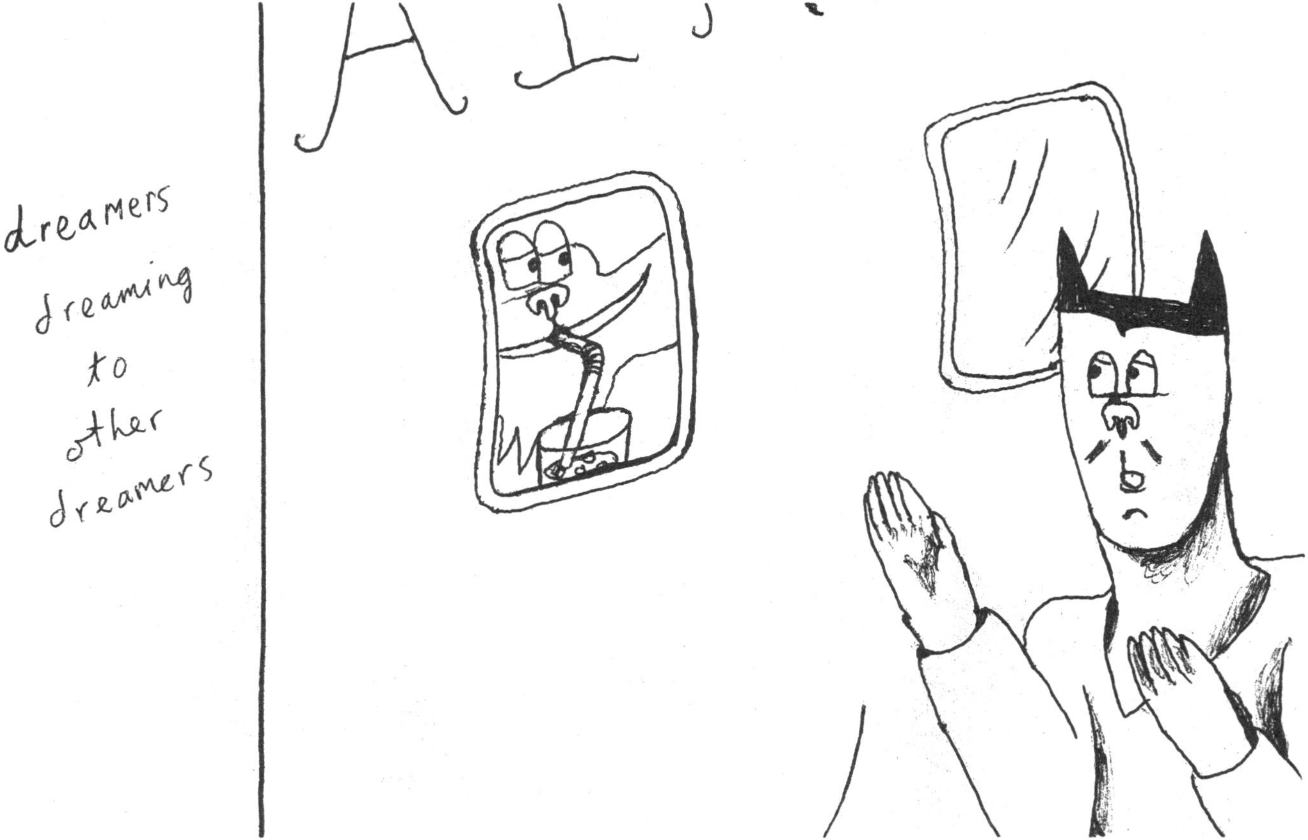
dreamers dreaming to other dreamers

dogwood
butter

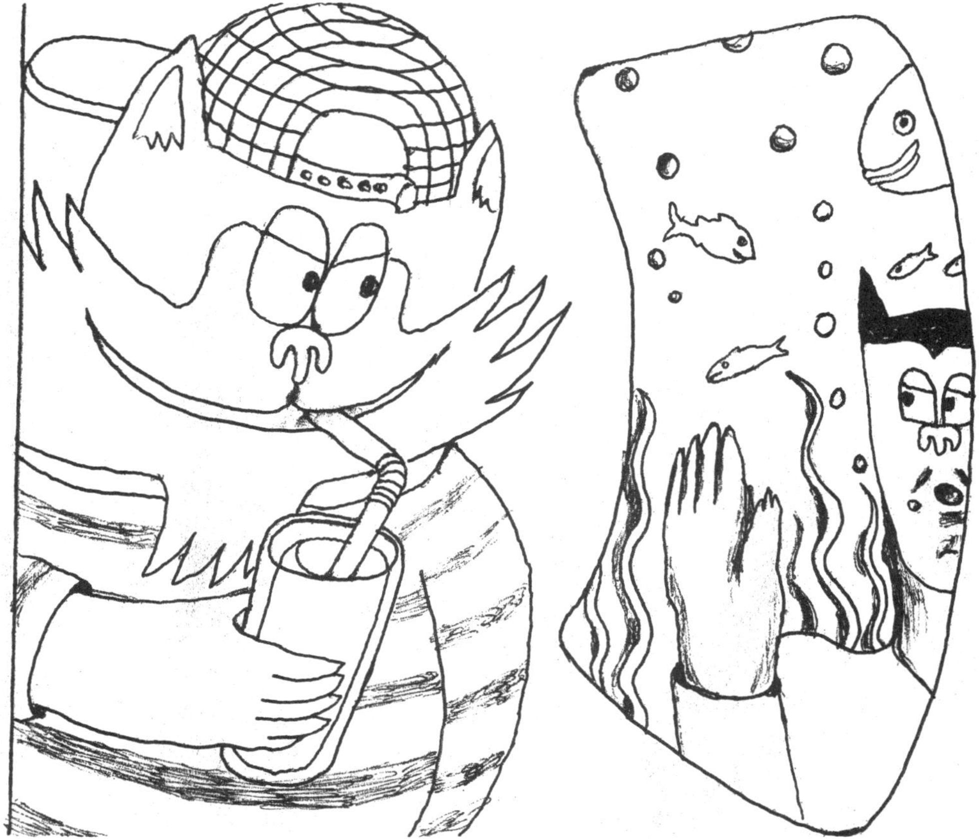

TOR

The Onion Route

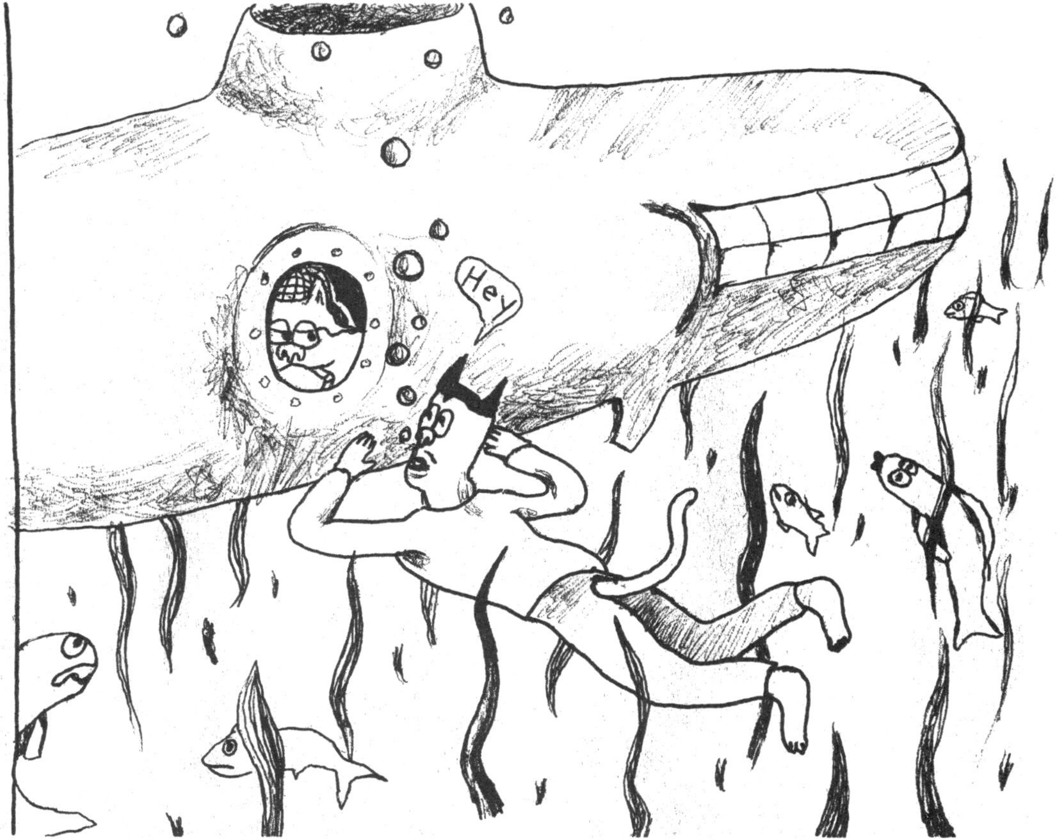
Hey

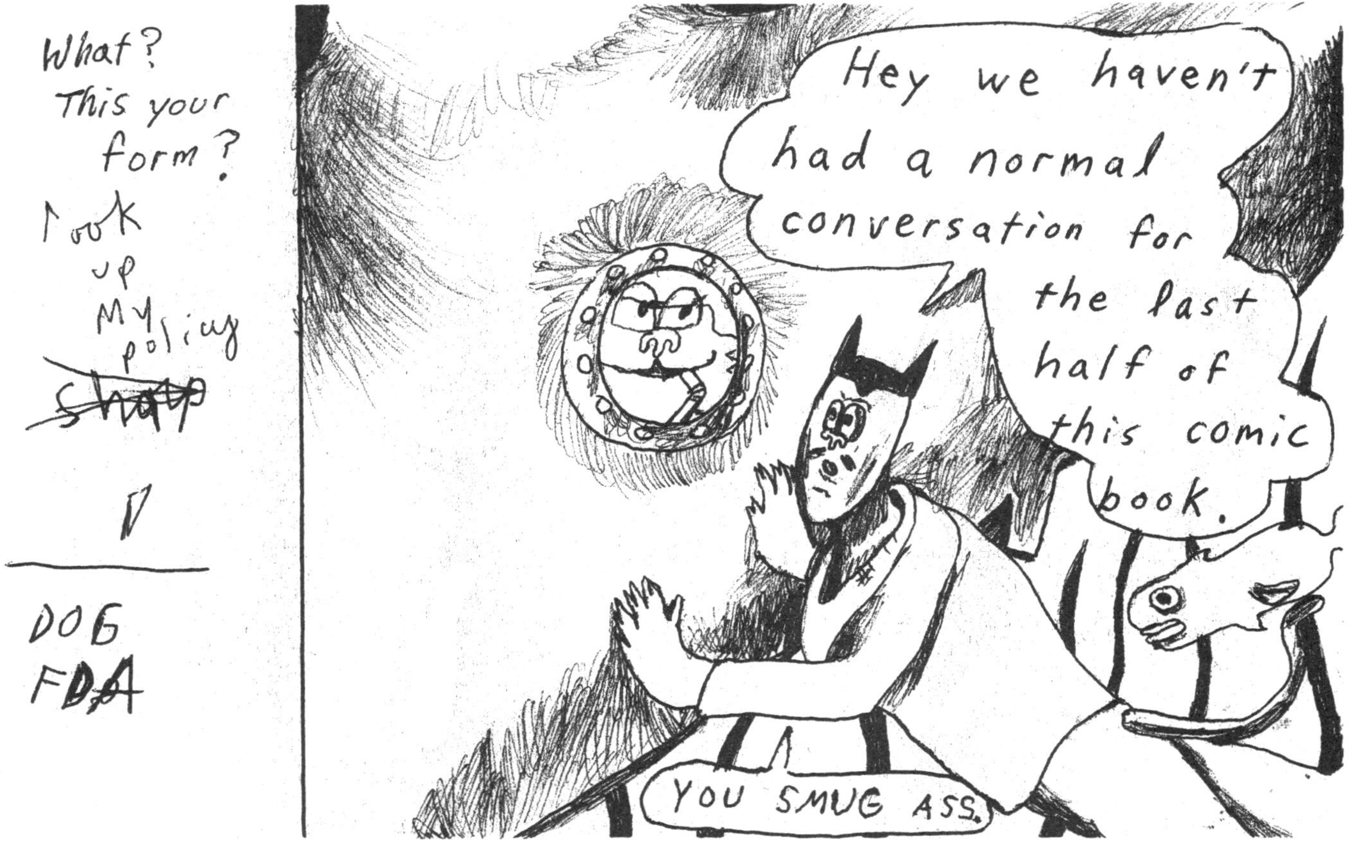
What? This your form?
Look up My policy
DOG FDA
Hey we haven't had a normal conversation for the last half of this comic book.
YOU SMUG ASS.

Verified bathroom reading

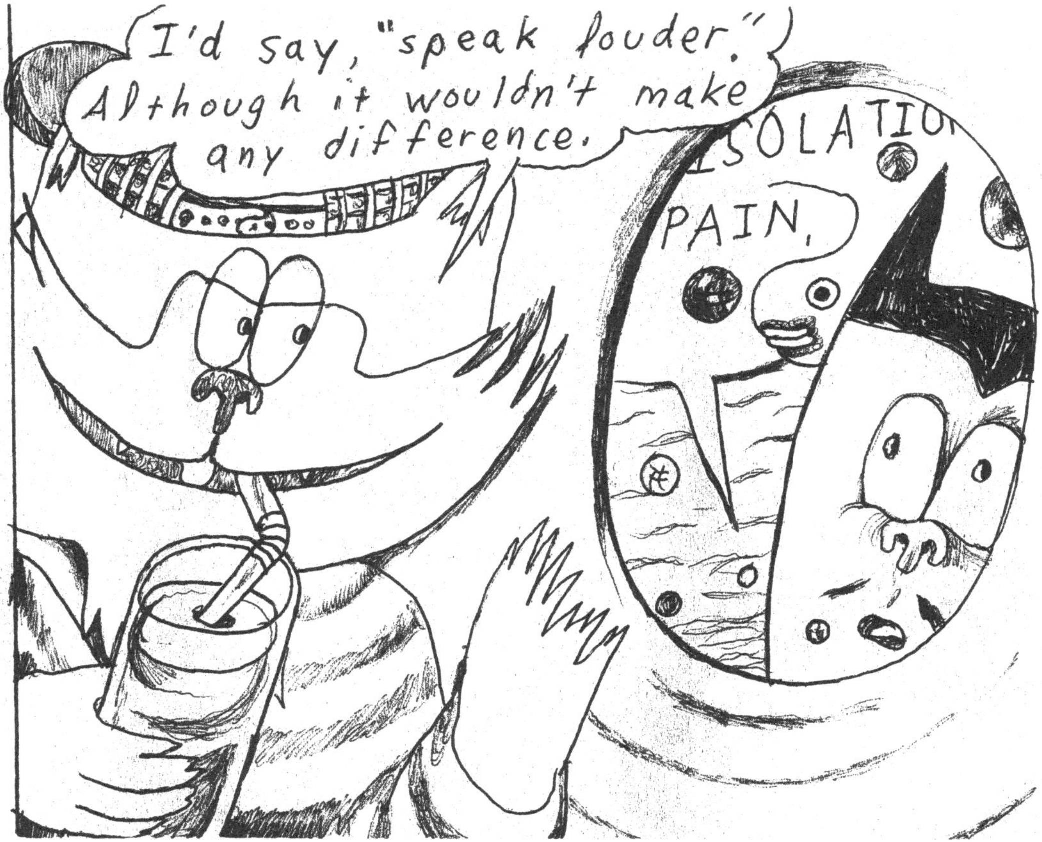
I'd say, "speak louder." Although it wouldn't make any difference.
ISOLATIO
PAIN.

P
into
the
wind

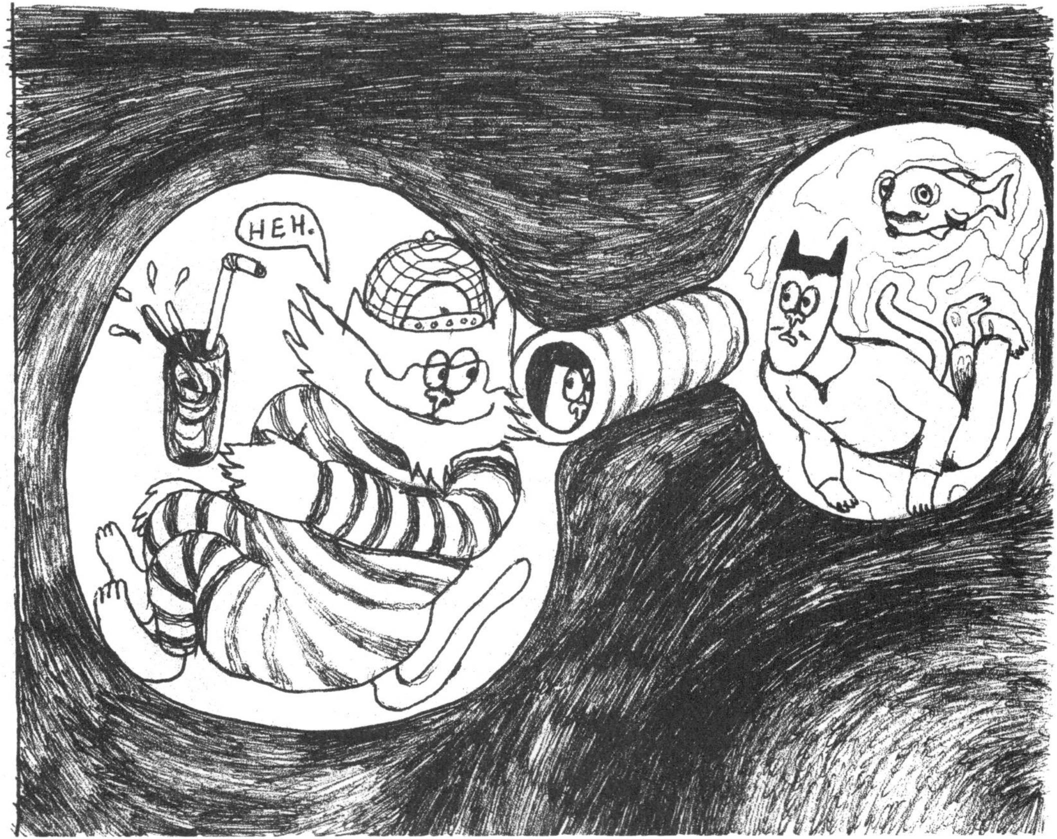
HEH.

Meta cat comic

creepy but cute

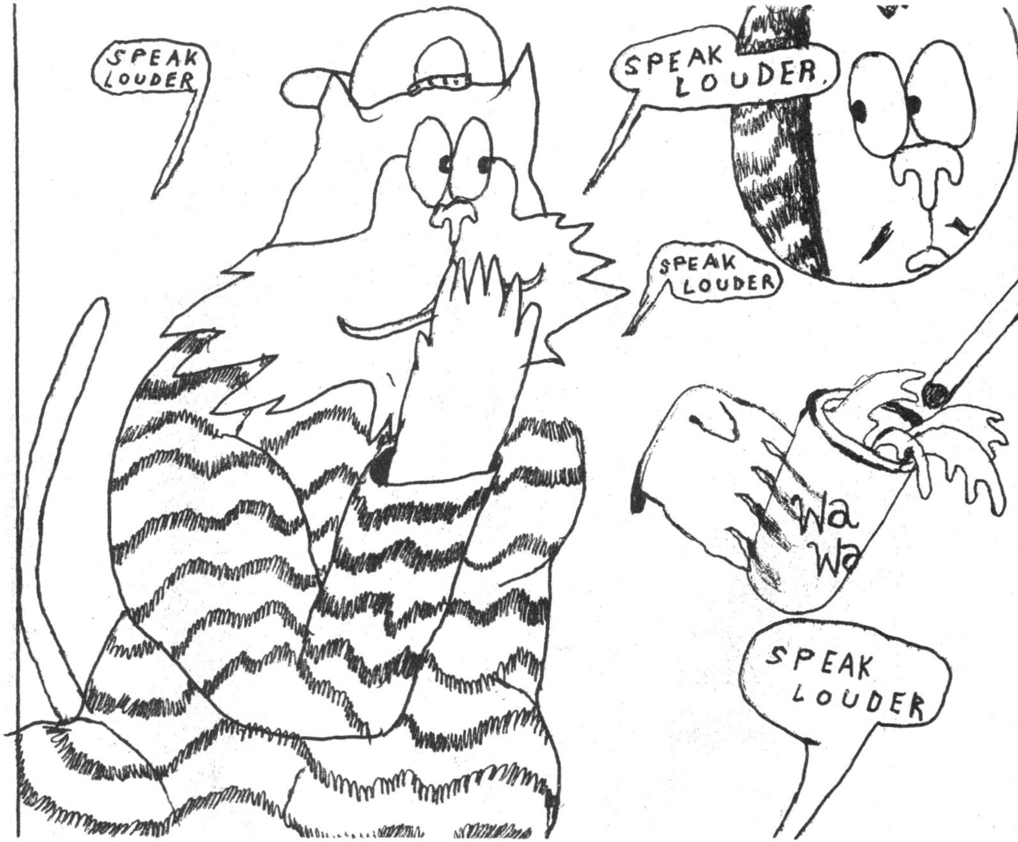
SPEAK LOUDER
SPEAK LOUDER.
SPEAK LOUDER
Wa Wa
SPEAK LOUDER

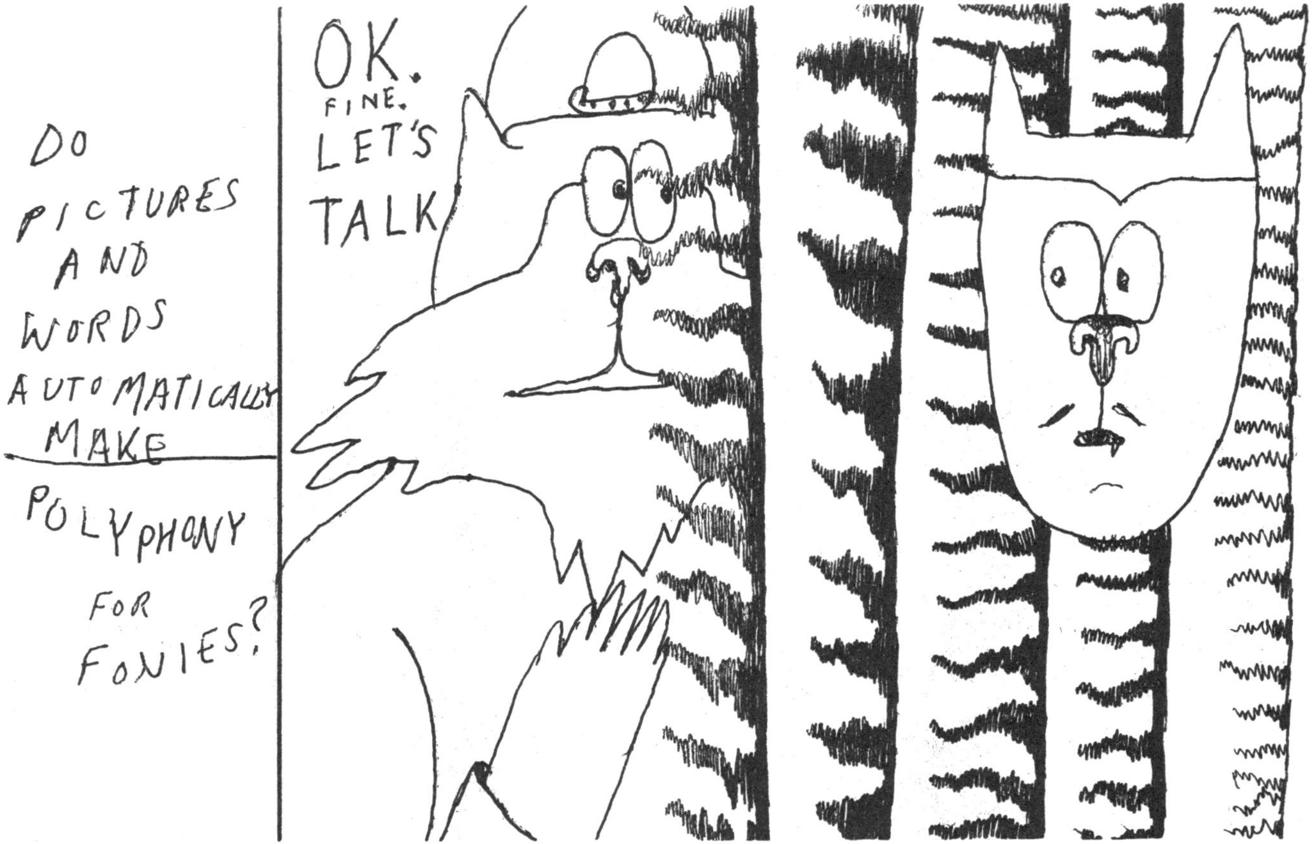
DO PICTURES AND WORDS AUTOMATICALLY MAKE POLYPHONY FOR FONIES?
OK. FINE. LET'S TALK

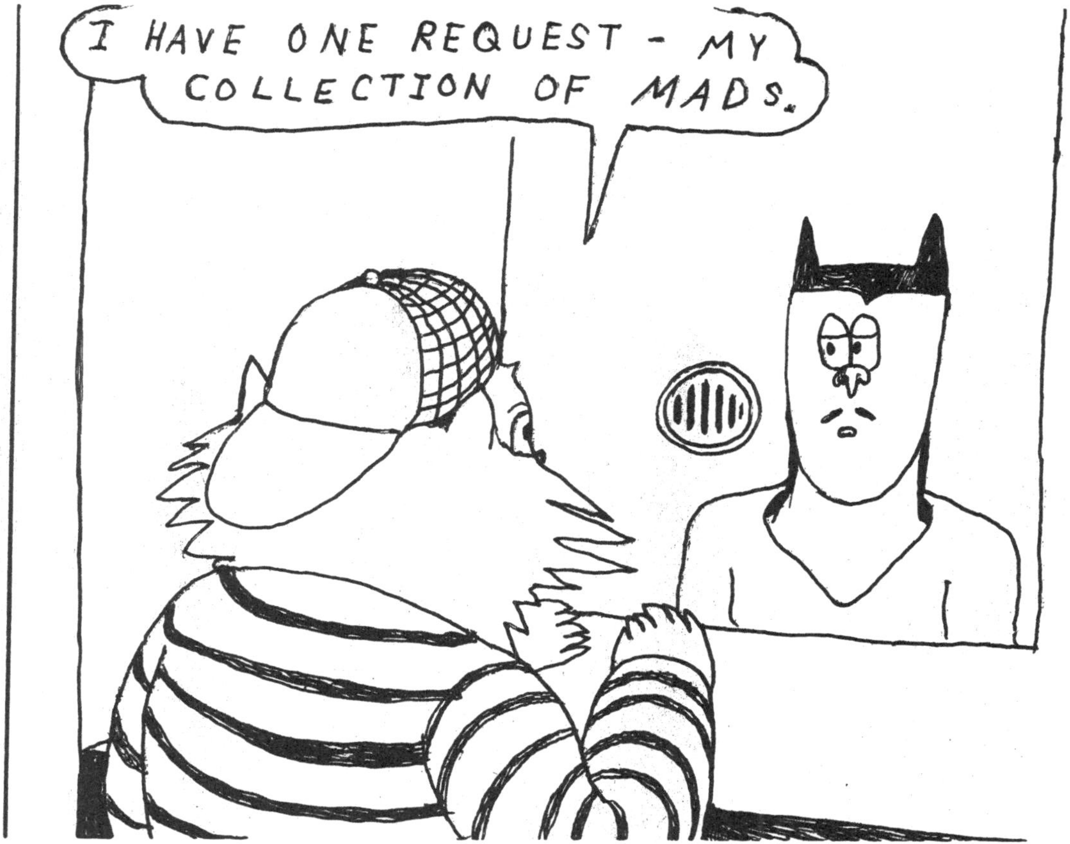
I HAVE ONE REQUEST - MY COLLECTION OF MADS.

Transparency of Material

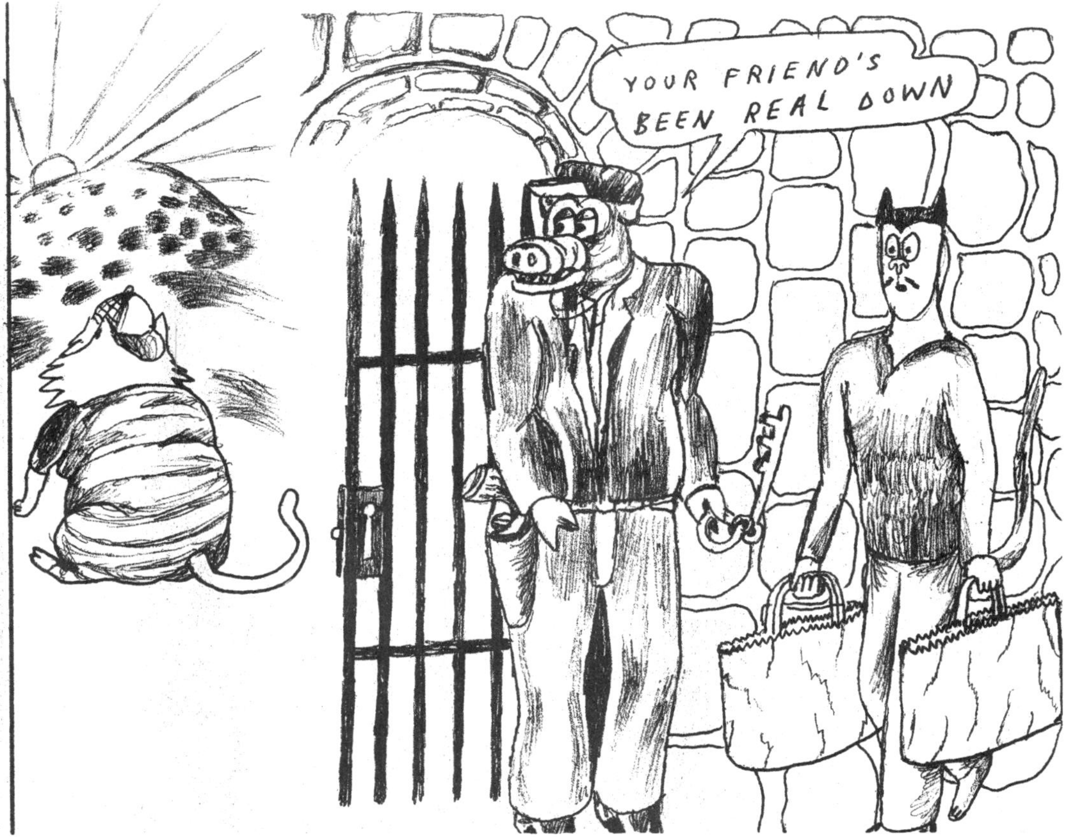
YOUR FRIEND'S BEEN REAL DOWN

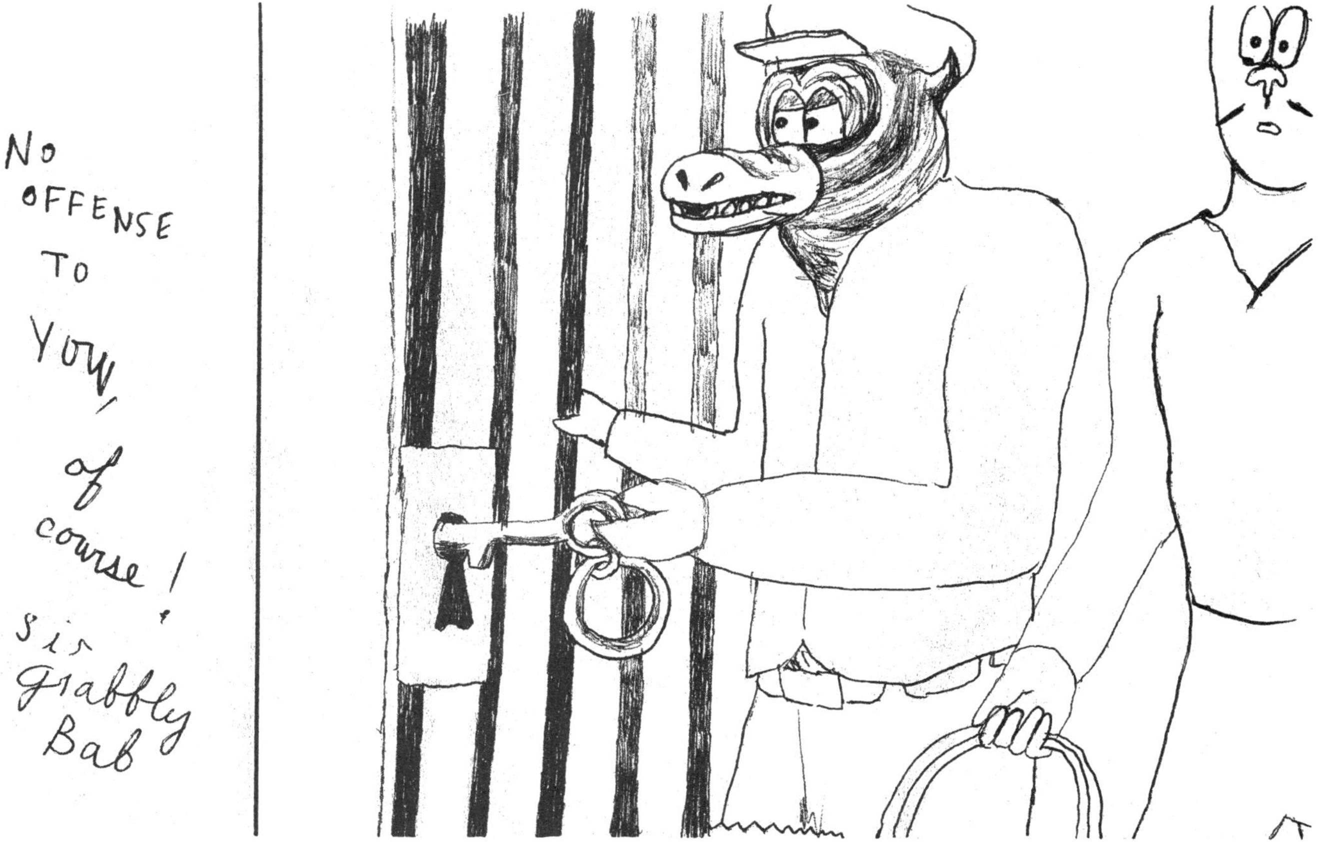
NO OFFENSE TO YOU, of course!
Sir Grabbly Bab

MATURE
=
IMMATURE

both
AS
equals

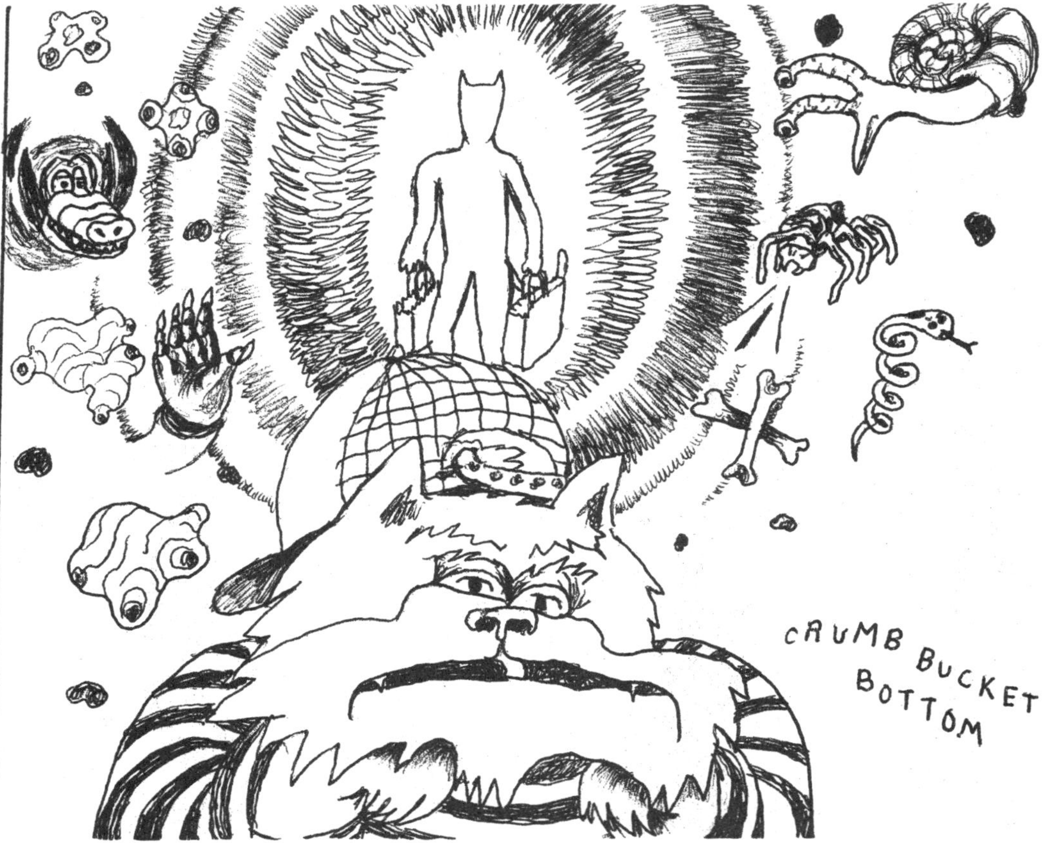

CRUMB BUCKET
BOTTOM

A life with out discipline

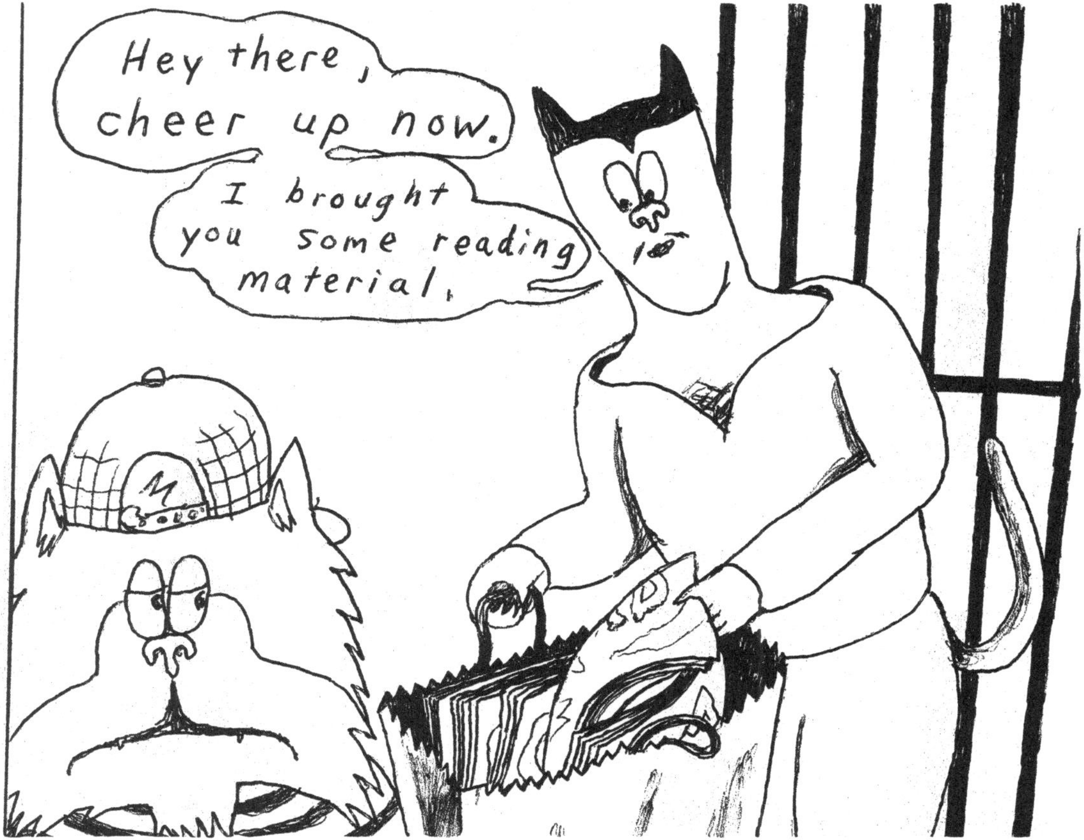

Hey there, cheer up now.
I brought you some reading material.

Jeuvenile Reading

Delinquant

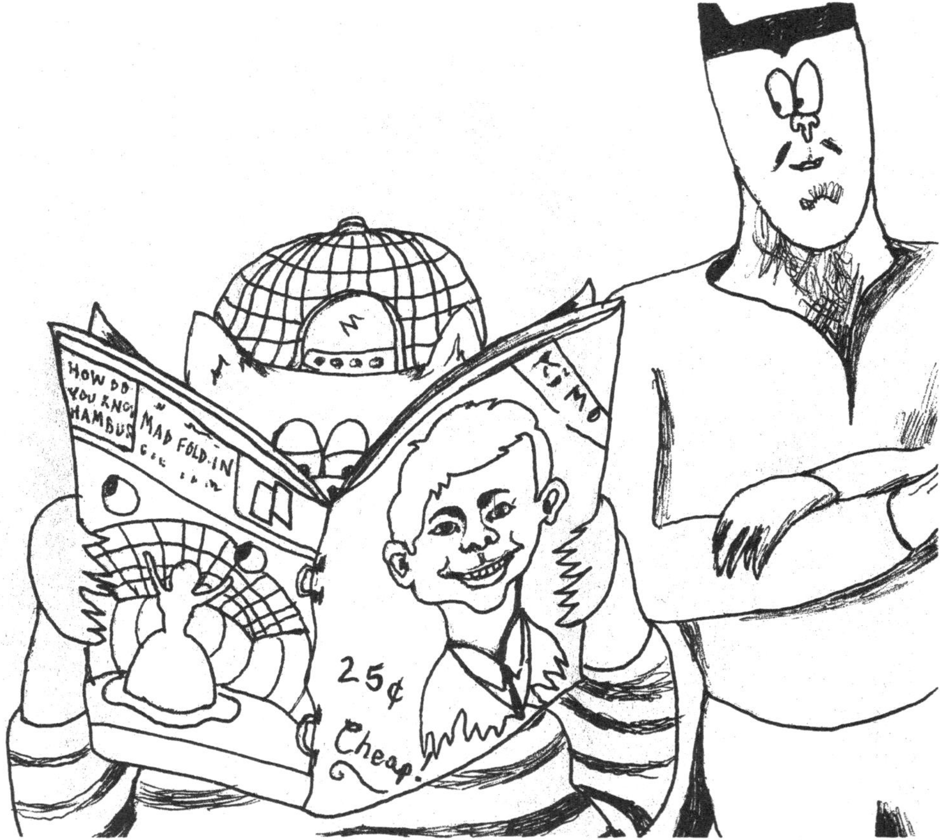
MAD FOLD-IN
25¢
Cheap!

Making something with NO GOAL IN MIND

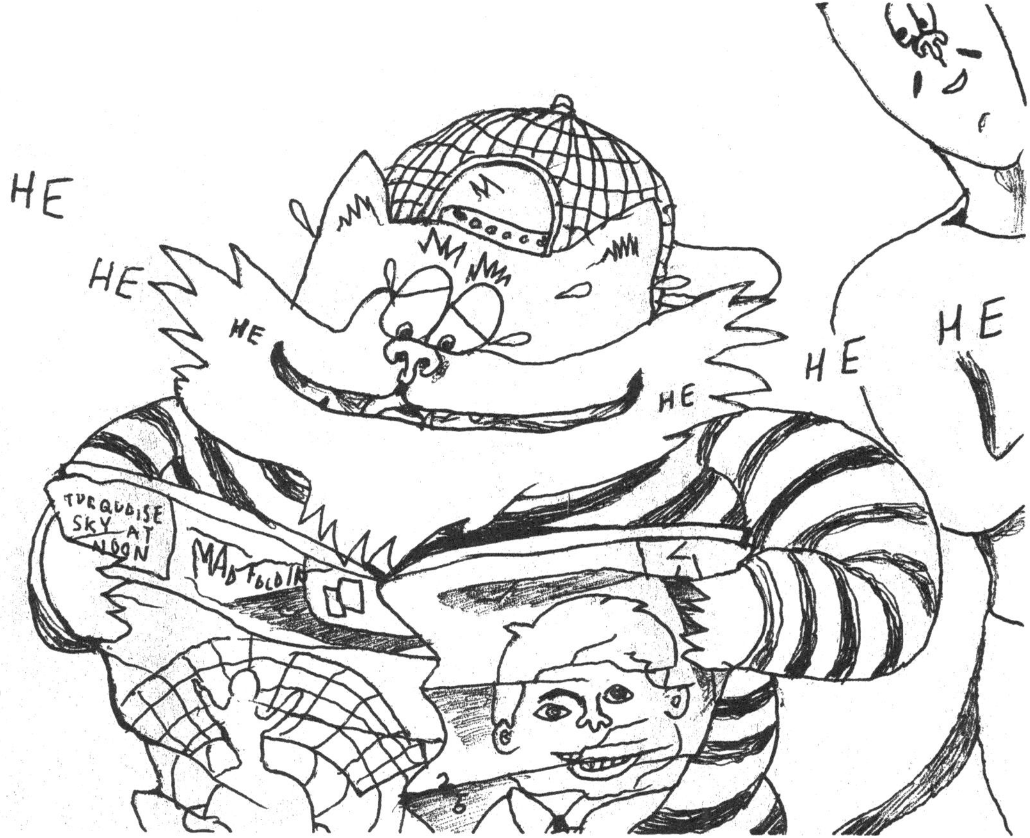
HE
HE
HE
HE
HE
HE
TURQUOISE SKY AT NOON

I ♥ MAD MAGAZINE

FUCK YOU

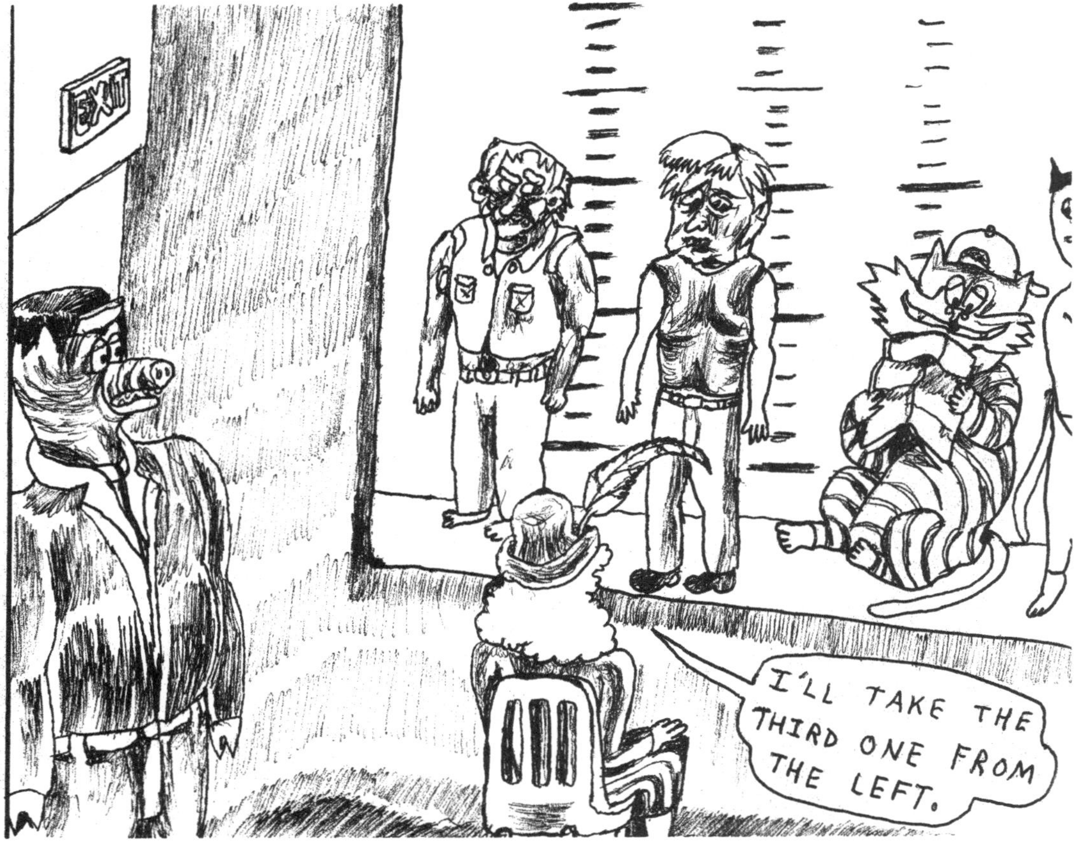
EXIT
I'LL TAKE THE THIRD ONE FROM THE LEFT.

DO NOT

Pretend

you're

SERIOUS,

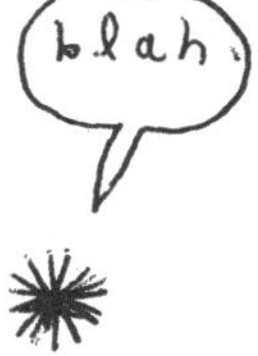
blah

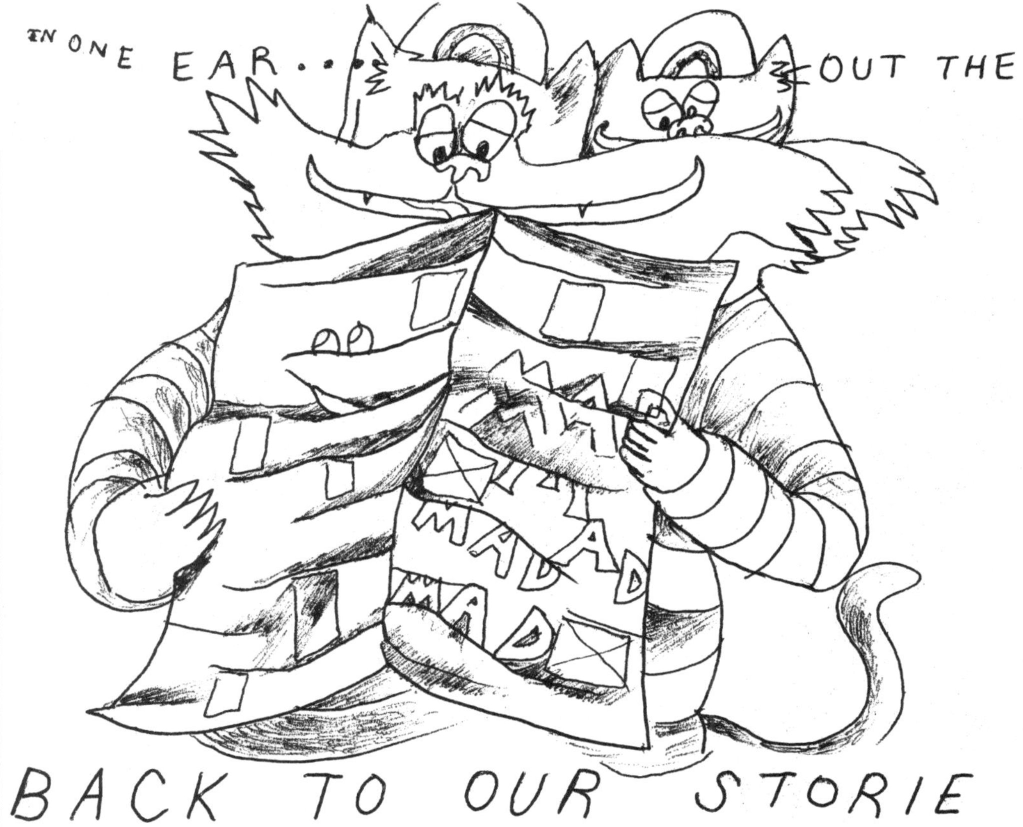
IN ONE EAR... OUT THE
MAD
MAD
MAD
BACK TO OUR STORIE

NATIONAL
"DC"
WASTE

DumComics
dum

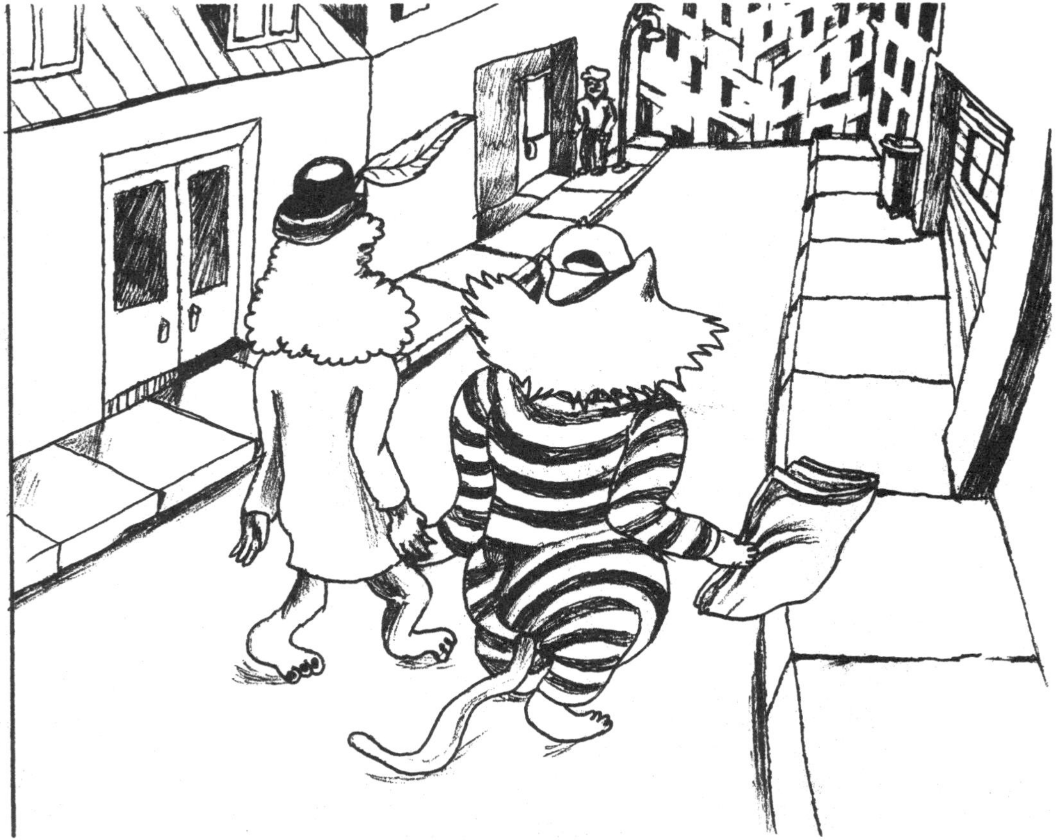

"Visual literature"

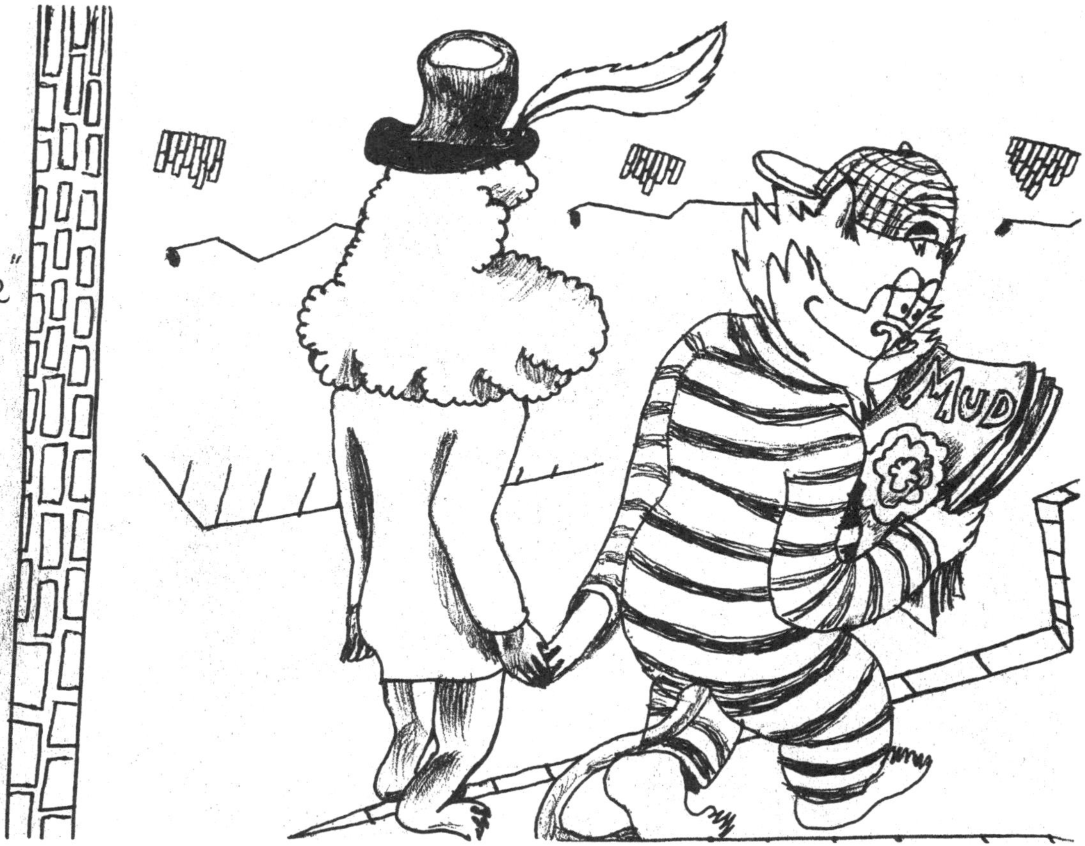
MUD

bringdown
for
teaheads

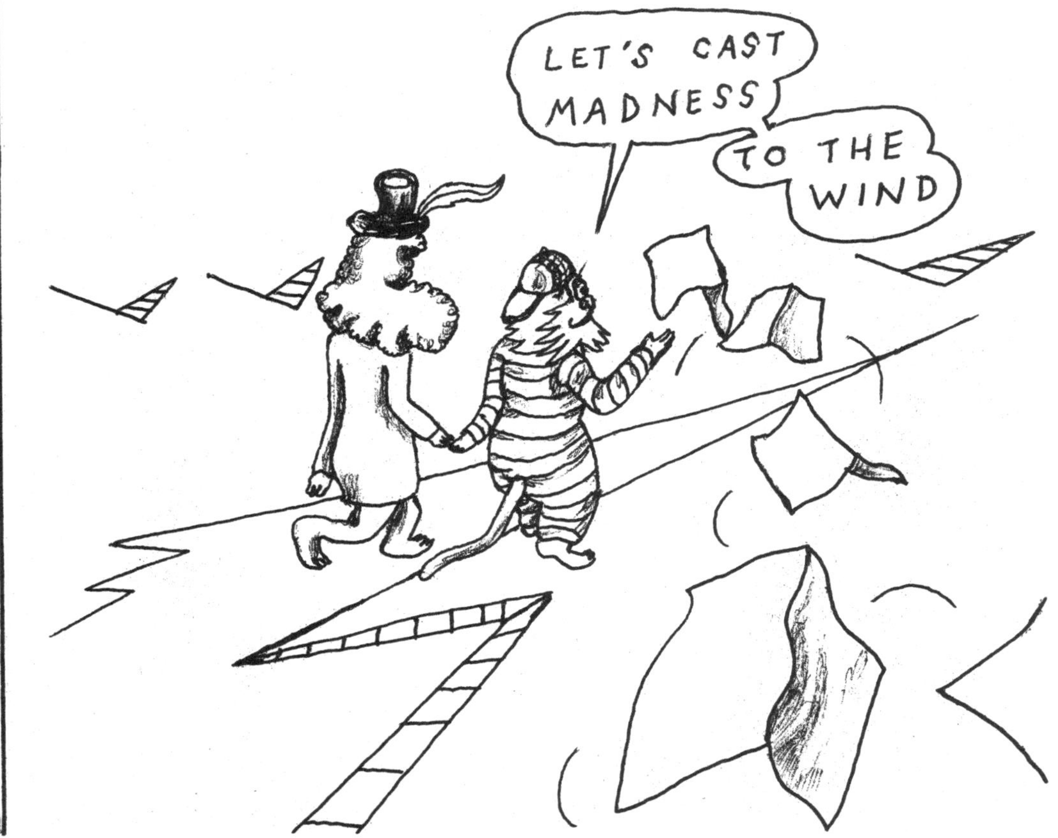

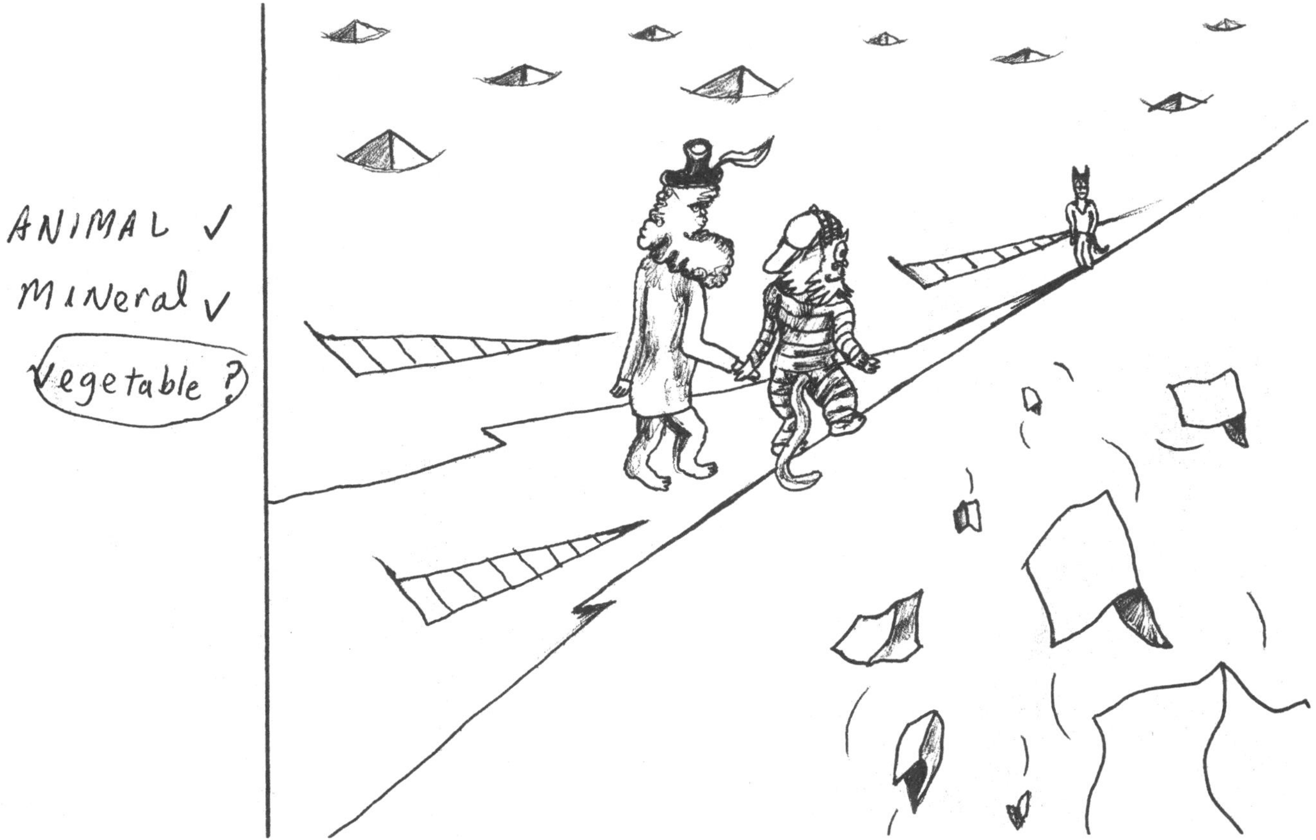
ANIMAL ✓
MINeral ✓
Vegetable ?

Goodbye SUN!

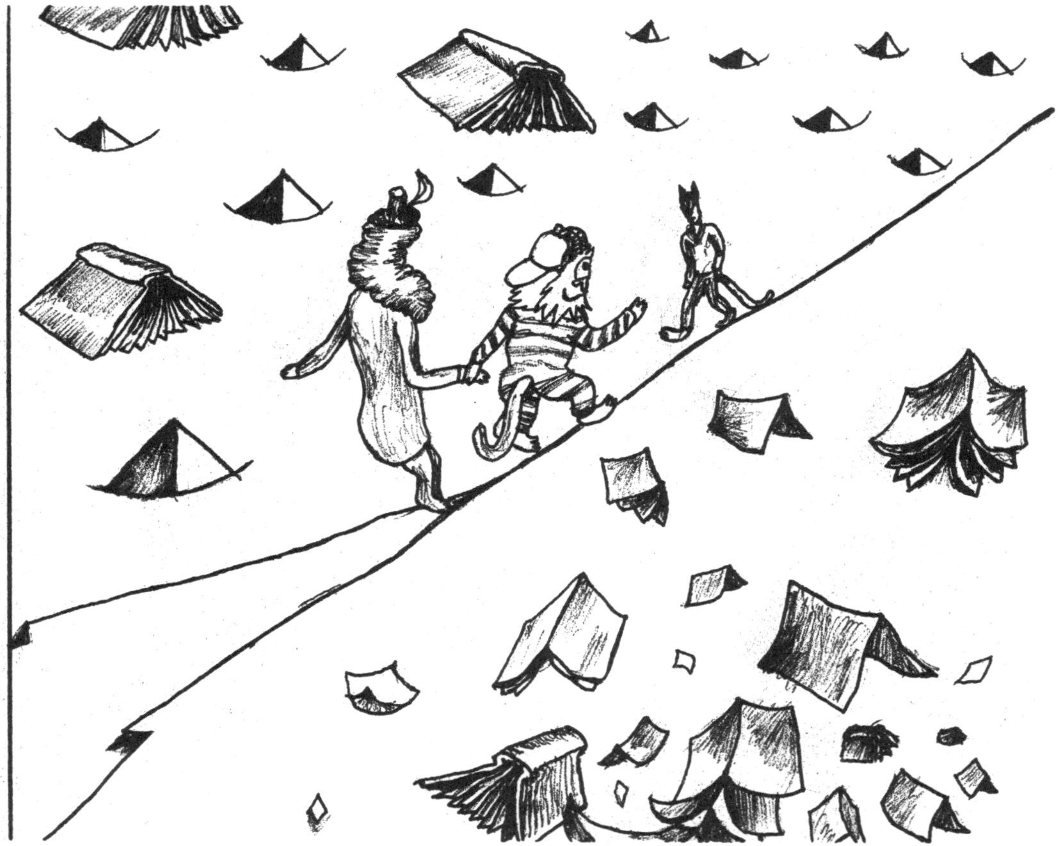

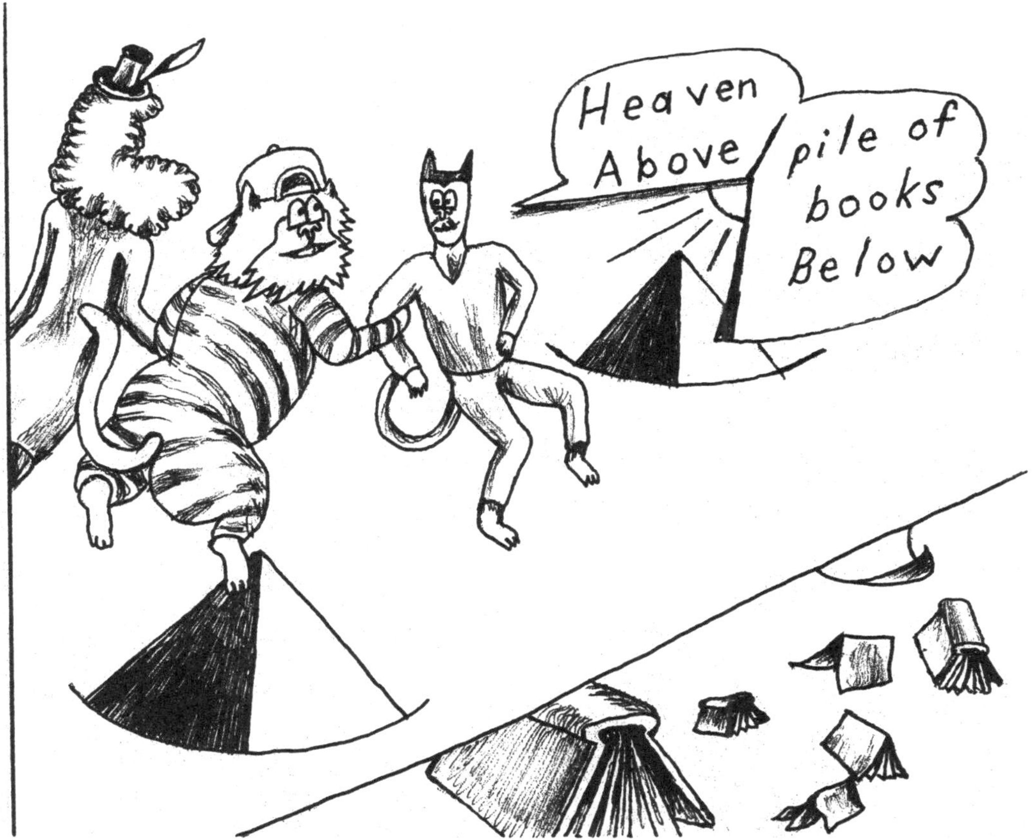

Heaven Above
pile of books Below

F-it let's FLY!

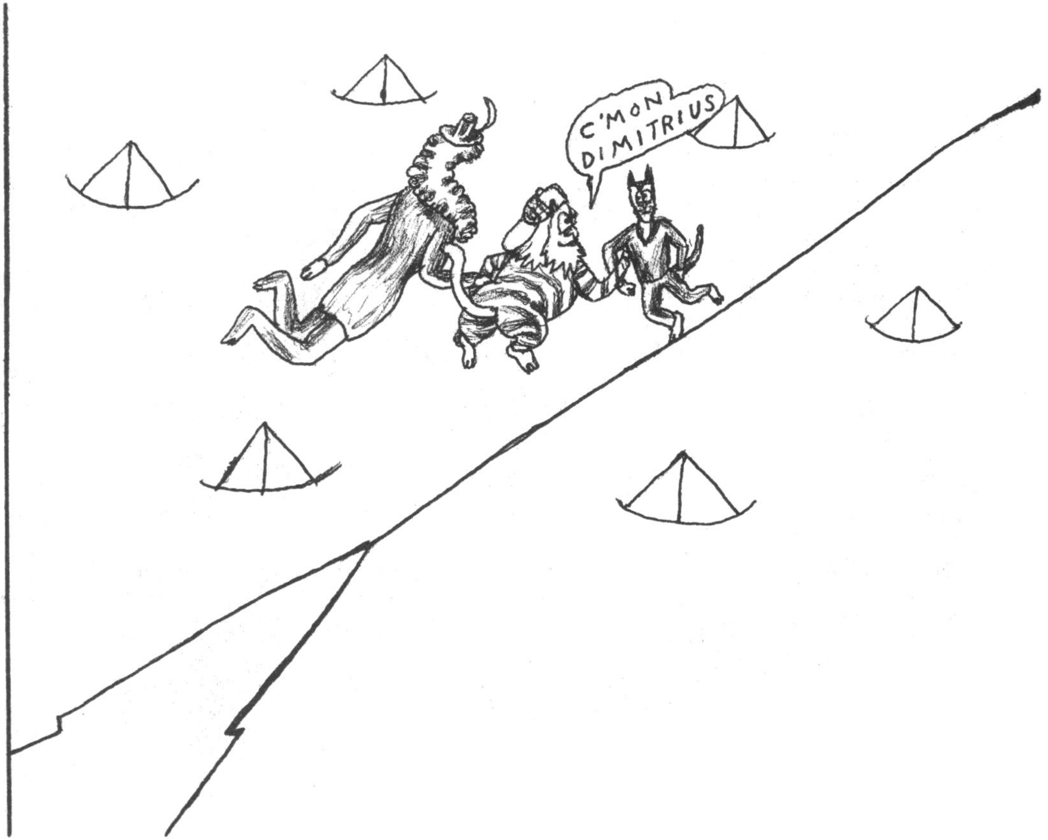

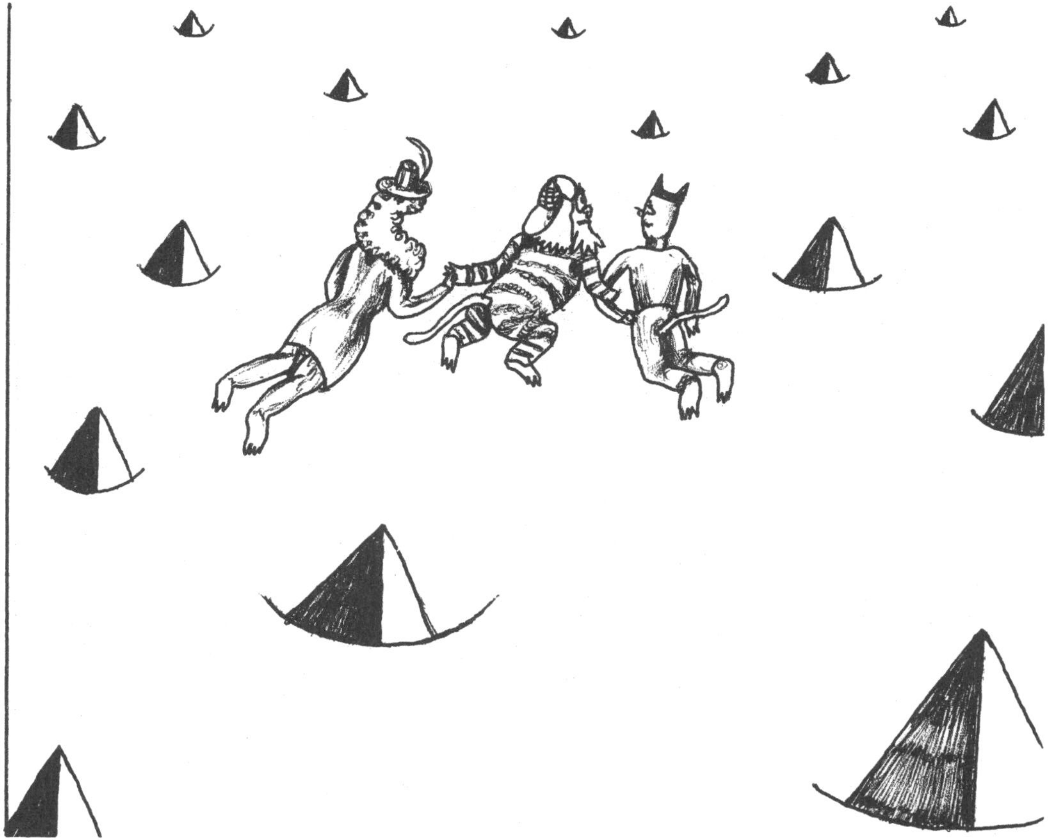

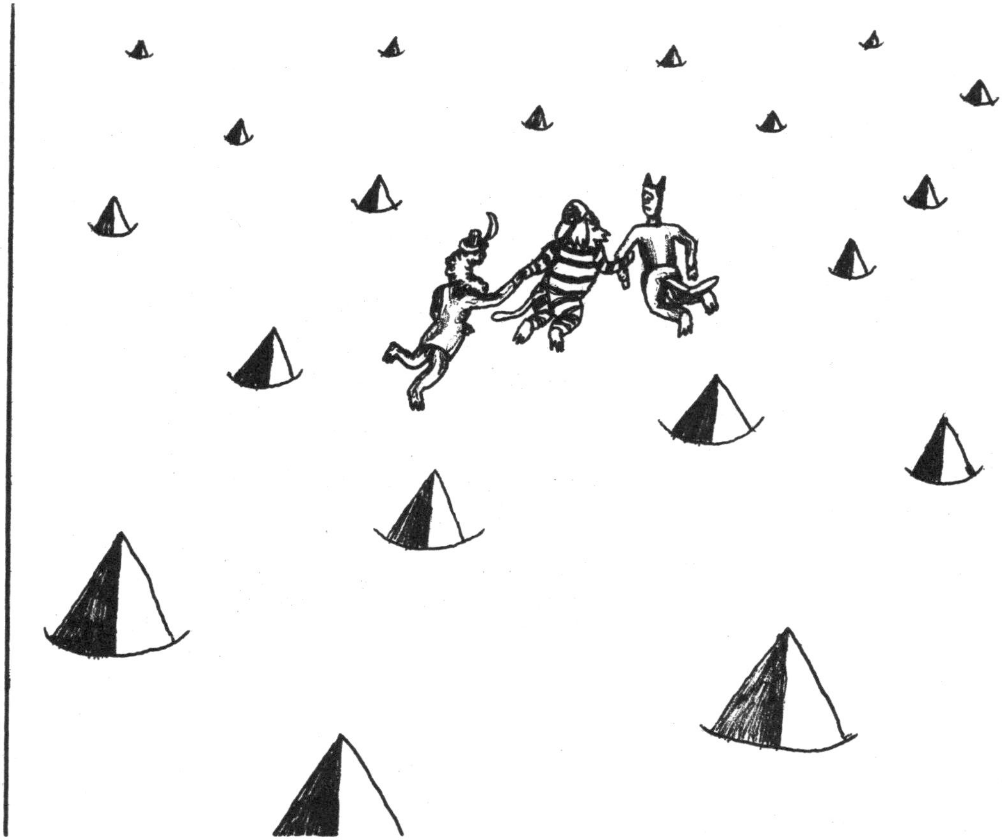

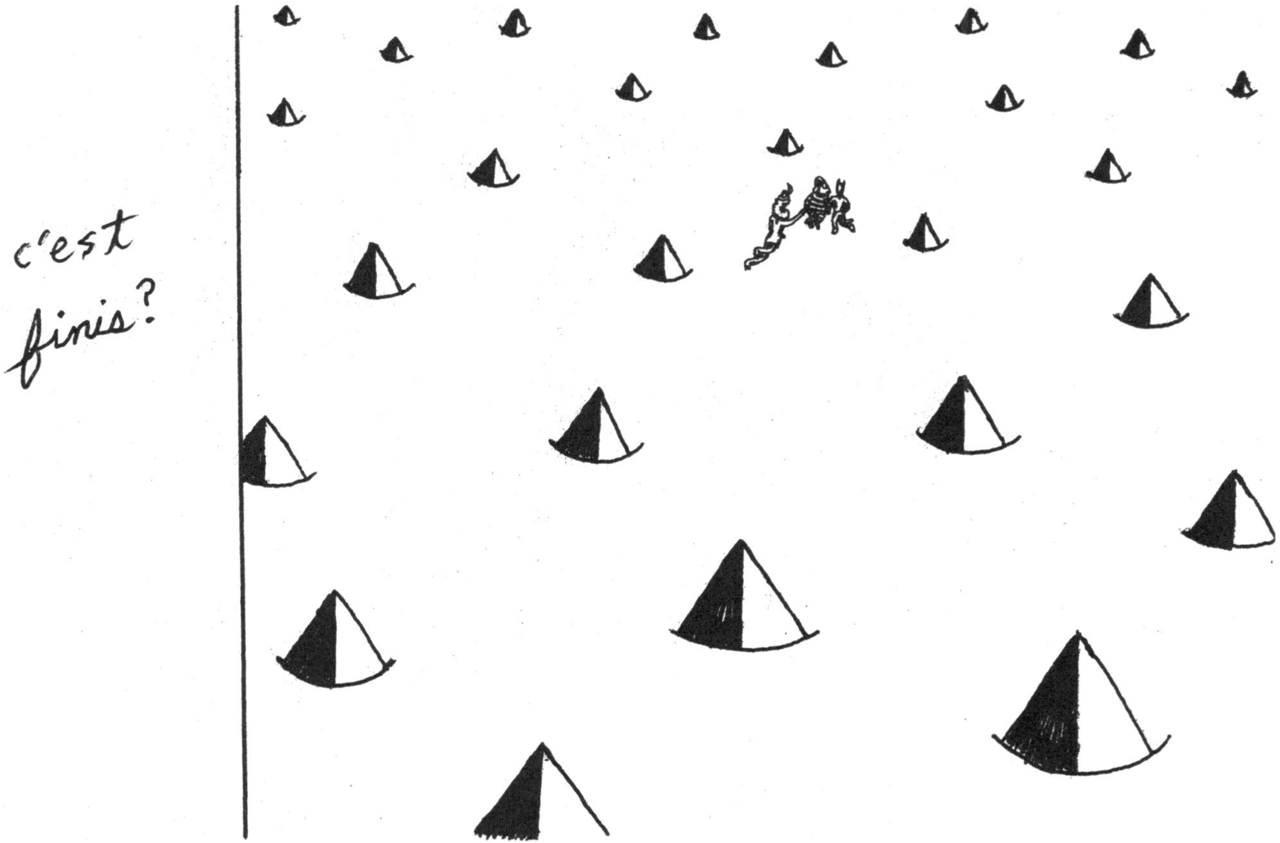
c'est finis?

just plain shitty. com

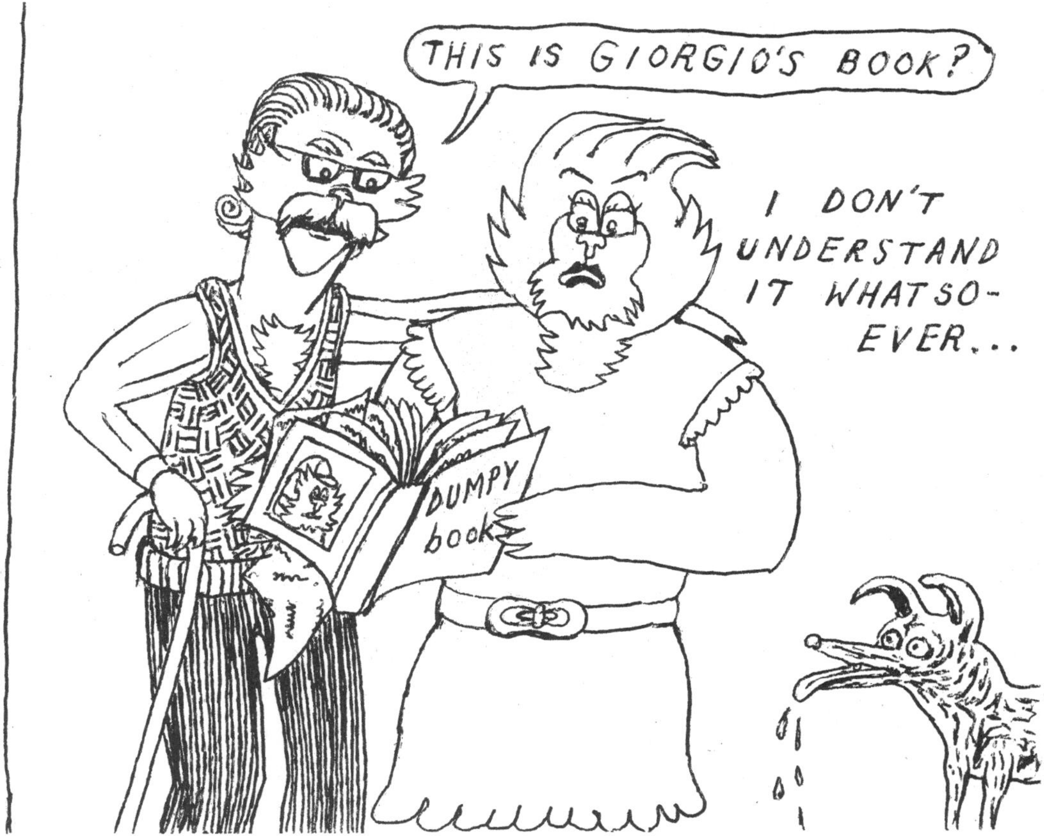
THIS IS GIORGIO'S BOOK?
I DON'T UNDERSTAND IT WHATSO-EVER...
DUMPY
book

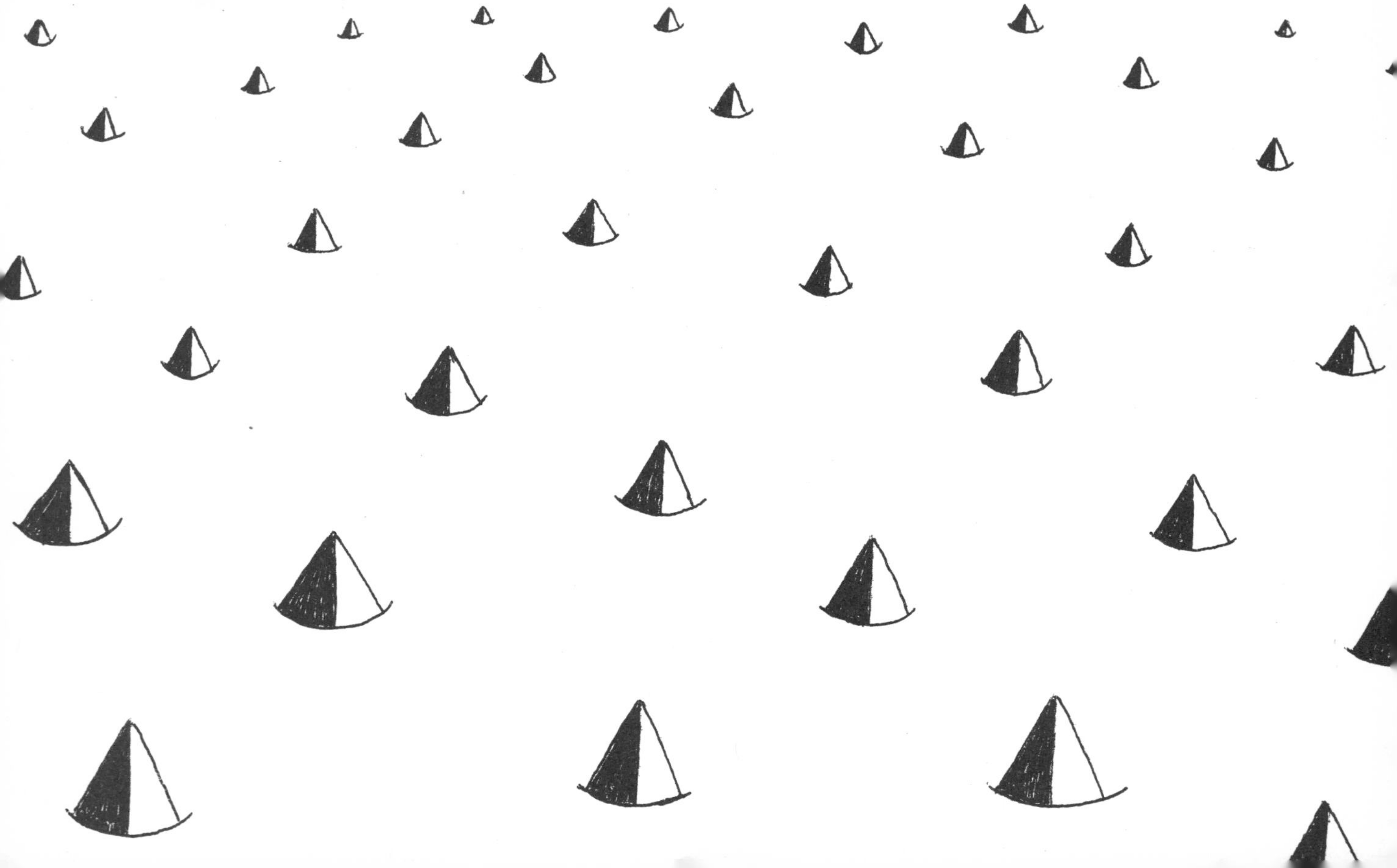